W9-BVU-946

STANDING ON TIPTOE

by Normagene Warner

*For Robin and Family —
Who walks their
own journey, helping
others along the way !
Enjoy each other
every day you have.
Love,
Normagene*

Woodhaven Enterprises
Carbondale, Illinois

Copyright © 2000
Normagene Warner

All rights reserved. No part of this book may be reproduced in any
form, except for the inclusion of brief quotations in a review,
without permission in writing from the author or publisher.

ISBN: 0-9701702-0-3

Library of Congress Catalog Card Number: 00-91778

Printed in the United States by:
Morris Publishing
3212 East Highway 30
Kearney, NE 68847
1-800-650-7888

The desperate fight of one courageous young
man against the insurmountable odds
of a formidable disease

ACKNOWLEDGMENTS

Without the patience and encouragement of my husband Bill and my children, Kathleen and David, this book could never have been written. And without the unabating courage and optimism of Stephen, I would not have felt the need to tell his story.

I also wish to thank Mara Lou Hawse for her patience and expertise in helping edit my manuscript and also to Imogene Beckmeyer as proofreader.

And of course, to all those friends, old and young, with whom we've been privileged to share life's journey.

CONTENTS

PREFACE

This is the story of the desperate fight of one courageous young man against the insurmountable odds of a formidable disease. It also deals with the rest of our family as we strove to regain the joy and meaning of life while we regrouped our family. Our story is poignant and moving but, I believe, ultimately comforting. Life is not a tale told by an idiot. Each family lends it meaning. Each family member is vastly important.

STANDING ON TIPTOE

How oft have you stood on tiptoe?
So filled with joy and delight
That you had to stretch up tall to breathe it all in?
To stretch and stand on tiptoe
Lest you should burst, with the sheer joy of it all?

A sunset so brilliant it hurts your eyes to look,
A sunrise so glorious it takes your breath away,
The sound of rain after a long drought,
The splendor of newfallen snow,
The tender holding of hands,
A lover's sweet kiss,
Sleeping babes in a cradle, moist curls on the warm, soft neck,
The wrinkled softness of a grandmother's cheek.

These are the things that stretch us tall.
We fling out our arms,
We stand on our tiptoes
Trying to take it all in,
Gulping in Life, with its feast-laden table.

Ah, to have had these moments!

We can never get enough.
There is never enough time nor awareness.

But to have had these moments. . .
Standing on tiptoe--
Falling on knees–

These are our growth rings,
A far truer gauge
Than the mere revolving of years.

OF HOPES AND FEARS

"Poptarts and lemon ice cream! Goodies for the sick folks," I sang out as I pushed the door open. "Sorry I'm so late, but I went to three places looking for lemon ice cream. I had no idea it was so hard to find."

I gave my daughter, Kathy, a quick squeeze and greeted her husband, Russ. "It's good to see you here," I said. Kathy and Russ had been married a year in June, and although we lived only five miles apart, it was always a treat to have them visit.

"Mama. . . ."

Something in Kathy's voice stilled my patter that Wednesday evening, October 10, 1973. I looked at her and noted the concern that had deepened the blue of her eyes.

"Mama, I know you're worried about Daddy, but I think . . . I think it's Stephen that you. . . ."

Kathy's voice faltered as she groped for the right words. "I don't like the way he acts. I've been here all afternoon," she continued, "and he's not been able to get any relief from his headache at all." Her voice dropped. "He told me that he passed out two different times today when he stood up to go to the bathroom."

Gone were all thoughts of preparing supper. I suppose someone else put the lemon ice cream in the freezer; I never saw it again. All my fears of the last few days came into sharp focus. My heart, for the first of what was to be hundreds of times, leaped to my throat, shutting off sound and breath. My shaking fingers finally found the number of the hospital emergency room.

"The north entrance? Yes. We'll be there in less than fifteen minutes."

I am married to a Methodist minister, and Stephen is our third child—our baby.

I met Bill, my husband, at Asbury College in Wilmore, Kentucky. I was a junior and he was the first veteran of World War

II to attend college there. I think I fell in love with him the first time I saw him striding across our small campus. Bill was a tall, lanky young man with curly, black hair and deep-set brown eyes, and even now—after twenty-seven years of marriage—my heart thrills as I catch sight of him. There's a little silver in his black curls now, but his eyes still shine with enthusiasm, and his ebullience and optimism have helped us through some lean, hard years.

At Easter break in 1945, Bill came home with me to meet my parents. I lived on a farm near Carbondale, in southern Illinois. Bill hailed from a small town in New Jersey.

We were married in 1946 and lived in a tiny duplex apartment during Bill's last year of college and part of his seminary training. His army experience had solidified his desire to become a minister. The Methodist Conference gave Bill a student appointment, and filled with zeal and enthusiasm, on December 7, 1947, we went to that first preaching engagement in Warsaw, Kentucky. While Bill was still in seminary, I lived alone in our rural parsonage, except for the three-day weekends ministerial students were given. As I worked with the church organizations, I felt that I, too, was part of his ministry. It has been a good life.

In the early years of our marriage, we talked about wanting six children—"Maybe a whole choir," we joked—for then we were blissfully unaware of the earth's burgeoning population and Malthus's dire predictions. All of our children were wanted, but none arrived when they were planned. After four years of marriage, the babies had not come, and the bills had mounted steadily, so we bought a car and I started to teach school, only to discover that I was pregnant. Our lovely Kathleen Marie was born on July 5, 1950.

When Bill graduated the next spring, we moved to Equality, a small town in southern Illinois. Two years later, just after I had enrolled in an artist's association, I found I was "with child" again—this time with our dear little David, who arrived on February 15, 1953.

Bill enjoyed his work with the church at Equality, and we were a contented, happy family. However, in those days, Methodist ministers were not expected to have long pastorates.

When David was only fifteen months old, we left the genteel country village and moved to Johnston City, Illinois, a coal mining town that had seen better days. Moving time was always sad for me; I was convinced I would never learn to love the new congregation as I had the one we were leaving. I could never quite believe that in five years or so the new home would be the old, and again I would bid friends goodbye through tears. All I could see that day as the van rolled into Johnston City were weedy vacant lots and closed stores.

However, the next three years passed swiftly. They were happy years, despite our failure to increase our brood. Finally I decided to return to college and finish work for my degree. But the very week I arranged for a car pool to attend classes at Southern Illinois University, I found I was pregnant once more. Fourteen more years would go by before I finally finished that degree.

We lived near Crab Orchard Lake in the Great Mississippi Flyway, winter home to thousands of Canada Geese and other waterfowl. While Kathy was in first grade that fall of 1956, the rest of us spent many afternoons at the reserve—Bill preparing his Sunday sermons, David finding treasures of rocks and cones and sticks and pretty feathers, I crocheting slowly on a baby afghan and reading a little, now and then. I was content to sit and bask in the warmth of my happiness. It was peaceful and quiet, despite the noisy backdrop of the honking geese and the mewing gulls. The mingled cries of the water fowl are surely among the most primeval of all sounds; I could almost hear the swirling of the waters as they were parted from the firmament. Words of an old nursery rhyme floated on the periphery of my mind.

I wish I may, I wish I might
Have the wish I wish tonight.

No stars, no night, just the wish—the wish that somehow these lovely sounds, the quietness of spirit and the deep joy, like golden honey, could be drawn into my unborn child like a blessing—a welcome and a benediction. The feel of the days and my body seemed one—both heavy and promising.

Three-year-old David ran on sturdy legs—to show me treasures or just to touch base and run again. I put a thin brown straw in my mouth and tasted the sun and the rain and the soil in the stem. The baby rolled and kicked as if he, too, were absorbing a part of our deep joy.

My sterner self stood up to gather yarn and books and said, "Don't be silly." But a gossamer winged thing, disguised as a butterfly, paused on my shoulder and whispered, "Who knows? Who knows?"

I remember Johnston City with a special fondness, for it was here, on November 9, 1956, that William Stephen was born. He came five days early, waiting neither for the delivery room nor the doctor. Nurse Bottom (her name somehow lent hilarity to the situation) sent Bill to "boil water"—in this case to ride the elevator down and hurry the doctor, and thus he missed the actual birth of that son. As the baby was laid, warm and wet, on my stomach, my heart overflowed.

When the doctor finally did dash in, I teased, "You're not going to get your money this time, Doc. Nurse Bottom and I did it all."

But the doctor did earn his fee. I developed complications—an ingrown placenta and phlebitis—and had a long stay in the hospital.

I worried about the baby, too. He stayed red longer than his sister and brother had. One nurse chided me, "Oh, he's a mite ruddy, but I wouldn't hold that against him."

Late one night during that enforced stay, when Stephen was three or four days old, I hugged his red, wrinkled loveliness to my breast. I promised myself that if ever those blood clots in my legs dissolved, I would never again take for granted the little happinesses that make up a lifetime.

I had learned that nothing can be taken for granted—that lovely, apparently well children can die. When Kathy was seven months old, tragedy had struck our family. My younger brother, Alan Dale, who was only twelve years old, died suddenly of post-vaccinal encephalitis. Because my brother Bob and I had both married and left home the same summer, five years before, that little brother had been almost like an only child. His death was extremely hard on my parents, particularly my mother.

Children became the source of my greatest joy. Life revolved about home and church, and in the very center were the children. Perhaps it was because I was twenty-seven years old when our first was born, or perhaps it was because my own little brother died when he was quite young, but our children—each one of them—were truly special.

I breathed my thankfulness. "Truly, my cup runneth over."

Finally, it was time to take the new baby home—home for Thanksgiving! Two bright-eyed moppets hopped around like elves, peeking at the little, red squirm-worm of a brother in his bassinet.

William Stephen was named after both his father and the first Christian martyr. We agreed the name would look equally distinguished on a book binding or on some scientific award.

Steve was a happy child—seldom angry, or even cross. Uncle Bob's nickname for him, "Chili Pepper" (he was born nine months after Bill came home from Mexico) was never appropriate. Once Bob asked, "Does that baby ever cry? He's a year old and I've never heard him cry once."

We had bought a movie camera to chronicle Steve's birth and homecoming, and when he was five months old, we decided to shoot a typical day. "A Day in the Life of William Stephen—April 9, 1957" was a funny, lovable movie that gave us joy for many years. Bill started filming when Steve awoke. I could hear the baby talking and gurgling—laughing to himself about his fascinating fingers and toes and the wonders of the World of Crib. He never needed time to wade through the limbo from sleeping to waking; when he opened his eyes, he laughed and reached for life. I always thought my babies were the most beautiful in the morning when they stood in their little long white gowns, perhaps pee-soaked, but eagerly reaching for the new day.

Kathy and David, willing supporting actors, slid down the wide banister as they did every morning. Later, with each showing, they begged Bill to run the film backwards so they could defy gravity by sliding up the staircase. Plink, plink on the piano as Kathy passed it, and then the familiar skirmish over the seating at the breakfast nook.

"Ummm, prunes."

Stephen's dimpled baby hands almost connected with the jar of baby food, but his coordination was still a little unrefined.

"Look at his mouth. He's already tasting it before I put the spoon to his lips."

"Mama, that's not fair—you smeared his cheeks with prunes just so it would look good in Daddy's picture," protested Kathy.

At bath time—always fun—Steve gleefully splashed water, getting a drop on the lens. His firm pink bottom dimpled over the crook of my arm as I dried him briskly while the other children cooed to him lovingly.

And so the day went—happily, routinely, quickly. Night time had come. But we were not satisfied. There hadn't been a tear—not one all day. So instead of turning off the camera and giving thanks for a totally happy baby on a totally happy day, we plunked him down on a pallet and walked away, saying in our sage stupidity, "No day is complete without a tear; into each life some rain must fall." Finally, he started to cry, and we rushed back to take his picture before we comforted him.

Those funny precious baby days. Steve watched Captain Kangaroo before he was six months old. Every morning he waited for his favorite character, Tom Terrific, who, with his dog, Mighty Manfred, battled evil in the person of Crabby, Rotten-to-the-Core Appleton. As the dog smacked his mouth, Stephen would smack his own soft slobbery mouth in mimicry.

I think he drooled for two years. He had such juicy kisses. He would hold our faces to zero in on his mark—slobber, globber, smack.

"It must do something for a baby's psyche to see his mother wipe off all his kisses," I laughed.

When Steve was nineteen months old, we moved to Karnak, still in southern Illinois. The small rural town held little resemblance to its namesake in Egypt, but it was a fine place for the children to spend a couple of years. It was there they acquired a lifetime interest in identifying trees, and it was there we met the Taylors.

Donald Taylor and Stephen became storybook pals. They could hardly wait until breakfast to get to the sand pile, or the tricycle race track, or the myriad other projects two- and three-year-olds must attend to. They cemented their friendship early, and as far as either family ever knew, the children never had a cross word—a record-breaking achievement for little boys—or for anyone.

Two years later, in 1959, when Steve was only three and one-half years old, Bill was appointed to an inner-city church. Once again it was moving time. Few people envied our move to State Street United Methodist Church in East St. Louis, a city with a long history of labor problems, unemployment, and racial strife. We loved it. We were just across the river from St. Louis, Missouri, with all its glamour and the opportunities of a big city. Our congregation was warm and receptive, and the work of the church was meaningful and exciting.

Our house had a front lawn that ended in a slope that went four or five feet down to the sidewalk—a wonderful incline for children to roll down, log fashion. Late one afternoon Stephen bounced into the kitchen with a tiny bundle of auburn fur in his hands. He had been sitting on the lawn, waiting for his Daddy, when "a man in a red convertible just stopped and gave me this little puppy *for free.*"

I did not accept this free gift gracefully and muttered evil things about an adult who would do this to a little boy. "We'll keep her until morning and then to the pound she goes," I threatened.

However, the puppy had a cunning, winning way about her, and by morning, we had named her Coco, since she was the color of chocolate and could easily fit into a teacup. Steve learned it was one thing to be given a dog, but it was another to take care of it. Every time there was a puddle on the floor, someone would yell, "Stephen, come clean up after your pup." After a couple of weeks, he thought he'd solved his problem. He simply tied a ribbon around Coco's neck and gave her to his sister for a birthday gift. I don't think we let him off the hook that easily, despite his ingenious finagling; but luckily, Coco was soon housebroken. Regardless of who owned her, Coco really was David's dog and followed him merrily on his paper route. We all grieved when, one day several years later, she did not see the truck barreling down on her from around the corner.

I can't remember when Steve started to talk about his energy spells—what he dubbed those spurts of activity that vented his joy. It seems he always had them. He strove so hard to be like David that truly, from twenty months on, he ceased to be a baby and became a responsible little boy. He would be sitting quite still—I don't think Stephen ever sat completely still—then suddenly he'd jump up and say, "I've got an energy spell. I've got to hug someone fast!" With that, he'd come running pell-mell with a bear hug. Occasionally his playfulness could be drained off by pummeling a sofa pillow, but usually it was converted into squeezes and hugs for everyone within reach. He must have kept up those displays of exuberance for nine or ten years.

Steve always had such candor that it was sometimes disconcerting to live up to his scrutiny. He seemed to have been fresh-born—clear of all the hang-ups and red tape and sacred cows most of us drag around. Once his father was trying to encourage more church members to participate in family devotions. In the sanctuary one Sunday morning, the program leader asked, "Are there any questions as to how this venture can be better implemented?"

A little hand went up. To our well-deserved embarrassment a childish voice piped, "What can a little child do if his parents don't come in and pray with him?"

I remember the titter that went though the congregation, but after that I hope I was a little more careful to be there, along with God, to hear "a little child's prayers."

I started to teach school again when Steve was almost five, and since his kindergarten was only half days, a wonderful black woman, named Willie, stayed with him. Steve and Willie were great cronies, but one day he told her that she was fat. When she retorted that his mama and daddy weren't too thin either, he confided, "I can't help it if they are, for they're not my real parents. I'm adopted you know." Willie never again wholly believed we were Steve's natural parents, and occasionally she would ask leading questions, trying to find out the little scamp's true identity.

Steve had measles that year and was very sick for several days. He did not break out in the thick measly rash, and each morning as I inspected him, I'd say, "I don't know why you don't break out more."

I didn't realize how this sounded to him until one morning he slipped his hot little arms around my neck and said, "Oh, Mama, when I'm so sick already, why do you want me to get worse?"

When Steve got a little better, I returned to school and left him with Willie. The first day, when I came in the door after work, they each had the same tale to tell.

Steve had told Willie, "My Mama reads me a story when I feel this bad."

So Willie had read a story.

He continued, "My Mama holds my hands and rubs my feet when I feel this bad."

So Willie had held his hands and rubbed his feet.

Then he'd said (I wish I could have seen his eyes, for even as sick as he was and barely five, he must have known he was pushing her near the edge!) "My Mama puts my toes in her mouth and nibbles them when I'm this sick."

At this point, they each reported, Willie stood up and said, "Well, there's lots of things your Mammy does for you that you don't pay other people to do!"

It was not just Steve's babyhood that was pleasant. He bubbled with good humor as he grew. He was tender and gentle with all things that were little and weak. In first grade he became friend and protector to Joey, a tiny boy, almost albino in appearance, except for big china blue eyes. Steve walked Joey home and protected him from the rougher boys. He was, simply, Joey's friend.

Then there was Mark. Big, awkward, slow-moving Mark had no friends in our neighborhood except Stephen. Yet, all summer long Mark kept slipping into our garage and taking Steve's tricycle. At least three times a week Steve would come in fuming, "Mark stole my trike again!" Or we'd look out to see Mark's father wearily bringing the tricycle back. Mark, though very intelligent, had trouble adjusting to school. One afternoon, as the two little boys were walking home, he did some strange, fey little meanness to Steve, who burst into the living room sobbing. "If Mark loses me for a friend, he'll be in bad shape, for I'm all he's got!"

How do adults keep in touch with mirth and whimsy if there are no children about? Children have funny little games with tightly drawn-up rules that have no meaning for anyone else. When Stephen was three or four, he insisted we play such a game each time we came home from church. He would go to our car ahead of us and hide in the back seat or under a coat, or he would crouch down behind the driver—the possibilities were limited. Each time we were supposed to wonder aloud, "Where is Stephen?" "I don't know," someone else would answer. Finally, Daddy would say, "Well, we can't wait any longer; we'll just have to go home without him." Although we usually heard a little smothered snicker, we'd keep up the pretense until we were a block from home. As we turned in the drive, he'd spring up crying, "Here I am! I was here all the time!"

We had many church potlucks, and people were always generous with their leftovers. Once, when I'd been given a large bowl of combination salad, already slightly wilted from the vinegar dressing, I placed it on the dashboard when I got into the car. This time Steve was hiding under the dash, where his Papa would have had to be blind and deaf not to detect him. As Bill drove out of the parking lot he had to jam on his brakes suddenly, and the big plastic bowl of salad came lurching back, falling directly onto Steve's head! He came up in a crying, sputtering, and fuming rage, lettuce and tomatoes dripping down through his hair and a pepper ring over one ear! That was the final episode of that childishly simple charade.

When the boys were very small they made up another game that lasted for a couple of years. They played this game while we rode in the car, and the rules were simple. "Let's play like all the cars we meet are trucks and the trucks are airplanes." They didn't play that game often, thank goodness, and no one but Steve and Dave ever seemed to know when a game was on. The very silliness of the pretense annoyed Bill beyond reason (which might be one factor that kept the game going so long—it can't have been that much fun, even for them). One particular incident put a cap on it forever. From the back seat, one of the boys called out, "There's an airplane right in front of us!"

Poor old Dad had temporarily forgotten the game and, looking frantically this way and that, shouted, "Where? Where?"

He sputtered angrily while the rest of us convulsed with laughter. That ended that game forever.

Most of the time, however, Bill was able to experience the wonder of childhood through the children's eyes. Such simple things were fun when we did them with kids—things like piling into the car and racing off into the face of a dark cloud to meet the storm, thrilling to the excitement of the drought-quenching downpour, or driving to the high bluffs that overlooked the Mississippi to watch the giant ice floes as they churned and crashed against the banks.

Steve was in sixth grade the winter after we'd first seen "The King and I," yet he pranced out onto the ice and did the "Run-Eliza-Run" dance, skipping over those ice floes with liquid grace. That was the winter the Mississippi froze over at Alton several miles north of our home. Occasionally he embarrassed his brother and sister, but more often they appreciated his zaniness. Once, when he was cavorting in the rain after a month-long dry spell, Kathy ran to take his picture. He was our happy clown.

I did not realize that Stephen and David played more agreeably than most brothers, but Grandma, for one, never ceased to marvel at how well they got along. In a week at the farm she'd never heard a cross word, just excited chatter about their plans from the moment they woke up until they fell asleep—how to rig a swing in the hay loft, how to build an elaborate road system with overpasses and tunnels. There was never an end to the things they found exciting. One summer they built a treehouse in the big spreading sassafras on the front lawn. Its bark was still slick from where my little brother Alan Dale had climbed it, and parts of David's and Stephen's tree house can still be found in the old tree. As they grew, their projects were more grandiose. We all took rides on the pontoon raft they rigged up in Grandpa's pond—even Grandpa!

Of course the boys did have quarrels and occasionally a regular donnybrook, but I never knew them to carry a grudge or have a scrap that lasted. Once, when he was about four, in a sudden, uncharacteristic burst of fury, Steve picked up a little pop gun and shot David with it. We were appalled. Guns are used to shoot rats and targets but not people, so we put the toy gun away for thirty days—an entire month. Steve carefully monitored his own time, counting the days until he could play with his gun again. That incident gave us new insight into his strength of character; he did the same thing when we limited his watching of "The Three Stooges" on television. I hated the show, but because Steve was particularly fond of its zaniness, we decided to allow him two shows a week. That was before he started to school, and it was amazing to see him feed all the variables into his mental computer.

He'd reason aloud, "'Beaver' is on tonight, so I'll save the 'Stooges' until tomorrow," or "David will stay for Scouts tomorrow night and we can't play, so I'll save the 'Stooges' until then."

He policed himself far more closely than we'd have done.

After five happy years in East St. Louis, we moved to Belleville, Illinois, a rather austere town of 35,000, with a rich German heritage. The first week in June was always moving time. That gave me the entire summer to enjoy a closeness with the children that I would no longer have once school started, with new friends, and clubs, and activities. Belleville had a high standard of living and an excellent school system; Stephen, who was in fourth grade, and David, who was in seventh grade, both took German. Kathy was a gifted pianist even then, so she had no trouble finding a niche in high school. When Kathy was a senior, we were a host family to Julie Stanton, an American Field Service exchange student from Sydney, Australia. For a year there were four spirited children in our household.

The week the girls graduated from high school, we moved again—this time to Cairo, the most southern town in Illinois, at the confluence of the Ohio and Mississippi Rivers. Cairo was a proud old town that had thrived when the rivers were an important means of transportation. Now, the beautiful southern-style mansions looked neglected. Cairo was not a happy place to be in 1968 when we were there. There were too few jobs, almost no industry, and a great deal of racial strife. I taught kindergarten, and many mornings my pupils would tell me they had slept under the bed because of the shootings that took place the night before. Bill had been sent there, supposedly, to combine the two United Methodist churches, but it soon seemed obvious that neither congregation wanted to unite. Only one year later, with a sense of failure, as well as great relief, we received a call to move.

Dr. Lee C. Moorehead, senior minister at First United Methodist Church in Carbondale, requested Bill as his associate. We moved to Carbondale in 1969. Lee Moorehead and his gracious wife, Betty, along with the entire church, made us feel loved and welcome. The warm, friendly congregation of about twelve hundred members was almost equally divided between old family residents and those associated with Southern Illinois University, both faculty and students. Betty and Lee had two children at home—Becky, in high school, and Tim, in seventh grade. Tim Moorehead and Steve, who was in eighth grade, became friends the night they met and remained so forever. Although Tim moved with his family to Green Bay, Wisconsin, in 1972, whenever the boys met after that, it was as if they'd never been apart.

Carbondale had been my home town, and our entire family loved it from the start. For the first time in twenty-three years we were near family; my parents lived just a mile away by the road, or half that distance if we cut through the woods, the pasture, and the soybean field.

We built a home on part of the land Mom and Dad bought when they were married. We all loved the house long before it was a reality. We could envision it, full-grown, when we tramped through the woods looking for a site. The rooms were already warm and welcoming as we laid out limbs and sticks to outline their dimensions. We planted daffodils where the stone walk would be. We would have a fireplace big enough to use all the special rocks we'd lugged home from every vacation.

We wanted a larger house than our purse allowed, so we did much of the work ourselves. But even the hard finishing work done by Bill and the boys did not often dampen their spirits. The children seemed to exult in country living, even that first year when we had to walk in from the blacktop when our road bed gave way and even that first cold winter when we moved into an unfinished, but promising, structure. We moved on January 3, 1970, a day when the temperature was a chilling zero degrees. We had to get to the upstairs bedrooms by climbing a ladder, and there was no water, except in the bathroom.

Once I overheard David mutter, "If I can just keep pretending we're on a campout!"

We never did hear any real complaint, though we did hear a squeal late one night as Kathy tramped through the mud after a late glee club rehearsal and almost collided with a 'possum that was scurrying along the same path.

Our life as a minister's family was lived in what others called a goldfish bowl. But we believed we led a perfectly normal existence—just one with an added dimension. I think all of us felt we were part of a larger, caring family—one that lent stability and relevance to our own close-knit clan. However, because we were a minister's family, other people's needs often took priority over family wants and schedules. We learned to cherish time as our most jealously guarded possession. I was always conscious of this garnering of our time together, this hoarding of our hours. Family trips and vacations were important parts of our lives.

The year Julie lived with us we had a delightful two weeks in Florida when Bill was guest minister at a church near Miami. We tried to absorb all that any place had to offer, so in Florida we went to the coral reefs, where the boys steered the glass-bottomed boats. We went shell hunting and coconut gathering in the early mornings. We watched the sunrises and the sunsets over the ocean, we marveled at the tides, and we went barracuda fishing. Never have fish tasted so good as that catch of barracuda, cleaned and filleted at 11:00 p.m., fried to a turn, and devoured at midnight!

But by eight or nine the next morning, as soon as I began to stir, I caught a whiff of a strong, offensive odor and hurried outside to see if the garbage had been overturned. Nine big fish skeletons, complete with tails and ugly prehistoric heads, swung from the clothes line!

Steve!

Of course, it had to be Steve! Who else?

Before we dispatched the bones to odor-proof bags, we took pictures of that smelly line of wash. We also pickled a couple of the heads to take home in a glass jar to show his classmates just how the bottom tooth of the barracuda actually fastens into the upper jaw, giving it a truly vicious bite.

Minivacations were another carefully planned part of our lives. Family members took turns selecting a site within a fifty-mile radius and assuming some responsibility for planning the day. Those times were kept simple and flexible—we could each take a book, or a pet, or, occasionally, a friend. We ate out—often picnicked. We took along games if we wanted, and we usually found that someone had included Steve's melodica, so we had accompaniment for the endless rounds and choruses we sang. Kids are supposed to hate doing things with their parents, so Bill and I could scarcely believe our good fortune—even the teenagers seemed to value those trips.

Bill planned one day with such flair that we referred to it forever after simply as "Daddy's Day." Memorial Day, 1971, exercising his parental prerogative, Bill flagrantly disregarded all limitations and almost quadrupled the fifty-mile limit before the day was over. But what a day it was! Not only Stephen and David, but Kathy and her soon-to-be husband, Russ, piled into the car.

We drove past miles of blooming hedge-roses and honeysuckle. There was the scrumptious taste of scrambled eggs and sausage cooked over an open fire, the echoing sound of woodpeckers getting their own breakfast, and the breathtaking sight of a scarlet tanager that allowed us to view his striking plumage. That was also the first day we saw a gallinule, the Emmett Kelly of all the wading birds, poking here and there in the dark green vegetation. We had not known that such plants as spatter dock and water hyacinths grew in southern Illinois, nor that we had palisades that could rival those famous ones along the Hudson River.

We gawked and climbed and poked, and when we finally had to drive on, the kids rolled down the windows and sat on the doors, hanging their long bodies out so as not to miss a single towering bluff. Their "hello-o-oes" rang out in the stillness, and the echoes reverberated, amplified by the surroundings, seemingly reinforced by the sound waves, until they reached back—all the way back—to the young red men themselves who had once inhabited Pine Hills. We arrived home a little too late and a little too tired, but it had been a wonderful day.

Besides our minivacations, we had long planned to drive south of the border for a fantastic vacation together. Now, at last, in 1973, it was going to happen. Christmas in Mexico. Our excitement mounted each week. In midsummer, when the idea really began to take shape, we began to read books and magazines and all the travel brochures we could find on Mexico. On my desk were a Spanish-English dictionary and a friend's practical, if somewhat optimistic, book, *Mexico on Five Dollars a Day*.

Everyone was going—even Kathy and Russ. This might be the last year when all our schedules were free simultaneously. Later there might be a baby to keep Russ and Kathy home. David was twenty and Steve was almost seventeen. This was clearly the year—now or never. We all agreed.

As we planned, I looked back over the years.

When Kathy was five or six years old, I exclaimed as I tied her sash, "Kathy, you're so tall; you're getting to be such a big girl!"

There must have been some dismay in my voice, for she said, "But Mama, don't you love big girls too?"

And then there were David and Steve. As they grew older and their personalities began to gel, they got along even better than they had as children; each had a healthy respect for the different strengths of the other. They seemed to complement each other, and Bill and I would say smugly to each other, "Aren't we lucky to have two such fine boys, and isn't it nice to have one of each kind?"

We would say, "Dave was born middle-aged and Stephen won't be middle-aged when he's seventy!" We recognized subtle and exciting differences—differences that led to strengths and that made a strong pair, just as the perfect but different fingers of the right hand lock into the equally perfect but different fingers of the left hand.

David and Steve were young men now, and the plans grew more exciting—the Appalachian Trail next year, rafting the Yellowstone, backpacking through the Rockies, climbing Half-Dome—maybe homesteading in Alaska, maybe a lifetime together preserving some rare wilderness.

My thoughts turned to Stephen. My brother, Alan Dale, had died just before he was thirteen, and at Steve's thirteenth birthday supper he had confided, "I never thought I'd live to my thirteenth birthday. I thought I would be the one in the family who would die when he was twelve, like Uncle Alan did."

I wondered where this idea had come from. Steve was not a morose child, and I never heard him mention it again, yet the idea had been there, hovering in his mind. It had not been a great fear, yet he seemed glad and relieved that somehow he had eluded fate.

Then, the night he was fourteen, he cried. I don't remember anything else about the day, but that night, November 9, 1970, when we were going through the ritual we still referred to as "tucking him in," his eyes filled with tears.

His voice quivered a little, and he said, "Mama, I don't want to be fourteen. I'm not ready yet. When I was thirteen I could act like a kid or I could be grown up. Fourteen is so old. I don't want to be fourteen yet."

We talked; I think we prayed together about the fullness, the roundness, the completeness of life with its varied gifts. I remember that we felt good together, and he seemed happy to be fourteen when I left his room. Maybe all he had needed was to be able to reveal a little of his vulnerability before he reached eagerly once more for the years to come. Life, with all the promise of its unfolding, lay before him.

The week of Steve's sixteenth birthday, I remember again being in his room and listening to him ponder about his age. He had spent his birthday in New York City, on a tour of the U.N. While they were there, he and some friends had a posh dinner in a big restaurant.

But later he said to me, "You know, I don't think there is a better age to be than sixteen, and I can't think of a place in the world I'd rather spend my sixteenth year than Carbondale, Illinois."

He glowed with contentment and joy.

It was a good town. It was a good year. Sixteen was a heartbreakingly tender, beautiful, and promising age to be.

Oh, Steve, just as the snowflake melts, even as I hold it in my hand and try to describe its beauty, no paper can capture and hold the image of your zest and drive.

We are at the north entrance of the hospital. It has taken less than fifteen minutes.

LOOK AT ME, MAMA

A nurse with a wheelchair waited for us at the hospital entrance. Stephen's pain was very bad; it had been made worse by the ride. The nurse whisked him down the corridor to be examined while Kathy and I sat, alone and scared, in the waiting room.

October 7, 1973—a Sunday morning—Stephen, our effervescent son of sixteen (almost seventeen) years, had taken his test for certification as a licensed scuba diver. I groused a little when he first told me that the class would meet on a Sunday. So many activities seemed to encroach upon the Sabbath, our day for worship and family.

When I protested that he would miss church, Steve explained with exaggerated patience, "Oh, Mom, it's just this once. I've got to take the certification test to get credit for the course. Passing this test means I can get my oxygen tank filled up at any marina in the country." He went on. "We'll be put through a lot of tests to demonstrate our ability and skills at various depths and under stress conditions. It's apt to be pretty tough. I don't know why the instructor planned to do it on Sunday, but it's not going to kill me to miss church one time."

I finally agreed, and Bill, David, and I went on to church. It hardly seemed possible that the scuba diving course was over. It seemed only a matter of days since it had begun in late August. Steve had long been interested in scuba diving. He and Tim had done a lot of diving without benefit of oxygen, using only their bursting lungs and whatever air they could take down with them in plastic milk containers. I think I was relieved that he was learning to do it right at last.

The diving class had met two evenings a week. I remember casual chatter about changed schedules and a little more hurry over evening meals, but overriding it all was the general feeling of excitement and pleasure Steve felt.

Sometimes it is hard to recall the tight structure of those days. We all were so very busy. I occasionally wonder—did we ever look at each other—really look? I thought we did. I thought we regarded each other deeply.

And yet, in retrospect, I ask myself, "If I looked, why did I not see the black cloud that loomed on our horizon? Was there no sign?"

When Steve was a freshman, he played Howie Newsome, the newsboy in Thornton Wilder's *Our Town.*

My mother had said, "Oh, that's too sad for high school kids. Steve did a wonderful job—the kids all did—but it was the wrong play. It was far too sad!"

I had felt that the play was exquisite and tender, and in some deep significant way, it taught much about our own lives.

Later, when the play was on television, I listened to each line with new sensitivity. How must it have seemed to Steve, a boy of thirteen, as he lost himself in the character he played? What had he felt? What had any of those young people felt as they played roles that dealt with life and death—full as they were of life, and confident as they must have been that death was far away? I cried, with new insight, at the poignancy of each role. How had this line affected him? What had he thought about that idea?

It seemed to me that the heart of the play was in Emily's words, when she was allowed to live once more the day of her twelfth birthday—"Mama, look at me. Mama, I'm here now. Won't you stop and look at me, Mama?"

I thought I looked. I thought I saw. But I did not look enough. I did not see enough. I used to whisper into the ears of my infants, telling them how lovely and delightful they were.

I always ended with, "And Mamas can tell. Mamas can see."

When we moved into our new house—the only house we ever lived in that was not a parsonage—the interior was unfinished. Late one night, in a fit of whimsy as we waited for Dave and Bill, Steve and I drew pictures and cartoons on the unfinished walls. Everyone liked them so much that even when the walls were plastered, Kathy and I drew cartoons all over the white wall of our downstairs hallway. One of our favorites showed a woman shaking her husband and saying, "Wake up, Donald. It's 1970 and the children are all gone." I felt a little like that that fall of 1973. Now that Steve was a senior in high school, Dave was in college, and Kathy out of school and married, we had so little time together.

Sometimes I felt like a pagan, fearing that the gods, jealous of our happiness, would strike us down. Words like "fleeting" and "elusive" were always in my awareness, followed quickly by "enjoy." Enjoy! Enjoy! Children are gone so quickly.

"Mama, look at me!"

I remember looking at Steve that fall, thinking he looked tired. His schedule was too crowded. I would be glad when the scuba diving course was over. It was not right for the young to be so busy. When those two nights a week were free, perhaps he wouldn't be so tired. There were work, school, and church—he was assistant director of the youth choir and president of the youth fellowship. Being drum major also meant extra practices for parades and the games.

A couple of weeks before, he had fallen asleep in the parlor at church, waiting for the second service to be over. His youth choir sang at early church, so after Sunday School he usually went with some of his friends to get milk and doughnuts or just walked around town, talking and waiting until we could all go home together. But that Sunday, everyone had other plans, so he just lay down on the sofa and went to sleep.

I remember looking at him and thinking that he looked thin. The occasional times that thinness made a dent in my consciousness, I had a pat explanation—he looked thin because he'd shot up so tall. He'd grown more than ten inches that year. In the pictures of Kathy's wedding the summer before, he was just as tall as I was; but here he was, a year later, almost as tall as his daddy! Bill and Steve and Dave all measured themselves on the door facing, and they were almost the same height. Six feet—all three of them! Size twelve shoes—all three of them! But Steve had never been thin until then. He was always the healthiest looking of the children.

"Mama, look at me."

I looked at Steve in his diving gear when he came home from class, and he looked so thin, so young, and so tired. Nothing had ever seemed to daunt him before. Never before had he seemed to have to work so hard to keep up. I remember him gray and cold and tired. He stayed in the water until he was chilled, and it would take him an hour to get warm after he got home. After he had rested a little—and maybe eaten something—he would tell us about the evening's class and demonstrate the equipment.

Once he said, "Slip these on, Mom. See if you can walk in them."

He and Dave laughed as I put on the long black flippers and clumped and spraddled across the kitchen floor. Then Dave tried them, looking like a bigger-than-life frog in a Disney cartoon.

"Man! I never realized the belts were this heavy."

David hefted the wide belt with the great leaden buckle that allowed the divers to sink. "I think I might get suspicious of a teacher who strapped one of these things on me and threw me into the water."

I gasped at that, for I could hardly lift the weighted band that had girdled Steve's skinny frame. He'd never looked skinny before—slender and lithe, but not skinny.

"I've read about gangsters who got rid of their enemies by giving them cement overshoes," David said. "But a whole class overboard at one whack—that's something else!"

The very fact that Steve's exhaustion was in such contrast to his usual energetic spunkiness made his total wrung-out appearance almost humorous. One night I looked at the skinny kid, steeped in weariness and slumped on the floor with his back to the cabinet, and I gently teased, "Lo, how the mighty have fallen!"

David interrupted. "Mom, I hear this is a really hard course and Steve is the youngest and the lightest person in the class. Some of the other guys are in my classes in college, and since they know Steve's my brother they told me the instructor kind of rides Steve—expects more out of him—makes him stay under longer, go down deeper—things like that."

"Why would he do that? Single out Steve, I mean?"

"Oh, I don't know. Just because he's the youngest kid of the outfit I guess, and well—you know how 'game' Steve is."

"Game?" Was that the word for him? David spoke as if he didn't like for the teacher to needle Steve—and yet as if he could understand it and even feel a little pride in it, too. Steve, the plucky, cocksure, younger brother.

But then the class was over. When we came home from church that October morning, Steve was already there. He didn't feel well. He had a severe headache, and he had been lying down.

"Is this normal?" I asked. "Diving's never given you a headache before."

The instructor had explained to Steve that he had experienced a sinus squeeze—not common, but not unheard of either.

"What's a sinus squeeze?" I asked. "I never heard of such a thing."

"Mr. B. says it's something that happens to some people when they go down pretty deep. He says it doesn't happen often, but there's no need to be alarmed."

"When did you know this sinus squeeze thing had happened?"

Steve gave me a rather baleful look. "I knew something was wrong right away because my head hurt so bad. Also, there was about a teaspoonful of blood in my mask when I took it off. Now, Mom, Mr. B. said not to worry."

Cheryl, a teaching colleague of mine who had become a close family friend, came to visit on that afternoon. Steve called her his "big sister." I knew Steve's pain must be very bad, because when Cheryl joined us for dinner at Grandma's, he kept very still, hardly even talking. Later, he passed up a bike-hike through Giant City State Park. He had planned to ride his new ten-speed bike of which he was especially proud because he had bought it with money he had earned. But his head hurt so bad that after resting, he settled for driving slowly around the park in the Valiant—the little brown car he considered his own.

Monday, October 8, was Columbus Day, so Steve and I both had a holiday from school. I was relieved about Steve's pain when

I awoke with a headache, too. My throbbing, dizzy, rheumy head convinced me that we both had a virus—one that just happened to coincide with Steve's sinus squeeze. My pain made his seem casual, ordinary. We decided it would be a good day to bring in the fish for the winter; we might as well be miserable all the way.

Steve had wanted the big bow window in his room to overlook a fish pond, so we'd put in a pool, surrounded by a rock garden. It proved nicer than any of us expected, and nearly every summer morning, spellbound by the colors of some prize guppies, I would sit quietly and let the fish take food from my fingers.

Once Stephen said, "Mom, I think you're the only one of us who has the temperament to sit and watch fish for an hour. I'll bet you know each one by name."

The fish had done well that summer. A lovely strain was developing from the offspring of a red-gold female guppy and the fancy-tailed males, so we separated these into one small tank for selective breeding. The job became endlessly more involved, and Steve had to make two trips into town to buy more units.

I will never forget the sight of Steve that day, grabbing his head as he bent over that stirred-up, smelly pond, scooping up fish. That last work we did together—that whole scene—seemed like madness later, but then he seemed only mildly ill, and the hint of winter could already be felt.

The next morning—Tuesday—my headache was gone, and as usual before I left for school, I tiptoed into the boy's rooms to bid them a quick goodbye—just a touch, a light kiss on the forehead, a squeeze of the foot, a gentle ripple of a water bed, always ending with, "Have a good day."

But that morning I left with a heavy heart. Steve still did not feel like going to school, so the chance that he and I had picked up the same bug seemed remote. Bill didn't feel well either. His chest was so sore he was having trouble breathing. His difficulty probably came from his strenuous work the previous Saturday—cutting up a dead oak tree. Saturday's breakfast table talk still seemed humorous.

"This morning I'm renting a chainsaw and by noon or a little after we can have that big dead oak tree down and cut into lengths and stacked. Maybe we can use it to put a rail fence down the lane. You boys can. . . ."

Never before had Bill met such adamant, unanimous protests.

Dave said, "Dad, did you forget that I'm going to Fountain Bluff today with my orienteering class? I have to meet them in about thirty minutes."

I chimed in, "Today is the day of the big flea market in the Arena. I want to go there this morning, and this afternoon I have to meet with the planning committee of the senior-high camp program. I can't help."

Between hurried bites, Steve said, "I've got the whole day planned, too, Dad. Mom, I'll take you to the flea market if you'll promise me you won't stay but an hour, and then I'm supposed to meet the guys at McAndrew Stadium to play football. Tonight is Debbie's birthday party. I have to get her gift this afternoon. Sorry, Dad, but my plans are pretty well set. This will be the last day I have to play."

Even then, before there was any hint of trouble, his words sounded a little strange. Not prophetic or sepulchral at all, yet they hung over the table for an instant, like a thought balloon.

I felt a little sorry for Bill—after all he'd had plans too. He acted a little miffed and finally said, "Well, I guess I'll do it myself."

"Yes, you're going to cut down that huge tree all by yourself, I guess."

I was trying to tease him out of his disappointment. None of us dreamed he could do all that work by himself. When I got home Saturday afternoon, the tree was down, cut, and stacked.

At school all day that Tuesday, I worried about both Bill and Steve. But when I got home that evening Steve seemed better. David, a junior at Southern Illinois University, was out working at McDonald's. Bill must be better, too, for he was staying in town to have dinner with the executive committee of the Kiwanis Club; he had just been elected president.

Steve and I were playing a lazy game of Scrabble after supper, when the phone rang. Bill was at the hospital emergency room, and we needed to go get him! He had developed breathing problems and, afraid it might be his heart, had gone to the hospital. They gave him such a heavy sedative that he couldn't drive home. Steve and I drove to the hospital to get Bill. Thinking he was going to be just a chauffeur, Steve went in his bare feet. However, no orderly was available to help his father to the car, and Steve had to go in to get him. I remember how embarrassing that was for a sixteen year old. Fortunately, Bill's problem was the result of the work he had done on Saturday. His rib cage was sore from a lot of muscle and cartilage bruising.

We were so concerned about Bill that Steve's condition took second place. The next morning—Wednesday—when I went to his room to tell him goodbye, Steve was feeling better.

"Be sure and put my drum major's whistle where I can find it," he said. "I'm going to school today and I'll need it."

I told him I'd leave his whistle by the bushel of Grimes Golden apples Grandpa had put beside our path, and, as I left, I called, "Bye. See you tonight."

"See you tonight."

"See you in the morning."

In our busy lives, the boys worked late at night, and I left early in the mornings, so I often left notes for them—a word of greeting, a funny cartoon, a message that told where a bite of favorite food could be found or some shared news of the day. Frequently, no more than, "How was your day? It's good you're home. See you in the morning. Love."

"See you in the morning."

That was our password, and we slipped it like a silver amulet from one member to the other—a loving ritual.

Months later I found one of those notes among some papers in Steve's room. I had tried to describe a rainbow I'd seen, flung across a great coppery sky. I suspect he kept it because it was written on the back of a *National Geographic* ad for a book about the Great American West—a book he might have wanted to order. The note was not unique, but at the time I found it, the words had taken on a new significance.

"I'll see you in the morning."

I'd scribbled as an afterthought, "That's a comforting thought, isn't it?"

Oh, my darlings, I thought I looked. I thought I saw. But even I did not appreciate the sacredness of our everyday.

After what seemed a long time, we saw Steve and the doctor coming down the hall from the X-ray room.

I looked at Steve, then. Anxiously, I noted that his face had a certain setness I did not like—the planes of his face, the very skin over his cheekbones, appeared leathery.

"Our tests were not conclusive, Mrs. Warner. You see, Steve passed out every time we tried to get a picture."

Surely the doctor did not smile or take this lightly, yet that is the way I remember his ridiculous statement.

"We tried several times, but all our findings were inconclusive. I advise you to take him to your own doctor tomorrow."

I remember that the bill was twelve dollars.

"Twelve dollars!" I exclaimed on the way home. "I didn't know you could get a splinter removed for twelve dollars."

Steve tried to smile as he commented dryly, "Well, at least I didn't cost you much."

I don't know when I had sense enough to grow angry over that emergency room examination. I remember being nonplused, and on the way home we discussed how they would have handled the x-rays if his back had been broken or if he'd been unconscious. Didn't they have tables where patients could lie down and be rolled to x-ray? Why had I stood like a ninny, accepting what they told me?

Yet, in some foolish way, I felt a little relieved. The doctor hadn't seemed too alarmed—not even concerned enough to take a proper x-ray! Was I reassured because he didn't send for the helicopter and pack us off to St. Louis the minute he looked at Steve? I guess that was the reaction I had feared. I was relieved when he was treated in such a casual, routine manner. A shred—a remnant—of the age-old awe and superstition with which lay people have always regarded the witch doctor must still remain, despite the

fact that it was October 10, 1973. The shadow of the Shaman had
fallen upon my child. It would hold the darkness at bay.

A virgin ice pack, still in its original box and demurely folded
away like the blossom of a Jimpson weed, had become a leaky sieve
over the years. I remember fashioning a make-shift ice pack to
replace it—a plastic zip-lock bag filled with crushed ice and tucked
into two new red velour washcloths I sewed together. I basted the
washcloths with blue thread. Such odd bits and details stick in my
mind when whole days are seared away.

Steve wanted to sleep on the sofa in the living room that night.
He complained that his water bed had been cold the last few nights;
he had added a heater for it to his Christmas list. He assured me he
would be all right; David would be on the first floor, too. I put a pan
and a big spoon on the floor beside him. He could use them to call
if he needed anything. With some misgivings, I went upstairs.

About 2:00 a.m., I heard a noise. When I came down to
investigate, I was horrified to find Steve crawling on his hands and
knees.

I rushed to him. "Son, why didn't you call me?"

"I didn't want to bother you, Mom." His eyes were glazed with
pain. "I was afraid I'd pass out if I stood up."

"HELL HATH ENLARGED ITSELF"

The doctor's office opened at 10:00 a.m., and we were there waiting. Steve was still in severe pain and was slightly nauseated. The slab-like, leathery look of his face had not changed from the night before. No one ever explained that expression to me—perhaps it was just due to lack of facial movement because of the pain. But I remembered seeing it once before—on the face of my young brother, Alan, as he lay dying of post-vaccinal encephalitis. A mask on a usually facile and mobile face is frightening.

Steve's doctor, Sidney Smith, was a pediatrician who had opened his practice in Carbondale a year or two after we moved there. Sid, his wife, Alice, and their two little girls became our friends and were active members of the church.

Steve didn't see Sid professionally often—the usual physical examinations for school and camp and an occasional sore throat—but, as Sid discovered later when he went back over the records, on nearly every visit, Steve made some reference to headaches. These headaches had never been severe enough to keep Steve from work or school, and when Steve mentioned them, Sid usually asked whether he had been wearing his glasses. And Steve often hadn't—confessing that he had broken them wrestling or playing football or basketball.

Sid always had the same admonition. "Young man, get those glasses fixed and wear them!"

Kathy, sitting beside me now, tense and worried, had occasionally complained of headaches when she was a teenager, and I cannot remember when headaches were not a part of my adult life. I had thought Steve's headaches were like mine.

"Normagene."

I jumped at the sound of my name and looked up to see Sid standing there.

"I would like Dr. Hamilton to look at Steve. He's a fine pediatrician here at the clinic. Is that all right?"

"Yes. Certainly. Whatever you think," I murmured. "But what is it? What do you think is wrong?"

"I'll talk to you after I've consulted with Dr. Hamilton."

Kathy and I stood just outside Sid's office. We could see the doctors as they conferred soberly. First one and then the other gazed long and deep into Steve's eyes, down that awesome tunnel called the optic nerve, to the very brain itself. I could not hear what they said, but I could see them nod occasionally, as if in agreement.

Finally, Sid came out. "Normagene, is Bill with you?"

This was the first of many times I was to watch a doctor look for my husband and see his eyes rove here and there—a little embarrassed or reluctant or sorrowful about what he had to tell me. It became a ritual I dreaded, for each time it was followed by some horrific diagnosis or prognosis or the request for some dangerous but necessary procedure—something so terrible that a mother could not be expected to stand it alone. Parents would need each other to cling to while they listened.

"No, he's home sick, too," I said, babbling something about cartilage and ribs. My voice trailed away thinly.

"Would you come in here, then, Normagene? I want to talk to you about Steve."

"Dr. Hamilton and I agree that something is causing pressure on Steve's optic nerve."

From then on I heard only disjointed bits of conversation.

"Choked discs are very evident. We both feel . . . in the brain . . . perhaps a tumor . . . an abscess could also cause. . . ."

At that moment, I felt as if I had turned to wood—a thing that somehow was still imbued with pulse and cold sweat. I prayed, "Oh, God—let it be an abscess. Abscesses can be drained. They are like boils, aren't they?"

Sid's voice went on. "Get him to St. Louis as soon as possible. I'll call to make sure they are expecting you. I'll have Steve's x-rays ready. You can take them with you and give them immediately to Dr. Guise, who is one of the best neurosurgeons in the country. I don't think an ambulance is needed, but I want him there as soon as possible."

I don't remember the details of the next hour. Did I call Bill, or did Kathy? She did most of the calling, reaching my parents and attempting to reach David who was not due at McDonald's until the next shift.

Two things I *do* remember. The first was calling the Morgans, steady, reliable friends from church, and asking to borrow their station wagon. It was the biggest, newest car I could think of. Their boys, Bob and Dan, were the ages of David and Steve. Steve had spent many hours shooting baskets at their house after school, while he waited for me to pick him up.

The second thing I remember was walking to a desk and saying firmly, "I'll need a pillow and some blankets. You see, we're taking my son to St. Louis from here. They think Steve has a tumor or an abscess in his brain."

It was unusual for me to behave that way—expecting rules to be laid aside—but this thing that had happened to Stephen was so horrible it never occurred to me that others would not comply. Mealy-mouthed and circumspect all my life, I suddenly was galvanized to take immediate action. We must get Steve to St. Louis—quickly.

It was as if my humanity had been compressed by fear into some dense and inanimate machine. I sorted essential from unessential with computer-like precision, and what was essential was what would get Steve help as soon as possible.

As I turned back to the examining room, Steve lifted his great brown eyes to me—eyes almost black with pain and haunted by unasked questions.

"Well?" he asked.

I leaned down and gripped his shoulders as he lay on the table. "Darling," I said, "Sid and Dr. Hamilton see something in the optic nerve that makes them think you have an abscess or a tumor in your brain. They want us to go to St. Louis right away. We're taking you to see a man at St. Luke's Hospital, and he'll take care of it."

Take care of "it." Even as I said the words, Steve and I both heard the terrible ring of them—an awful echo. "It" was unknown and unidentifiable. "It" was in that most vulnerable of all the parts of the body. "It" could surely kill.

In that first dread encounter, the evil that beset us was personified. The sound of my voice, like tolling, hung in the air in that little room—like the dialogue of some macabre comic strip.

Tucking Steve into a wheelchair—attempting to move him without jostling—served to steady my hands and somehow steadied my mind for the tasks ahead. As I wheeled him out to the lobby, Kathy came running to us.

I was amazed by the evenness of our voices as we talked, and especially by the calm resoluteness of my young son. Not once—not then nor in the months to come when he absorbed shock after shock that should have felled strong, brave adults—did I ever hear him ask, "Why me?"

"There is nothing we can do except walk through it," I said. Kathy nodded.

"It." There "it" was again. Through the weeks and months to come, we watched "It" grow from a menacing incubus into the full-fledged maniacal demon that slew us.

"Hell hath enlarged itself" is a frightening passage from Isaiah. "It," our Adversary, our Hell, would enlarge itself daily, gorging on its own venom. But we did not know that yet.

As we wheeled Steve out of the clinic, we saw Bill and David walking toward us. Welcome sight! Later, Bill explained that he had been at home watching the World Series when Sid called with his frightening diagnosis. Then, Kathy phoned to tell him about our plans to borrow the Morgan's car and ask if he felt like making the trip with us. If so, he was to meet us immediately with the station wagon.

Kathy had called David at work, and there he was, beside his brother, pushing the wheelchair. My parents were there, too, looking tense and apprehensive. A detached part of my mind remembered their own race to St. Louis with my brother, twenty-three years before. A desperate race, to no avail.

But this was 1973. Medicine had made great strides. It wouldn't be that way again, I told myself. Angry, I pushed all other thoughts and comparisons away.

Our leave-taking was fearful and poignant. Farewells can be hard, but haste was our friend as we bade my parents and Kathy and Russ goodbye. The trip seemed to take hours, though the clock showed only ninety minutes. Steve stretched out in the back of the station wagon, on the pillow and blanket I had commandeered; David knelt on one side of him and I on the other, to support him and try to keep him from moving. The least motion caused him great pain. Dave and I sat so rigid that our rib cages were sore for days afterward.

Sid had given Steve a strong sedative, but we were three-fourths of the way to St. Louis before it helped. Then he opened his eyes—eyes that were clearer of pain than they had been for almost four days—and said, "I'm hungry." He had not been able to eat for forty-eight hours.

It seems strange, but we stopped. I don't remember what he wanted to eat. It was something quite ordinary, but the restaurant didn't have it, so I bought Jello—or was it ice cream? Steve ate most of it and said it tasted good.

Huddled there in the back of the speeding station wagon, we placed each spoonful to his lips with all the awesome ritualism of our own Last Supper. We were acutely aware of what "It" could do; that small meal was a sacrament, pure and meaningful.

Watching David then and in the months to come, as he looked at Steve, as he touched him gingerly and did the few little things that he could do to help, I was reminded of the kids with little animals—the way they cooed as they cradled soft baby chickens under their chins. How gentle they were with an occasional tiny rabbit the dog brought in, or with a fallen fledgling bird. When Stephen was very little, we told him that he sometimes purred. He still had that same little purring burr when he spoke to the very old—not patronizing, but respectful and gentle. Now Steve had become the recipient of just such tenderness. The rough-and-tumble little brother had become a wounded bird—infinitely helpless, infinitely precious.

We were met at St. Luke's Hospital by a retinue of doctors and other medical staff. Steve received glucose while he was still in the hall. I seem to remember a doctor at each corner of the gurney, examining him as he was being wheeled to his room. We were impressed by the speed and apparent skill with which the staff tackled his problem. Odd details stand out in my mind—the muttered scolding of a nurse as she criticized the way a doctor inserted the IV. There was blood on the sheet, and that distressed her.

Experts probed and prodded Steve. They did not say much. There were just the sounds of sages making sage marks in their books. We sat in Steve's room, tense and still, as the doctors talked to him. I tried not to interrupt. I did not like it when, on registration day at school, a mother would answer when I asked a student, "What's your name?"

"This child of mine is a sharp young man," I thought. "Allow him the dignity of answering their questions. Let him play the man's role while he can." I snapped the door shut on that line of thinking. I refused to let forebodings—like a swarm of gray buzzards circling, circling above me—settle in.

The experts questioned Steve about his headaches. Bill and I winced with pain and guilt. We had not realized they were so frequent.

"When did the pain become severe?"

"Sunday, following my scuba diving test."

"How far down did you go?"

"About forty-five feet."

"That's pretty deep, isn't it?"

"Not really. A friend of mine and I went down over sixty feet without a tank. The instructor kept me under almost twice as long as the other boys, though. That might make a difference."

"Why was that?"

"I don't know. He said he was putting me through the stress test. There was about a spoonful of blood in my mask when I took it off.

He said not to worry about it—it was caused by something called a sinus squeeze. He told me I might have a headache for a few hours, but it wasn't serious."

"Doctor," I interrupted, "is there anything about firecrackers that could throw light on his headaches? An allergy to gunpowder or something? Two or three years ago he had a severe headache the day after July Fourth."

The examining doctors did not pause, or even respond. It was as if they had not heard my tentative and timid questions.

"It probably has no significance anyway," I finished lamely.

The woman who, so short a time ago, was galvanized to do battle, had turned meek in the presence of experts—awed by their apparent knowledge and skill. The tiger was once again a rabbit.

Oh, my son, I look at you now as they query you about every phase of your health, and I cannot swallow the lump of fear that chokes me. Your very breathing out and breathing in is not too small to be taken note of. They go over your beautiful body with their skilled fingers and their little rubber mallets. Often they murmur things to each other that your daddy and I cannot hear.

After a lengthy examination, the doctors conferred like players in a huddle. When they turned to us, they wore those guarded, enigmatic medical smiles that seem designed to instill confidence but stopped somewhere short of creating actual hope. The best they could tell us was that there was no conclusive evidence—they needed to run extensive tests the next day.

We felt some release from the dread that gripped us. Surely if something had been there, they would have found it. These people were "the best." Sid had said so.

Bill and Dave and I spent that night with Chuck and Barbara Cogswell. The Cogswells had been members of Epworth United Methodist Church in Belleville, Illinois, when Bill was pastor there. Through the years our friendship had grown beyond the usual closeness of pastor and parishioner—as they demonstrated in the months to come. When Bill phoned to tell them about Stephen, they insisted we stay with them. Belleville, a suburb of greater St. Louis, was about fifteen miles from the hospital. And so, that first night, after we left Steve alone in his hospital room, we drove across the Mississippi River, to sleep at the Cogswell home. To sleep? Maybe a little, in the flat, hollow hours just before dawn. But mostly we talked and cried and remembered and hoped. There had been many happy, golden, funny years when our children were growing up together; many shared theological discussions and counseling sessions. Now it was hard to tell who was preacher and who was layman. Our son was ill—desperately, perhaps mortally, ill.

Again and again, Bill and I went over what the doctors had said, and we asked ourselves a thousand times how we could have missed symptoms of something so horrible. How could Steve have been so beautiful and acted so normal if something was there?

Then "something" became "Something." Was there really Something—anything—other than man in the universe?

For generations the Christian faith had been part of our heritage, yet that night we felt pitifully alone and scared. The peril that threatened our child brought all the doubts and questions we'd ever had about God crashing and tumbling about us. Were we alone, or were we surrounded by Eternal Love?

We talked and wept with Barbara and Chuck until three in the morning. Surely, Someone was there. I had to believe that. Yet, what kind of God would allow this to happen to Steve?

Something was there. We didn't know what.

Was Something—Someone—there, too?

REPRIEVE!

"Something is there. We don't know what."

Perhaps it was those words, uttered that night at the Cogswells, that intensified my struggle with semantics, for from that night on, every spoken word and random thought took on double meaning. Throughout the months of Steve's illness much of what I saw or heard became allegorical.

Signs that I saw—Exit Only, Travel at Your Own Risk, Danger, People Crossing—seemed written in letters larger than life. Beside the elevator phone in the hospital there was a sign that read, "If there is trouble, call Security No. 1." More than once in the months to come I was tempted to pick up the phone and call for help. I never did; I could recognize the sharp edge of hysteria in contemplating this macabre joke. And besides, had I not been calling on Security No. 1 with every prayer?

This super-sensitivity persisted for at least a year, until I, who have always been thrilled by the subtleties of words, feared a kind of madness. Would I always be plagued by the double entendre? Elizabeth Barrett Browning said that we who could not see an earth crammed with heaven, must sit around and eat blackberries. Was there no alternative?

The tension did not lessen for three days and nights. We were told little about the endless charts and exhaustive tests. The answer to all our questions was the same. "Our findings are not conclusive. We will let you know when they are."

It was Sunday, October 14. Bill had returned to Carbondale to preach, and David had gone with him. The Cogswells had gone to church, and I was alone, ready to leave for the hospital, when the call came. It was Dr. Guise himself.

"Mrs. Warner, we have good news for you. We have found no evidence to warrant Dr. Smith's suspicion of either an abscess or a tumor. However, we have found that Steve has an infection in the frontal sinus. That bears watching, so we are switching him from

neurosurgery to Dr. Hardy, our ear-nose-throat man who will be in complete charge from now on. Thank you. Goodbye."
I laughed. I cried. What a reprieve! How lucky we were! I ran throughout the house—simply because there were no fields of clover. I swung my arms wide in exultation as I danced around the rooms. It was like Steve's childish energy spells that caused him to run and hug someone.
I called the family to give them the joyous news.

This, thy son which was dead, is now alive. This, thy brother which was lost, is now found. Rejoice! Rejoice! Rejoice!

But Steve was still in great pain. He was a very sick boy. That morning I met Dr. Hardy, a tall man, about sixty years old. Dr. Hardy patiently explained that pressure on the sinus—caused by Steve's diving test—had forced some type of bacteria into his sinus cavity. And there, in the closed warmth of Steve's body, they were flourishing and multiplying. The infection created pressure on the eyeball and the thin membranes that separated the sinus from the brain, and this had brought on the unrelenting pain.
Steve and Dr. Hardy liked each other from the first. During the next few days, I waited at the foot of Steve's bed, tense and tight, with sweaty palms, until the meticulous daily peering and probing was over.
The doctor carefully examined minute amounts of fluid drawn from Steve's sinus cavity with hypodermic needles. Then he would either turn to me or speak to Steve.
"It's about the same as yesterday. I'm going to treat it conservatively for a while longer . . . forty-eight more hours . . . at least another. . . ."
I did not understand the words "conservative" and "radical" in this context, but I learned. To treat the problem "conservatively" meant to give medication by mouth or injection, or just allow the infection more time to run its course. To treat it "radically" meant surgery. The doctor always took so long and appeared so serious

during the examinations that, each time, I was afraid he would say the condition was worse and he must operate.

But each day, the verdict was the same. Steve was holding his own. Dr. Hardy said that he had had a frontal sinus infection himself and could remember the intense pain, so he felt great empathy for Steve. In fact, he seemed surprised that the pain was not worse.

Once during an examination, when a particularly blatant commercial for Dristan came over the TV, Steve teased, "Now that's what I need, Doctor! Why didn't you think of that?"

Dr. Hardy seemed not to have heard Steve, but fifteen or twenty minutes later, when he had finished his examination, he asked, "Well, do you want the drops or the tablets?"

"What?" Steve asked, puzzled.

"The Dristan—shall I write the prescription for nosedrops or tablets?"

That week at St. Lukes was a time of hope and expectation—a time of wonderful closeness. Bill, David, Kathy, and Russ came whenever their school and work schedules permitted. The hospital was most considerate about visits, so every morning at about nine o'clock I arrived for the day. I always carried some treasure with me—a new story, a funny episode of a favorite cartoon, a plant from the florist, something good from the Cogswell kitchen.

The leaves were turning, so Kathy and David brought bright red branches of dogwood and sour gum from our woods. Kathy and I made a quick shopping trip and bought red and white checked pajamas and bright red jockey shorts. We thought Steve would think the shorts were funny, but he folded them away to wear when he got home.

"The nurses will think I'm some kind of weirdo," he said. He liked the pajamas but remarked, "They look so much like a tablecloth the nurses won't know whether to give me a shot or set me for dinner!"

I knew he dreaded being caught with the wrong underwear, so I should have guessed his reaction to the red shorts. The boys had always worn "long johns" on the coldest days—except when the coldest day also happened to be PE day; then they would freeze their tails waiting for the bus rather than be caught with long underwear in gym class. Oh, the pain of not dressing like your peers! Now we joked about our poor timing. I think it was during these days that we began a mental list called, "Things We'll Laugh At Later."

After Dr. Guise assured us that the trouble did not involve Steve's brain, we were no longer consumed with fear, and the time passed quickly and rather pleasantly. We made frequent trips to the gift shop on the first floor to buy magazines, newspapers, and stationery.

Steve set himself the impossible goal of writing a thank-you note to everyone who sent him a card or letter. He had never been sick before, and he was surprised and delighted that people took the time to wish him well. Later, many thoughtful people gave us back the notes he'd written—charming, funny, witty notes, some with caricatures of his many doctors and clever sketches of the things that filled his days in hospital. But, here and there, the underlying fear he felt leaked through.

He found a little simulated ivory chess set in the gift shop. "See how each piece fits in a hole on the board? That will be good when I have to quit playing for awhile for an x-ray or something, and it'll be just the thing for me and Dave to use when we drive to Mexico at Christmas."

That past summer, Steve had offered me a dollar for every pound I could lose before our trip to Mexico. He didn't know it, but I was saving the ten dollars I'd cost him so far to buy a real onyx set at our first Mexican market. Once I'd heard him say, "Sometime I'd like to have a chess set that's really made of what it looks like, and not white plastic for ivory and brown plastic for onyx."

We also made occasional trips to the hospital tea room. Steve was not on a restricted diet, so although his appetite was poor, he sometimes found things that tasted good. Other times, old friends from church took us to lunch. The younger people seemed to enjoy the relaxed atmosphere of the tea room more than they did the hospital room.

To pass the time and to soothe ourselves—and just because we'd always done it—we played games. We played guessing games and made wagers about hospital protocol, the pecking order of the staff, the number of times in a day a table top would be washed. We even ran races. When we traveled from one floor to another, we kept score according to who arrived in the shortest time. Because he was so weak, Steve was usually in a wheelchair and had to ride elevators, but I preferred the stairs. Its surprising how often the races were tied. Occasionally I would beat Steve and could watch him propelling his pajama-clad figure down the corridor, his long, brown arms making the wheelchair fly.

Although we all were sure now that Steve was going to be fine, his pain was still severe, and his weakness was scary. The fluid drawn painstakingly through his nostrils was still full of pus. The sinus walls were so thin, and the brain was so close, so near. Our greatest fear was that the infection would break through.

Finally the day came when Dr. Hardy said, "I can't wait any longer. I believe we must now treat the infection radically."

"What does that mean exactly?" I slipped from the chair at the foot of the bed to hover near his elbow.

"It means I'm sending him to Barnes Hospital this afternoon. He will have surgery tomorrow. The man I want to operate is on the staff at Barnes."

Steve took this as he took everything else. As long as he could register any response at all, it was one of unflinching, unblinking optimism. He possessed a sense of realism—he did not minimize his danger—but it was realism coupled with hope and courage. Even though the time came when he knew he was desperately, dangerously ill, I think he always expected to get well. And since he expected to get well, that miracle must lie in the next treatment, the next procedure, the next surgery. So it seemed he was always eager—almost impatient—to get on with the treatment.

During Steve's time at St. Luke's, the hospital had taken on an air of the familiar. In a sense, St. Luke's was Steve's hospital—a place where he'd felt almost well enough to enjoy himself and where the news had seemed good. And now we were leaving—going to Barnes for surgery.

I was surprised by the speed with which we moved, once the decision had been made. It was like breaking camp. Someone else made the plans; we just walked through the maneuvers. There was time for only a few scribbled addresses and hurried goodbyes to other patients on the floor. There was Louie, an irascible old man with giggly, red-cheeked, teen-age granddaughters (Louis had broken his leg chasing a mule, and his brusque son, who always wore three-piece suits, seemed unduly embarrassed by the old man's thick brogue and constant swearing); the plump white-haired woman whose son, a school teacher, had a brain tumor (the second in eight years); the young wife with the bright henna rinse who'd just been told her husband had inoperable lung cancer.

I felt so sorry for them all. I think my compassion was fed a little by the sweet relief that had flooded us since Sunday, when our own dread of a tumor had been lifted. We were giddy with relief. We were not yet home free, but in comparison, anything was less sinister.

Bill had driven up the night before, and the car was waiting in the loading zone. Steve hurried up and down the corridors, looking for his special nurses, to say goodbye. In the months to come we learned there were other stricken young people, but Steve's bright, young face was still an unusual sight on the eighth floor, and the nurses loved him. One nurse always tried to wind up each day's duty in his room. She helped him tape his cards to the wall, then found string to criss-cross from wall to wall so he could hang them up, clothes-line fashion, when the walls were full. Much of the staff gathered at the nurse's station to give him a hearty send-off. It was a gay occasion, full of hope and good will.

"Come back to see us, Stephen." "Get well soon now, you hear?" "Best wishes."

The October sunshine was warm and benign as we walked to the car—more slowly than common, for Steve was weak and shaky. This caused us some worry, but I recalled hearing that if a well man went to bed for a week he would become too weak to walk steadily across the room.

I couldn't believe how tall Steve looked in his street clothes—or how handsome! He wore navy slacks and a blue chambray dress shirt with a faint iridescent sheen and tiny red stitching around the collar and cuffs—his second favorite shirt.

Barnes Hospital, where Dr. Sessions was on the surgical staff, is one of the great hospital complexes of the nation. It was not far from St. Luke's. Since we did not have to be there until two o'clock, there was time for lunch. I remember only two things about that meal—the huge bowls of popcorn sitting on the tables, and the fact that Steve could not eat anything. Restaurant food tasted no better than hospital fare.

We particularly cherished those few hours sandwiched between hospitals. We had a little time—not much, but enough for a little sightseeing. Bill drove slowly. We saw the St. Louis Zoo train and decided to ride it—to go the whole loop. Ah, the zoo. What fun we'd had there. We'd ridden the train when it was brand new, but later had spurned it, preferring to dash or saunter (depending upon age) to those exhibits that most fascinated each of us.

That day, however, Steve did not have strength even to walk up the little hill to see Siegfried, the walrus. We'd watched Siegfried grow from a flipper-sucking infant to a behemoth who fed upon clams and whipping cream, and the year before, we had taken a picture of Steve leaning far out over Siegfried's pool, scratching his great bristly face. The polar bear pit was near the train station, so we went to take a last look at those great white beauties.

There were not two seats adjoining in the little open air car, so Bill and I sat in one and Steve sat several seats away, by himself. I can still picture his casual air as he sat, back to the side for support, arm over the back of the seat and one long leg drawn up beside him. I suspect his posture originated from fatigue, but I cannot help thinking that his studied air of nonchalance must have been fed by the side glances and giggles of two young women who sat nearby. I know he was acutely aware of their flirtatious glances, for several times he flashed his eyes up to us (never with any recognition of us as parents, of course) to see if we were witnessing the little tableau in the back. It always makes me happy to remember that.

"Look at me, Mama," Emily had said.
Oh, Steve, Mama looked. Surely I looked. Surely I saw.

WHO'S TAKING MY PLACE
AS DRUM MAJOR?

We had a long wait after we arrived at Barnes Hospital. We faced long, long lines—or short lines that never moved. Two people who had been sitting patiently at 10:00 a.m. were sitting on the same chairs at 4:00 p.m.

There was no room on the eighth floor where Ear, Nose, and Throat patients were assigned. Finally, Steve was given a temporary room in Pediatrics, and we met Dr. Session, the surgeon who was to operate.

Steve wasn't usually conscious of age, but at sixteen (for another three weeks anyway) he was still close enough to childhood to be embarrassed by the little pink and blue furniture, the cute curtains, the crib-like beds, and, especially, the manner of the nurse in the children's ward. And there was another problem. Steve's headaches were still bad, and his roommates, toddlers waiting for tonsillectomies, were noisy.

Relief came on Monday, when Steve was moved to the eighth floor of the East Pavilion where his roommate was an Internal Revenue agent and part-time professor of economics at Sangamon College. Later, there was such a succession of roommates it was hard to keep them straight.

Although Dr. Hardy thought Steve's surgery would be scheduled for Friday or Saturday, October 19 or 20, we learned it would not take place until the following Tuesday, October 23. Until then, he would still be treated "conservatively." Monday, October 22, we again saw Dr. Session, who was to operate. We had talked only briefly with him before. Dr. Sessions seemed to be a gentle, caring man, and he came with the highest credentials. We appreciated the almost leisurely conversations he had with Steve. On Monday, he explained in detail what he planned to do.

"I will make an incision just above Steve's left eyebrow, close to the nose and go in and find out exactly what we're fighting. I'll scrape the cavity clean, and then I feel certain we'll see a rapid recovery."

Dr. Hardy seemed confident of success, and so did Dr. Sessions. Steve underwent an unbelievable number of examinations, not only during the day, but often at night. Amidst the fear and pain, I think there was also a sense of excitement—it was a little like being a celebrity. Frontal sinus infections are not common, and here was this tall, good-looking young man laid low with one acquired from scuba diving—somehow the scuba diving provided romance. This was no mere sinusitis caused from blowing his nose too hard! Wryly, I recalled that John Steinbeck once said that nothing is too poor for people to boast about if it's all they've got.

During the two days Steve waited for the operation, doctors we had never seen brought whole classes in to look at him and listen as their instructors read all the data on his charts.

One said, "Now fellows, this is what can happen to you when you go diving in dirty water."

Steve bristled immediately and retorted, "That's not what happened! I took my diving test in Devil's Kitchen Lake, the cleanest lake in all of Illinois. It's well below the safety requirement for scuba diving."

I doubt if he convinced anyone, but at least he tried. He wouldn't take that lying down. Not Steve!

While we were all eager to have the surgery over with now that the decision had been made, no one was as pathetically eager as Steve. He was chafing at the bit to be back where he belonged.

"What a way to start my senior year!" he complained.

Another time he said, "Did I tell you Debbie and I are singing a duet for the winter concert? Mr. Biggs said he thinks he also has a solo part for me. I hope he doesn't give it to someone else. It must sound dumb to everybody back home for me to be in the hospital for sinus trouble."

"Oh, they know you don't have a mere sinus headache," I assured him. "There's sinus trouble and there's Sinus Trouble! One of Grandma's friends told her this week that her son had this same thing happen to him while he was in the army."

Still, Steve fretted. "The only class I'm worried about is Government. All the rest I can catch up on easy, but this is just for one semester, and the teacher has to cover a lot in a hurry. It's really kind of interesting—it's so different from anything I've ever had. The teacher's pretty neat, too."

Every day he talked of school. "Wonder who's taking my place as drum major? At least I got them through the two big parades. It was so hot you could have fried an egg that day in DuQuoin when we marched at the Hambletonian. I told you that one girl passed out from the heat, didn't I?"

"Yes," I said. "It's a wonder to me you all didn't drop."

"The Apple Festival was fun—that was a neat parade. Man! It scares me yet when I think how I almost led the whole parade down the wrong street! I was just ready to cross over when this girl next to me gave a low whistle and I realized what I was doing. Kathy and Russ said they saw me hesitate, but I don't think anyone else caught on."

Steve always became weak with laughter when he recalled that event. What if he had marched his band down the wrong route, away from the parade? But as he began to laugh, he grabbed his head. It hurt too much to laugh out loud.

It hurt me, too—not only to see him in such pain, but because I felt such remorse. I had not watched his parade. I wonder what I did do that morning? Perhaps I bought groceries or ran a load of laundry.

Steve mulled over his job at McDonald's. "I was due for a promotion," he said. "I hope this won't delay it 'til the next review. It'll mean a ten cents an hour raise, and with Christmas coming I could use that extra money for Mexico. I'll bet things have gone up a lot since Dad was there. That was before I was born."

I had been thinking of Mexico, too. It was less than two months until our departure date—until we would pile into that motor home and drive south of the border for one last fantastic vacation together. I must add my Spanish-English dictionary to the list of things to bring. It would give Steve and me something to do, and it might perk up his spirits.

We felt little real concern about the upcoming surgery; the doctors assured us it was fairly routine. But it is never easy to read and sign a waiver of responsibility. I never got used to it. In the following months, emergencies arose when Bill was gone, so I had to sign—read and sign. Always, my mouth dried out and my hands became so sweaty I could hardly hold the pen the doctor had conveniently at hand.

At last it was time. We were frightened despite the doctors' encouraging words. We knew little about surgery, and the operation seemed to take forever. Actually it was quite a long operation, though the exact time eludes me.

It is merciful to have something elude me. Sometimes I fear I will be cursed with perfect recall of every horrific detail as long as I live!

In the afternoon, when it seemed to be taking much longer than we'd expected, Bill got out a notebook and said, "This seems like a good time to figure what we have to do to finish the house. Let's take the rooms, one at a time, and put down in detail everything that needs to be done."

"I don't think I can keep my mind on it," I protested.

"Come on. Let's try. It will make the time pass. Let's start in Dave's room."

I remember the giddy feel of talking animatedly about door facings, window wells, and door knobs while our minds were constantly on a boy in an operating room—while we were silently pleading, pleading.

Finally, we looked up and saw Dr. Sessions and Dr. Hardy. They had come to tell us the surgery was over. Steve was in Recovery. Dr. Sessions seemed pleased at the way the operation had gone.

"We found just exactly what we expected," he said. "An ugly pocket of pus had accumulated. That could have caused big trouble if we hadn't gotten it. I scraped the cavity clean, so there should be no more problems."

Dr. Hardy added, "The infection was caused by an influenza virus, called hemopholous. I had suspected a more virulent virus because of the length and severity of the symptoms. I guess Steve was particularly susceptible to this one. I agree with Dr. Sessions that your fine young man is going to be all right now."

Dr. Hardy seemed happy. I think he had grown genuinely fond of Steve.

Bill asked the question that was on all our minds. "When do you think he can come home? He's been here a long time."

Dr. Sessions answered, "I see no reason not to expect a quick recovery. I think he should be dismissed within a week."

Dr. Hardy nodded his agreement.

At last the gurney rolled down the corridor and turned in at our door. Here was our boy—a little wan and sleepy still, but it was good to see him stir! His head was swathed in bandages. He grimaced as his hand went shakily to his forehead and he touched a drainage tube that protruded through the heavy gauze compresses.

"You mean I have a rubber hose hanging out of my head? I must look like an escapee from a monster show!"

The nurse spoke up. "Don't worry about that, Steve. The doctor left that in to make sure the infection won't build up again. He'll take it out in a few days. Would you like something to eat?"

By now it was midafternoon, and Steve was a little hungry. The nurse named some things she could bring from the cafeteria and pretended to be a waitress taking orders. It pleased Steve, being able to sidestep the hospital kitchen, and he ordered a turkey sandwich and a raspberry shake. We watched him eat the thick slab of white meat and drink the shake. Then, we tiptoed out as he fell asleep.

The doctors had assured us that Steve would recover quickly, and indeed he did feel so much better that when the kids came up to spend the weekend with him, I went back to my second graders, leaving Bill to stay with him. Every evening I called and chatted a while.

The following Tuesday night, when I called Steve's room, another patient answered the phone. He couldn't tell me anything more than that Steve was not there and he knew nothing about him. Calling the switchboard I got little more information—just that there was no William Stephen Warner listed as a patient in Barnes Hospital.

I couldn't understand what the problem was. I had talked to Bill and Steve the night before. How could anything have gone wrong? Steve was to come home on the weekend. Could he have been transferred to another hospital?

Oh, God. Could he have died? Wouldn't they have notified me immediately?

Bill always told me that I never believed the children had a simple sore throat; first I had to rule out leukemia and rheumatic fever.

Panic set in, and I could not finish supper. I could do nothing but worry and wait.

Half an hour later, in they walked—Steve and Bill. All my worry flared out as anger at Bill.

"How could you do this to me? I've been frantic. I had no idea what had happened. I couldn't get any information from the hospital."

"I told her there was bound to be a logical explanation," countered David. "But you know Mom."

I almost ruined Steve's homecoming. Their story seemed so reasonable as they told it.

Steve had begged, "Doc, why don't you let me go home? They're not doing a thing here that can't be done at home."

When Dr. Sessions explained that the drainage tube had to be changed every two or three days, Steve insisted that he could come back for that.

"Dad will bring me, won't you, Dad?"

He knew his father pretty well. Of course Bill would have done anything to get him home.

Steve had continued, "Do you realize how sick I am of being sick? I've been stuck in some hospital since October 11, and tomorrow is Halloween. Come on. Have a heart. Please let me go."

Bill assured the doctor that he would be glad to drive Steve back, every other day, if necessary. We lived about 110 miles away, but Bill, too, felt that Steve had had enough.

When I had recovered enough to exclaim over him appropriately, we settled Steve on the living room sofa. It made a good bed, and he would not be so far from the family. Steve and David chattered like magpies the whole evening. Eventually we learned that Bill, wanting to celebrate, had taken him out to dinner and to a movie before they left the city.

"I'm sorry," Bill apologized. "I guess we should have phoned, but we thought we would be home before your evening call."

Steve added, "When Dr. Sessions gave the OK, I couldn't get out of there fast enough. And we thought what a neat surprise it would be for me just to walk in the house with Dad."

WINTER SETS IN

Steve came home on the eve of a Hallowe'en party David hosted for the Wesley Foundation, a religious group on the SIU campus. He watched with interest while the young people carried in corn shocks and scattered leaves about our family room. Steve planned to attend the party and said wryly, "I won't need a mask. Can't you just see someone opening the door to a trick or treater and seeing a man standing there with a rubber hose hanging out of his forehead?"

But in spite of his intentions, Steve was too weak to stay with the revelers. He and Eric Robb, one of his best friends, spent most of the evening in Steve's room.

After that night, Steve continued to recuperate at home, and I went back to work. Bill and David were in and out, and occasionally Russ came to spend the day. Our old tin mailbox, the one we had put in the woods, hoping vainly to woo the bluebirds, still bears the pock marks of their target practice. Some days Bill or Dave took Steve to visit my parents and have lunch with them. To sit docilely and let himself be driven was a far cry from running swiftly on a woodsy path worn slick by eager feet—Steve's usual method of getting to Grandma's. He was still so weak, yet the doctors assured us it was just a matter of time until he recovered completely.

Twice a week Bill took Steve to Barnes Hospital to be checked. Before one of these appointments I noticed that Steve's right eye pulled ever so slightly to the outside. Alarmed, I urged Bill to call this to Dr. Hardy's attention.

Steve's eyes had always been beautiful. Large and lustrous—so dark that sometimes the black pupils were lost in the sable-brown iris—they were fringed by heavy, black lashes that looked as if they'd been freshly oiled. How his pretty blonde sister envied those black lashes and neatly etched brow line. Steve complained that when he played in the snow, he had to keep batting his eyes to unload the snow that accumulated on his long lashes. But his true beauty was in the wit, the charm, and the eagerness behind those eyes.

I worried all that day about his eye. I could not imagine what made it turn outward. When Bill and Steve returned, I was afraid to ask what the doctor had said, but I laughed out loud when I heard the diagnosis.

Unsure himself, Dr. Hardy had sent them to an ophthalmologist, Dr. Robert Drews. Bill had liked him, and I liked his diagnosis. Steve's right eye had been bandaged so long it had gone lazy and was not seeing at all. How simple! Nothing to worry about! Why, my cousin's boy had worn a patch for a year because of a lazy eye.

Dr. Drew's explanation seemed logical and beautifully simple. Steve's right eye had always been weaker than the left, and that summer, when he was tested for new glasses, his vision had changed from something like 20-70 to 20-200.

In the months to come, I was to wonder whether the optometrist who fitted Steve's glasses should have been alerted by that drastic change—if he should have warned us that something dreadful might be causing it. But for now, Steve had to keep a black patch over his stronger eye. He wore it jauntily, looking as debonair as Captain Hook or Moshe Dayan.

When, after two weeks, the rubber drainage tube was removed from his forehead, Steve said jokingly, "Well, I've graduated from a hose in my head to a black patch over my eye. Wonder what the next step will be?"

Time passed swiftly. The doctor told Steve he could return to school the week of November 5, and he did try to go. Once he called Bill to bring him home because he just didn't feel like staying; another time, a week later, the school nurse called to tell Bill that Steve was in the infirmary because he'd become nauseated. Many days he did not even make the effort.

Once I chided Steve a little. "I know it's hard to get back into the swing of things, but the longer you put school off, the harder it will be. You've just got to go the minute you feel like it."

I will always remember his low, even voice as he said in a most definite way, "Mama, I don't *feel* like going to school."

I believed him and never prodded again.

Steve was still very weak, he had no appetite, and his headaches persisted. We were not exactly frightened, but we were puzzled—uneasy.

Dr. Hardy had not expected the hemopholous virus to be so stubborn in yielding to treatment. But the doctors seemed to keep a close watch on him and assured us of his eventual complete recovery. We had to remember that Steve had had a severe infection and had been in bed for almost a month.

It never crossed our minds that he was not getting well. These men were the best in their field, we were told. Surely they would know if something was wrong.

Months later we were to learn that Dr. Sessions had no knowledge of Sid Smith's early diagnosis of a brain tumor or an abscess. This seems unconscionable! Surely the information was there in that slim file that was to grow so voluminous. I do not know how those other doctors had ruled out a tumor, any more than I know how we, his family, had accepted their less serious diagnosis so unquestioningly. The explanation for Steve's symptoms was always the virulence of the infection.

"Look at me, Mama."

Oh, yes, I looked. I drank in the sight of him. But I was powerless to speed his recovery.

The time from Hallowe'en to Thanksgiving—three short weeks—is frayed and indistinct. It seems blurred because it went by so quickly. The days themselves seem out of focus. So many things took up my time.

Our church had scheduled a Lay Witness Mission for November—a time when laymen would witness to other laymen about their own spiritual experiences. One afternoon Steve himself felt well enough to host a small party for the youth.

Then, I spent two evenings making pressed flower pictures for the annual church bazaar. I heard later that they sold for forty dollars. I'm glad, for they cost me a great deal.

I write about that time—those three precious weeks when Steve was home—only to show how much we believed he was recovering. Someone else could have done all those things if we had thought it necessary. But we all felt it was just a matter of settling in for the long haul of Steve's recuperation.

I keep plucking at the threads of that time, but there is never any substance to it. We did not know—no one knew—how ill Steve was.

There seemed to be no end of distractions. My father was seventy-two years old on November 10, and we celebrated with a family party. My niece and her two little children came from Florida. It was a small gathering, but it required a couple of days of preparation time—that precious commodity that was running out.

Oddly, my memory of that day remains sharply in focus, and it is one that I do not begrudge—perhaps because Steve was pleased with it. The children were smitten with love of him—a tall, lanky, dark-haired cousin who did not rush off like other "big kids," but seemed content to sit and talk and listen to them. The three of them lay on big floor pillows and talked quietly. Steve brought out a little wooden balancing man from India and his perpetual motion machine. He kept the fire going, and they played about the hearth, fascinated by the flames.

Later, as Bill and the boys and I basked in the day's afterglow, Steve said, "Those kids are really nice. I've been around so many bratty kids lately I was beginning to wonder if I'd even like my own. But I had fun with Jeff and Julie."

Steve's seventeenth birthday had been the day before, and he had had his own celebration on Friday. That day—his actual birthday—was the only day he felt really well during his time at home. He was able to stay at school all day.

His youth group at church was having a party that night and I teased him, "Of course you stayed; you knew you didn't have a ghost of a chance to go on this hayride if you weren't able to stay in school!"

He just grinned his slow grin.

The hayride was also to be a surprise party for Steve's birthday. The girls made two big chocolate cakes, and if Steve had not been able to go on the hayride, the kids would have brought the party to our house, to surprise him there. Kathy and Russ were youth sponsors that year. We all were so delighted when Steve felt like going that, in a sudden burst of enthusiasm, Bill and I decided to go too. We couldn't bear not to be in on the surprise.

In the late afternoon it started to get colder, and by six o'clock a wintry cold wave had clamped down on us. Dressing as if we were going Christmas caroling, we pulled out long handles for everyone—and we still froze.

"Look at me, Mama."

What a night to look at him! I had the same glow I'd felt many times throughout the years—myriad times I'd seen him in a crowd or with a group of his friends—times of my exulting that he never knew about.

Watching Steve that night, I wondered. Did he really feel as well as he seemed? Or for this one day, his birthday, had he psyched himself up—his great spirit and bubbling enthusiasm momentarily quelling the dark mutterings of the flesh? I'll never know. I only know that this night was good, very good.

Except for David, who had to work, the people Steve loved best in the world were with him—wishing him well, rejoicing in his regained health. Sitting quietly in a corner of the wagon, Bill and I laughed at the fun Steve was having. How good it would be to have him well again. I hadn't realized the depth and persistence of my concern until I tasted the sweet relief of seeing him looking almost normal.

For this hayride, the group had spurned a tractor for the glamour of great prancing work horses whose broad backs glistened in the moonlight. Quite often as we rumbled down the back road at a gentle trot, they delicately lifted their tails and noisily expelled great gusts of wind from those fat rumps. The deliciously gross sounds caused the town-bred kids to howl with laughter. All of it was good. Even the piles of warm horse manure, dropped on the road where they lay steaming in the crisp cold air, gave forth a not-unpleasant odor when blended with the smell of the clean straw piled about us.

Steve had been away for more than a month, and everyone was glad to see him. It was, "Steve, here's a place." "Steve, come sit by me."

Steve had on so much warm underclothing that he needed only a white hooded sweat shirt to keep warm. It shone almost blue white in the moonlight as he moved from place to place.

His spirits were high, too. Sometimes he and some of the other boys ran alongside the wagon. A couple of times he sprinted ahead and ran beside the horses, prancing and pawing the hard ground in broad pantomime.

The fire that night was marvelous. We were taken to the luau pit—a deep glowing hole big enough to bury a car—a wonderful gathering place for a wagon load of cold people. Logs had burned in it for hours. The man in charge of both the horses and the fire wore a lapel pin that said, "Licensed Farrier." He told me that a farrier was a shoer of horses, a blacksmith.

Later, one of the doctors who would work closely with Steve was a Dr. LeFarrier. I wondered if his forebears had been blacksmiths—if they had ever shod fat draft horses and, if so, how many generations had it taken for horny hands to become so refined that they could gauge the delicate calipers that measured an ominous pressure. How long from horseshoe nail to surgeon's knot?

We roasted the wieners until their skins popped and juice spat and fried in the fire. We toasted marshmallows until they became swollen and pendulous or else crisped themselves with a black sugary coating.

Next came the cakes. They'd been well hidden. Steve was surprised and delighted that the kids had planned this party for him. There were presents, too. One friend had knitted a neat, dark red cap for him. We sat around the fire and sang camp songs.

Before we piled on the wagon to come home, someone began to sing "Happy Birthday . . . And we wish you many more."

Seventeen! I could not remember what it had been like for me, but surely it would be good for this handsome man-child of mine—this cavorting half-man, half-child who still was able to dip from either side. Seventeen was the age to savor—the best of both worlds. His senior year had gotten off to a rotten start, but somehow we would make it up to him.

The nagging cloud of worry began to lift.

The year before, when he'd studied Booth Tarkington, I told Steve how much I had enjoyed reading the book, *Seventeen.* We decided that when he turned seventeen, we'd have to read it together. We never did. I suspect you cannot appreciate reading *Seventeen* when you are busy living seventeen.

Steve had always been popular with the kids from church and school. One friend said that Steve could be standing in a crowd, bare-footed and wearing ill-fitting, frayed cut-offs, and somehow he would still be the center of attention. You would be pleased if he came over and talked to you. I never quite understood his charisma—his easy grace. I do not know how to describe his specialness. It was just there.

Months later, Mrs. Lee, of the Children's Literature Department at Southern Illinois University said, "You know, I never had children. I just have to borrow a special one here and there. And your Steve—he was special! I'd watch him whenever the youth of the church put on a program or when he was singing in the choir, or just when he was with his friends. He always stood out. There was just one word for him, and that was radiant."

I smiled. I agreed, of course, but I was also amused to think how Steve's comment would almost surely have been, "weird," for he would have associated her beautiful words with Wilbur the pig, in E. B. White's novel, as Charlotte the spider spun the word "radiant" over the pig in the stable.

Did I look at him? Ah, yes! He was radiant, whether he realized it or not.

The next morning, Saturday, we went to Injun Creek where Grandpa showed us where to pick up black walnuts. Later, the boys went off to a geological formation overlooking the Mississippi River—a place called Fountain Bluff. David had been there earlier, and he was eager to share it with Steve. When they got home, Steve did not complain, but he was very quiet.

Dave seemed disappointed. He said, "Mom, Steve must really be weak. Can you believe he stayed at the bottom of the bluff while the rest of us hiked up? He didn't feel like climbing—not even when I told him about that broad wheat field between the bluffs. It's really a sight. I sure wanted him to see it."

"I guess he pushed himself too hard last night," I said. "He seemed so well on the hayride. I know he's disappointed, and disgusted, too, that he's not gaining strength any faster. Never mind. When he's stronger, we'll all go. We'll all go before winter sets in for good."

The Pale Horseman Mounts

But winter came faster than we thought possible. Steve's weakness grew more frightening. Every day we looked at him, and every day we grew more anxious. Did we just imagine that his eye was turning more?

Medical check-ups took a frightful precedence. We saw both Dr. Hardy, the ear, nose, and throat specialist, and Dr. Drews, the ophthalmologist, twice a week. Stephen wanted to stay home and we wanted him home, so Bill laid aside all other plans in order to make those long drives to St. Louis. It was then that Bill's great sense of enthusiasm and his innate optimism upheld us all, for he tried to turn each trip into an outing with some special sight or a special place to eat.

Bill had an innate gift for embroidery—that rare gift of being able to see life in larger-than-life dimensions. Once, ages ago when he'd done something (long since forgotten) that I judged highly extravagant, I'd complained, "I swear we'll wind up in the poor house yet!"

Stephen, who was about eight, saved the day by singing out, "But it will be fun to be in the poor house with Daddy!"

Bill's optimism was infectious, and although life had not always been easy and there was never quite enough money on a minister's salary, there had been many friends and much laughter and singing. I had to agree with Stephen. It probably would be fun with Daddy!

During the visit on Tuesday, November 20, Dr. Drews was surprised that the black patch had not had a more immediate effect on Steve's lazy eye. He even suggested that his right eye might always have wandered and that we had grown so used to it that we did not notice it.

How ridiculous! As though I would not know the face of my own child—as if I would not be intimately aware of every feature! That crowded month included Thanksgiving—November 22, the earliest it can ever be—and we were eating at Grandma's house. She was fixing all the things the boys liked, and I went early to help. I was surprised to see Steve come in wearing his blue pajamas and robe.

"Son, didn't you feel like dressing for Thanksgiving dinner?"

"No, I didn't." It was that same short, decisive, let's-not-talk-about-it-anymore tone with which he'd told me he didn't feel like going to school. However, he seemed pleased to help with a short Thanksgiving worship service, and, as he blew out the turkey candles in the centerpiece, he said, "Let's save these for another year." But he ate very little—just picked at his food.

Worry nagged at me and brought a hard knot to my stomach. Steve had no appetite at all. He didn't seem to be gaining strength, and I had begun to doubt Dr. Drews' beautifully simple explanation about the turning eye. The week before, I had been so scared about his eye that I wrangled a work-in appointment with Dr. Peterson, Carbondale's own highly reputable ophthalmologist. Steve had had to wait in the office three hours, but after only a five minute examination, Dr. Peterson said he thought Dr. Drews' diagnosis was correct. Steve was so worn out by the long wait that I was almost sorry we had put him through it, but we were greatly relieved by the doctor's words.

The Friday after Thanksgiving, Dave took the day off, and we all made the trip to St. Louis. It felt almost like a family excursion. As we walked from the living room, on impulse I grabbed up a photograph of Steve to show the doctor what his eyes were supposed to look like—lovely, large, clear eyes that were perfectly steady.

The comments of both doctors were disappointingly the same. Steve needed more time. Dr. Drews conceded that Stephen's eyes had been clear and straight, but that seemed like a small victory since he had no new theory as to what was causing the problem or how to correct it. We wished for some new drug—some wonder vitamin for our wunderkind.

Steve had felt pretty well all day. We even did a little shopping, buying him some clothes for a belated birthday gift. He chose a beautiful, tan, fine-wale corduroy car coat. He really liked it and looked good in it—very grown up and handsome.

We considered a movie or a dinner out, but nothing seemed better than another night with everybody home. We arrived in time to watch "The Odd Couple"—another good evening, another quiet, ordinary family time.

On Saturday Bill performed a memorial service for Scott, the nineteen-year-old son of Dr. and Mrs. Jack Taylor. I had not known the young man, but I knew his parents. How could one stand to lose a child?

Ever since my brother died, I'd prayed, "Oh, Lord, anything but that. I can take anything else you send my way, but I can never bear the loss of a child."

Now, here were Jack and Rosemary, somehow having to bear that loss.

Because of the funeral, Kathy and Russ and the boys and I went alone to Cairo, about 60 miles away, to Cheryl's house, for a second Thanksgiving dinner. Everybody liked Stephen's new coat. The tan lent a little color to his cheeks. He ate quite heartily, and I could feel my worries slip away again—he was going to be all right. It was just taking longer than the doctors had anticipated.

Before we left for home, I was aghast to see Steve clowning around with his double vision. Russ would toss him grapes and he would try to catch them in his mouth—first with one eye closed, then the other, demonstrating graphically how distorted his vision had become. It was hideous, yet it did not seem to appall anyone but me. Steve did not really seem sick; he was just clowning.

Coming home we stopped at a shoe outlet store where Steve filled out a card to be notified when a certain style of hiking boot came in. He and Dave were going to walk the Appalachian Trail the next summer. Steve ordered a size 12; he was going to be a big man.

Nearer home, we stopped at a gift shop that featured handcrafted Christmas items. As I waited at the counter to pay for some tiny carved trees and other wooden ornaments, Steve said, "Mom, I'm getting tired; I think I'll go sit in the car."

Russ and Dave joined him. The cashier took forever with my charge card, and Dave came in, exasperated and a little angry.

"Mom, I think you should come right now. Steve is really in a lot of pain."

We left immediately. About half a mile from home, the odometer crossed the 89,999.9 mile mark.

Steve watched it and said, "Dad always likes to see this happen. If I didn't feel so bad we'd walk home and leave the car 'til morning. He could come and drive it in."

When we walked into our living room, I gasped. I knew Steve had been in a lot of pain, but in the dark I hadn't been able to see any physical change. Now I could see not only that his eye was swollen shut, but that the eyeball itself was bulging out of its socket. It looked as if some great malevolent thumb were pushing at it from behind. It seemed as big as an egg and was threatening to burst through his eyelid.

Bill, who was at the door to welcome us, was also greatly alarmed. We put Steve to bed immediately with the same old rag-tag, make-shift ice pack. Oh, why hadn't I gotten a proper one?

The rest of the family hovered near him while I started to call doctors. The three or four local doctors who knew something of Steve's problem were out of town for the Thanksgiving weekend.

When I had seen his swollen eye, I began to shiver. Now, my hands shook, my voice broke, and my teeth chattered as I strove to speak coherently.

I thought, "The night he was born, my labor also started with a hard chill."

Angered that my mind should leap to any comparison, I prayed, "Oh God, spare us. I cannot bear these thoughts!"

Finally I called Dr. Hardy in St. Louis. He told me to keep ice on Steve's eye all night and to bring him to St. Elizabeth's Hospital first thing the next morning.

At 7:00 a.m., Steve was lying on the back seat of the car, as comfortable as we could make him with blankets and pillows. He was wearing his new coat.

The pain had yielded a little to medication, but it was still bad. The leathery, frozen look once again imprisoned his features. We drove swiftly down the lane and once more headed for St. Louis.

I was glad there was no time—or sentiment—for him to look long and lovingly at his dog Lumpi, or his cat Zanzibar, or his woods, or the house he'd helped build, or David, or his life.

Winter was here in earnest.

The Eye of the Hurricane

As the hospital bracelet was clamped about his slender wrist, Steve commented wryly, "I'm getting quite a collection of these things. I bet not many people are trying to beat my record though."

While Dr. Hardy examined Steve in another room, I said to the one other woman in the waiting room, "This is hard when you are just seventeen!"

"It is hard when you are seventy-one, too," she replied in a scared, flat voice. I recalled then the older gentleman who had preceded Stephen and the cankerous black sore on his huge swollen hand.

On this quiet Sunday morning, I recognized our fear as the same tight atmosphere of "vigil" we'd known before. It had not ended—not ended at all. The weeks at home were just a respite—only the eye of the hurricane—a time-out. Now the adversary seemed even more formidable, and we had been unaware of its stealthy approach.

Dr. Hardy spoke to Bill—Steve stood behind him looking very sick and scared. "You are to take him to Barnes and have him readmitted. I want Dr. Sessions to see him immediately. I think the pressure is from the infection, and it must be building up at an alarming rate."

"Immediately" is a word with an indefinite meaning. It meant one thing to Dr. Hardy; it meant a sense of frantic urgency—of *now*—to Bill and me; and apparently it meant nothing at all to the admitting office of Barnes.

It was absolutely the worst day of red tape and endless, needless waiting that I have ever experienced. A nurse took away Steve's medication, so there was no way to ease his pain. The pain became intense, and occasionally a scalding tear slid from his closed eyes. I begged for just one pill, but was refused. We were never told why—or why there was a delay in admitting him.

After a couple of hours, when Steve became very nauseated, I ran and begged for a towel.

I was asked, "Why is your son nauseated, Mrs. Warner? What is the nature of his illness? Has this happened before?"

By the time I got back with the towel, it was too late.

It took more than three hours to get Steve to a room where he could lie down. We did not see Dr. Sessions that day. Once he was admitted, though, things happened quickly. Doctors were everywhere. We were met by Dr. LeFarrier.

Apparently things were not going well for him that Sunday either. The first examining room we went into had not been cleaned; he wheeled Steve to another, and it, too, was cluttered and messy. Dr. LeFarrier muttered something. With an angry flourish he tipped everything off the table onto the floor and rubbed the table clear with his coat sleeve.

Dr. LeFarrier was a man with deft hands and a genteel manner—whoever his ancestors might have been. He would work with Steve closely for a couple of days, keeping an almost hourly check on his blood count and the amount of pressure on his eyeball. Like Dr. Hardy and Dr. Sessions before him, he seemed deeply concerned about the acuteness of the infection and came back repeatedly to gaze silently and worriedly into Steve's eyes. I never knew what he was looking for. I never knew what he saw. Even after Steve was no longer his responsibility, Dr. LeFarrier continued to inquire about him.

That afternoon we also met a technician who wore a knee-length white coat and had Peter Falkish hair and mannerisms. When he turned his back to us, Steve mouthed, "Columbo."

That man, with his calipers and other highly refined devices, measured the fluid in Steve's eye so that he could predict the rate of increased pressure and decide whether surgery could be delayed until the next day. He checked and re-checked his measurements. He seemed so concerned about Steve—so careful and concerned—it made me even more scared. But he decided that surgery could wait.

The surgery on Monday, November 25, was like a replay of the surgery in October. Dr. Sessions operated again. He had been out of town the day before, when Steve was readmitted. The operation did not reveal anything particularly sinister—just more of the same. Steve's sinus cavity was scraped and cleaned again, and another rubber hose was inserted to drain off the excess fluid that had caused the frightful swelling.

Once again we were assured it would be only a matter of time until Steve was completely well. It wasn't so funny to see him with that tube in his head this time—if indeed it ever had been.

Hallowe'en was over.

Thanksgiving was over.

Christmas was approaching.

It didn't feel now as though we were keeping vigil. This was familiar territory—scary, but a route we'd traveled before. We could do it again.

This time Bill stayed with Steve while I went home to teach. I came back to visit on weekends, so there is much I do not know of the closeness they shared. They both enjoyed TV, and though Steve could not read, Bill finished several books he'd brought along.

Their relationship had always been unusually close. When the children were little, Kathy and David would wake up and stumble sleepily to my lap, where they "simmered" for those few moments between sleep and waking. Not Steve. He always made a beeline for his daddy's lap. The same thing happened when they'd been at Grandma's for a few days; the other two would run to me, but Steve would run for Bill's outstretched arms. For a long time he thought that Bill was God; and when, at about age thirteen he discovered he wasn't, it was hard for both of them for a while.

Their time together at the hospital must have been rich, for Steve and Bill were a great deal alike. They shared an innate enthusiasm and optimism that buoyed them along. Steve had the gift of living each day largely and in confidence that all the rest of life would come his way.

As the intuitive Mennonite author, Nathaniel Willis said, nature called him with a "thousand songs to share the general feast." And Steve was eager to accept every invitation.

They did tell me of one funny but poignant incident. Steve's doctors were confident he would bounce back quickly. When his bounce was slow to return, Dr. Sessions implied that there might be a degree of malingering.

"Now Steve," he said, "you're going to have to stand a little pain, Buddy. You're never going to get any stronger lying here on your back. No wonder you don't eat—you don't get enough exercise to give you an appetite!"

Perhaps this made Steve a little angry, or perhaps it gave him hope that he really was on the verge of recovery and he just needed to push a little harder. Whatever the impetus, he rode the elevator down eleven flights of stairs and walked back up seven different times that day. Later, he started at the bottom, rode up and walked down five more times.

Although by now the outward swelling was gone and the pain could be held to a bearable level, this was a great deal more exercise than the doctor would have allowed. Only three days earlier, orders had been for "bed rest only."

Flushed from exertion, Steve asked Bill, "Do you think Dr. Sessions will think that's enough exercise?"

The next day, Bill said, Steve asked whether he could think of any medication or anything that would cause the calves of his legs to ache. After nearly two months without much use, those muscles must have been screaming in protest. That man-child was still so young, so trusting, so naive.

Even before Steve's second surgery, Bill and I had decided we could not go to Mexico.

"Not this year," we said. "We dare not take him out of the country."

December 20 would be too soon to be sure the infection wouldn't flare up again. The decision was easy; the risk was unthinkable.

But Steve took it hard. "Why, in three weeks I'll be well," he argued. "Dad's already rented the big motor home—we'll never have everything this perfect again. Don't call off the trip."

He tried to convince us. Three weeks? It had already been seven, and we were still a long way from being home free.

Every day the same tests were followed by the same puzzlement—the infection was still there, unshaken by massive doses of antibiotics. Could this infection account for his pain and the inexplicable weakness?

It was beginning to feel like a vigil again—the territory was becoming strange and shadowy once more.

Finally, Dr. Sessions told us of another procedure—an obliteration—a drastic surgery resorted to in extreme cases. He explained that when a sinus infection cannot be eradicated, the entire sinus cavity can be opened, scraped, and packed with fat taken from the patient's abdomen. He thought Steve's case warranted it. There was always the threat that the infection would seep through that thin partition to Steve's marvelous brain.

We were frightened, and so we agreed to the operation, as bizarre and gruesome as it was. I do not know what else we could have done. Two doctors on the staff of one of the finest hospitals in the United States recommended this procedure to us.

Steve, typically, was eager to have it done, saying things like, "Well, I'm sure not getting well this way." Or, "Now I'll be able to scuba dive again. If they do away with the sinus, I sure can't get another sinus squeeze."

He was heartbreakingly eager to get back to school. Every weekend a carload of friends came to see him. Dozens of cards and letters still came every week. Before his hospital stay was ended, he must have received two bushels of them.

Once Steve put down a letter and grinned ruefully, "Well, that may be the only good thing that ever comes of this whole mess."

"What do you mean?"

"Mr. Hayden has announced that if I can't be back in two weeks, he's going to have to put in someone else as drum major. That will suit me fine."

"Oh no!" I said with a pang. "I haven't seen you enough."

I'd driven him to practice often, but I had seen only one half-time show. Guiltily I wondered what I had been doing while he was leading his first parade. Had I washed a couple of sheets or perhaps cleaned the kitchen?

"I thought you liked being drum major." I added, "I thought you looked cute."

"That's just it. Who wants to look cute their senior year?"

"I didn't mean cutesy cute. I just thought you looked pretty sharp. Won't you miss it?"

"Oh, it's not so bad I guess. Still, I won't care if he gives the job to someone else. I think I'd rather play the sax again. If the doctor does do this obliteration, I wonder how long it will be before I can be back in school? I sure don't want to go to summer school."

"That wouldn't be so awful, would it? Even if you miss the whole year, you're barely seventeen—almost a year younger than most of the kids in your class. At the most, you might have to pick up civics. You wouldn't have to go all summer."

"I hope not. Summer school—Ugh!"

It wasn't easy to sign for the obliteration. We read the fine print, trying to understand all that it meant, when all the time we knew. It meant we would not blame them if things went wrong. It meant we would not sue them if Steve died.

The procedure seemed simple as Dr. Sessions explained it. Simple, yet bizarre.

"I will cut under each eyebrow and across the bridge of the nose so I can lift the forehead back. Then I will take fat from his stomach and pack the entire sinus cavity solid, leaving no room for infection to thrive. It sounds gruesome, but it should heal nicely."

"Steve doesn't have enough fat in his stomach to pack a sinus cavity," I said, envisioning globs of yellow chicken fat. "He's always been thin, and I bet he's lost twenty pounds since he's been in here."

I babbled on. "I hate to have this done to him. Will he have an awful scar?"

"No, not really," Dr. Sessions explained. "You'll hardly be able to see it after a few months."

"He's had a scar in his right eyebrow since he was eight months old, when the car seat pitched him onto the dashboard."

"I doubt if this scar will be that noticeable."

Fortunately, I have only a few memories of that third surgery. I remember that Steve's entire face was terribly swollen. I remember he was in great pain. He was expected to be in the intensive care unit for about five to twelve hours, and he was kept there two days instead. I remember he had visitors from Carbondale, and one girl, Cathy, threw her hand over her mouth and started to cry when she saw him. Sometime after he had been transferred to a private room, the National Hot Air Balloon Race started at St. Louis's Forest Park. When eight huge balloons sailed past his window, I tried to get him to look. He said he hurt too bad and did not even try to see them.

Not watch eight hot air balloons sail past his window? Steve? My adventurous son? He must be very sick—worse even than I had feared.

Yet, somehow, my fears were allayed by the staff. Reassured, I returned the next week to my teaching, again leaving Steve with his father. All of us spent each weekend with him, and one week Russ stayed a few days with Steve, letting Bill go back to the church.

Russ never said much about their time together. Once, he had walked through a light snow to the Planetarium, and Steve had kept him in sight the entire time with his binoculars. I wish I knew more of what they talked about.

Progress was slow—so much slower than the doctors had expected. Where was wunderkind? What had happened to the boy with the derring-do? The boy who could always lick anything? Perhaps because he had always been a wunderkind we never doubted his complete recovery.

Yet, unwanted, unbidden, half-forgotten stories whirled in my mind. Poe's sailor in *Descent into the Maelstrom,* whose hair had turned snow white without his knowing it, and poor Samson who "Wist not that his strength had departed from him" gnawed at me. Unable to do anything—impotent—but still thinking ourselves capable, we were deep within "vigil" and still thought it merely "episode." Like the men of old, our hair was turning—our strength was ebbing.

So was Stephen's. I could tell he was worried. One day, on a particularly obnoxious TV ad, a woman simpered, "If you've got your health, you've got everything."

Wistfully, Steve said, "You know, she's right. I've been sick enough, long enough to know that without good health, you've not got very much."

Steve often discussed scuba diving. I had come to despise the sport that had brought him such pain and danger. I wished I'd never heard of it—that he had never signed up for the stupid course. Not so Steve.

Several times I heard him say, "I'm in another world down there. It's worth all the pain of all three of these surgeries."

He meant it, but I hated the very words.

Steve still could not eat much, and he still looked tired and thin when I left him on Sunday afternoon, December 9. We talked on the phone every night. Sometimes his voice was shaky and he sounded homesick, but usually the conversations were satisfying. Sometimes they were a little stilted and bored.

Bill's reports, too, were always the same. What could they tell us they hadn't told us last night, and the night before, and the night before that?

"Then another ant brought in a grain of wheat."

The words were as unchanging as the tales of little Scherazade.

Sometimes I could tell I had interrupted a crucial moment on television. Steve had cable TV and watched a lot of old re-runs of things he'd seen as a little boy—"Leave It to Beaver" (he and Dave had once seem themselves as Beaver and Wally) and "Star Trek" were two favorites.

TV Trivia was big at home, and one day Steve exclaimed, "No wonder Morgan (Bob Morgan, a friend of both our boys) can always beat me at Trivia. He's got cable TV at home. I bet I've stored up as much as he has while I've been here. Just wait 'til I get home!"

We weren't going to have to wait long. Dr. Sessions said Steve was progressing. Finally! Then the night came when Steve called home and there was no boredom in his voice, no fumbling around for something to say.

"Guess what? I'm going to come home! I'm coming home Friday!"

"IT" IS AT THE DOOR

The Psalmist says there is a river, the streams whereof shall make glad the city of God—a river of joy flowing through the city of our Lord. I like that. Those sinewy desert people of the Old Testament never took water for granted. The Hebrews spoke of God as springs in the desert—rivers of living water to a thirsty people. I have felt the flow of this stream—have exulted in the swelling surge as I sensed my life given deeper meaning by being aligned with some great eternal purpose. If only the current didn't sweep us along so fast.

Events are like that current—always it seems that events propel us too quickly. Ever since I was a little girl I've felt my life was speeding by too swiftly. I never tear pages off a calendar without a sense of loss.

Some people say, "Oh, I wouldn't be young again for anything in this world," or "I certainly don't want to live my life over," or "I'm so glad I've got my children raised."

I seldom believe them. Until Steve became ill I would have liked to have each span of my life last twice as long. There was hardly a day that I did not want to prolong—to savor.

I remember especially a day in Johnston City, where we lived when Stephen was born. I was sitting on my front steps, late one afternoon, as gentle spring rain fell. Across the alley, the neighbor's peach tree was in full bloom. All at once, despite the rain, the sun broke through, limning the peach tree and the bright green grass in a kind of earthly halo. Suddenly, I realized I was crying. My cup was already full—and then that. But the beauty passed me by too quickly. Even as I watched, the sun began to fade.

And now—now that Steve is better, actually coming home—oh, how I will savor our every day.

The calendar on my classroom wall was turned to December 13. I jumped at the intrusion of the loudspeaker. "Mrs. Warner," the disembodied voice called. "Please come to the office. You have a long distance call. Your husband is on the phone."

I hurried down the stairs. Why would Bill call me at school? "Today is Thursday, and Steve is coming home tomorrow." I thought, "Maybe he's bringing Steve home today! I bet that's it. They've remembered how scared and worried I was the last time, and they want to prepare me."

"Hello. Bill? Is that you?"

"Honey...." Bill's voice was muffled. It hardly sounded like my husband.

Then I realized he was crying.

"Bill, what's wrong? What is it? I can hardly hear you."

Fighting for control, he continued. "Honey, they think Steve has a brain tumor."

The world stood still as he went on.

"You know the doctors have not been satisfied with his progress, and this morning...." His voice broke. "Something in the way he walked this morning made them call in another doctor. He had them run another series of tests, and just a little while ago they gave me the report. They're sure it's a brain tumor."

"How is he?"

"They haven't told him yet. Of course he knows something is wrong. I told the doctors that I would not leave him here a day longer; he'd had enough. I was going to bring him home tomorrow as planned, and then we'd see about this latest diagnosis at another time. Well, I learned what happens if you ever cross them. Within minutes a swarm of doctors called me out and said there was no way I could do that. Honey...."

Again that struggle to form the words. It was from my gentle, compassionate husband that Steve inherited the tendency for quick tears.

He went on. "Honey—they say he will surely die if we don't let them operate."

A portion of one's mind can be frozen—numb—and the rest can function at a reflex level.

"Is Kathy with him now?"

"Yes. I met her train this morning, and she's been with him ever since."

"It's almost time for school to be out. I'll just wait for the carpool. Will you call David so he can be ready when I get home? And Russ—Russ will want to come, too. We'll be there as quickly as we can."

"We'll just walk through it," we'd said back in Carbondale, on October 11. "We'll just have to walk through it together."

But "It" was like a snowball that had been gathering force and mass, silently enlarging itself until now it was a veritable avalanche of blank, smothering whiteness. "It" was now at the door.

I had thought I always would be able to reach out and touch my life river—to thrill to a thrush's trill, to see a wayside violet. But oh, what could I do if the river had been filled in and even the pools dried up? What could I do if my life-giving river disappeared.

I arrived home about five, and David and Russ and I headed for the hospital with all possible speed.

"Well! What are you all doing here?"

Steve looked pleased to see us—especially David and Russ, with whom there was the usual gentle cuffing that's an acceptable greeting among young males.

"Why did you decide to come tonight? I'm coming home tomorrow."

Did our presence alarm Steve? Probably so, because of the new tests that had been run. Although he had been told nothing, he was sharp enough to know he'd been seriously ill. On November 19, his last day at school, he and Mary Beth had written notes to each other in English class. Months later, she shared those notes with me.

After some boy-girl chit-chat, she had written, "How are you, really?"

Steve had written back, "Me? How should I know? Don't you know, the patient is always the last to know? Russ and I were talking the other day, and we're sure I'll have to have the operation.

I'm convinced I may be blind, but I'm sure after a great deal of thought and MUCH PRAYER [sic] I can handle it!"

Blindness had not once entered my mind, but I had no idea of the intensity of his pain. I saw only the strabismus or wandering eye that the doctors assured us was a minor symptom.

"I'm sure after a great deal of thought and MUCH PRAYER I can handle it!"

In the midst of all his optimism, his courage, his interest in every technique and procedure, there must have been a gut fear (not quite covered by the gay and noble banter) and a dark foreboding. Steve was no fool.

He told us about the new tests. "Would you believe they gave me the drunk test this morning and I failed? I couldn't walk a straight line!"

Bill told us that Steve had also made a mistake in counting backwards by sevens, from one hundred. An awesome and vastly intricate thing, the brain.

We learned that Dr. Sessions had called in Dr. Robert Racheson for consultation, and he had administered the tests. Dr. Racheson, one of the eminent neurosurgeons of the Midwest, was on the staff of the Barnes Hospital Complex and was also a teacher at Washington University School of Medicine. He was to be Steve's surgeon. That night he told us of his grim discovery in unrelenting detail—our son had a brain tumor.

The image of a broken plate—a plate with a great piece missing—floated before me. That's what our family seemed without Steve.

When we plied Dr. Racheson with questions as to how such a thing could have been overlooked—when this was the fearful diagnosis that had caused us to rush him to St. Louis two months earlier—his answers were noncommittal. His best explanation was that indeed Steve had had a sinus infection, and for some reason the many doctors who had examined him had seen that and had not looked for other causes. He was careful not to incriminate others—doctors close ranks—but he told us with evident tenderness and sorrow that he was positive surgery was Steve's only chance.

He must have our immediate approval to proceed with plans to operate on Tuesday, December 18, if Steve's condition remained stable, or on Monday if he could not wait. We did not understand the delay—five days seemed an eternity—but Dr. Racheson explained that his best crew worked on Tuesday. We needed the best.

How does a doctor manage to give you hope without actually saying anything definitely encouraging?

John Gunther, whose many books include *Death Be Not Proud,* the story of his own son's losing battle with brain tumor, said after countless interviews with his son's doctors, "I'm sure of one thing. Doctors tell you nothing."

I don't remember exactly what Dr. Racheson said about Steve's chances. I'm sure he did not lie; yet I remember leaving him with the feeling that we had a chance—a good chance. We just had to hold together until Tuesday.

I turned to Bill and the children and said, "I won't tell him. He's had enough. We can't tell him that he has a brain tumor." I babbled on. "We'll just let him go into surgery thinking he's going to have another sinus operation."

"Mama! I don't believe you!" David's voice was tight and shallow, his knuckles white as he gripped his own hands. "I can't believe you'd do that to Steve. If you won't tell him, I will. We've always sworn we'd be honest with each other if anything like this ever happened. He's got to be told. He deserves to know the truth!"

David's voice broke. "Would you believe he told me last winter he thought he had a brain tumor?"

"Why? What made him think that?" We all asked at once.

"I don't know exactly. His headaches, I guess. And last winter, when Steve and Tim and I were camping, he thought the fire had scattered and he jumped up to put it out before it caught the woods on fire. But the fire hadn't scattered at all; he was just seeing two fires. I think it must have been this same double vision thing that's been so bad lately. We didn't think any more about it. Tim and I laughed and told him it was just his eyes playing tricks on him. But it was more than that; most of all I guess it was just a feeling he had."

Why hadn't he told us? Why? And why hadn't we been intuitive enough to know? Why couldn't we see something was wrong? Where was that inmost eye that mothers are supposed to have?

"Let's go tell him," I said wearily, and we went to Steve's room.

"Well, what is it?" His voice was a little clipped and brittle with urgency.

"Darling," I said, trying to keep the terror out of my voice. "They have found something—a tumor in your brain—and they think that that's what's causing your pain and your weakness."

I don't remember what Bill said, or Kathy, or David. But somehow we found a tiny island of sanity amidst a whirling maelstrom, and that gave us the strength to endure.

After a while, Steve said, with a hint almost of triumph in his voice, "I knew my headaches must be different from the kind other people have!"

Yet, when we searched our memories, none of us could remember much mention of headaches—maybe a few that summer, but none that we did not attribute to lack of sleep, too much time spent in the water, or some other logical cause.

It seemed as if events were out of control—like a raging current—sweeping away the stuff of life. Bottle—diaper change—lullaby—bottle—nap time—bottle. Events propelled us. The child was grown. And so quickly we are through. This was the reality. My river of joy was the illusion.

"No! I won't believe that. My stream is not an illusion! Even with Steve so ill, I will not believe it."

In those halcyon days before Steve got sick, I knew there was a stream. And even then, in that awful drought, I knew, with some primal understanding, that there was a river—a river of joy. It was not just a current of events that tossed us willy-nilly from eddy to whirlpool to sandbar, finally losing us forever in some monstrous and inescapable maelstrom.

I remember nothing clearly—except that we were all there and all in that maelstrom together. But Steve was in it in a different way—in a way that we could not know, though Bill and I ached with our yearning to save him from it.

Oh, Steve. Mama thought she looked. How could she not have seen?

FIVE LONG DAYS AND THEN—TOMORROW

In five days Steve would have surgery. What is the best way to say, "I love you?" How do you say those words to someone who is dearer to you than life itself? That's how our family spent those five days.

Soon after Dr. Racheson made his diagnosis, Steve was moved to the tenth floor—to neurosurgery. His new room was more like a fine hotel room than a hospital room—if we could ignore the charts and emergency equipment.

As we made the move, I tried not to look at the lackluster faces of many of the patients as they shuffled up and down the corridors on their endless exercise rounds. Surely our son would never be like that. Dr. Racheson had told us. . . . My mind stopped. I was not sure exactly what Dr. Racheson had told us.

On Friday, December 14, this almost-grown male child of ours—this child who in so many ways had been so much an adult since he was three years old—looked at me and said, quite matter-of-factly, "I don't want to be left alone again."

And so we stayed. His daddy one night. I, another.

As soon as Steve was in his new private room, Kathy bought a string of lights and shaped a Christmas tree on the window. This lifted our spirits a little. Then, after the shift changed, a nurse stopped by.

"I saw your Christmas tree from the street—it's beautiful." She paused, "Now, I have to tell you to take it down; it's against our rules."

She seemed sorry.

Undaunted, Steve had us save all the little medicine cups and make a plastic pyramid tree out of them. Soon there were so many that a large triangle shape stood on the window sill. Someone said, "We'll spray them gold or green and make a tree that will always remind you of the Christmas you spent in Barnes Hospital."

In retrospect, our routine seems mundane. Doris Lund, in *Eric,* the story of her son's fight against leukemia, says that when her son-in-law, who had not been to the hospital, saw how the disease had so wasted and ravaged Eric's young body, he fainted dead away. She wrote, "that is the only honest and proper response to such a thing." I agreed.

Yet, we tried to be normal—whatever "normal" was under such conditions. It was not easy to escape from so awful a reality.

Conversation was easier when Steve's brother and sister were there, and they came often. Bill and I were there all the time. Bill read fiction. I could not follow the thread of a story, so I worked endless crossword puzzles. Steve's particular evasion seemed to be television. Once I scribbled on a flyleaf:

Hospital Inanities
"What's a three-letter word for Roman Bronze?"
"I've seen this re-run fifty times."
When all the time we want to cry,
"Why am I mortal?
When will I die?"

It bothers me that we did not talk more of the ordeal Steve was facing. I gain some comfort from the fact that he asked us to be with him and that we never left.

A stream of doctors examined Steve—probing, measuring, checking. One of our favorites was Dr. Michael Ryan, whose time on the neurosurgery ward coincided with Steve's. Unfortunately, his stint was over in January, and ours was not. Dr. Ryan was a wild-eyed young man, thin and gaunt, whose mop of black curly hair made him an easy subject for caricature.

In an attempt at humor one day, Dave drew a picture of him with the caption, "How would you like to wake up at midnight and see this character leaning over your hospital bed?"

Steve retorted, "Hey! Cut that out. You're making fun of my doctor."

Sometimes Dr. Ryan would come in just to chat with Steve—man talk about backpacking, canoeing, ambitions, plans. Sometimes he would stand at the foot of Steve's bed or by his side and watch him—just look at him for fifteen minutes at a time. There were endless tests and exercises.

"Can you touch your nose with you right forefinger? With each successive finger of your right hand? Can you do the same with your left hand? Touch your right ear lobe with your left hand. Can you touch the fingertips of your right hand to the fingertips of your left hand without looking?"

Skills so easy and done so unerringly that sometimes Steve grumbled.

"What's wrong, Doc? Do you think I'm crazy? Is this supposed to be hard or something?"

Dr. Ryan would just smile a little and put Steve through other similar tests, or else he would turn and leave without a word.

Saturday morning Steve fretted because his hair was dirty. He had always been fastidious about his hair. He was proud that although McDonald's had a general rule that boys' hair should not touch their collars, he was allowed to keep his hair longer because he kept it so clean. It was dark brown, but the sun lent it reddish highlights. It didn't look bad, but since it bothered him—and since it was something to do—Kathy found some dry shampoo in the hospital gift shop and "drycleaned" him.

Steve's comment was, "Well, it'll never take the place of a hot, sudsy shower, but it's better than nothing."

Our family's base was now at the home of Bob and JoAnn Gordon. While visiting someone at the hospital one day, Bob, pastor of Grace United Methodist Church, in St. Louis, had seen Bill. Hearing of our trouble, he had graciously offered us their home, only seven minutes away from the hospital. We moved our bags from the Cogswell's, across the Mississippi River, to the Gordon's. JoAnn and Bob, like Barb and Chuck Cogswell, were wonderful friends at a time when our need was great.

Steve was elated when the Mooreheads called on Friday to say that Tim was coming to visit. Tim and Steve. Steve and Tim. Best friends forever. Steve said he was going to name his first boy after Tim—Timothy Lucas. Tim flew down on Saturday from Green Bay. No gesture of friendship was ever more eloquent or more deeply appreciated.

Because the tests were all completed, Dr. Racheson prescribed powerful pain medication. With his brutal agony eased, Steve was able to enjoy most of Tim's visit.

It was good to see Tim with the boys—laughing, making jokes. Once we were all asked to step out of Steve's room while the staff performed some lengthy procedure. Thirty minutes later, when we went back in, there was Steve's form, still and straight, with the sheet pulled over his head! We could not help but gasp until we saw the bed shaking. How Steve laughed as he threw back the sheet.

Tim spent Saturday night alone with Steve. I'd wanted David to have that privilege—he was entitled—but never mind. There would be a lifetime of nights for David and Steve to be together. If Tim was apprehensive, he did not show it.

In the morning we learned that the boys had not slept much; Steve was sick several times, so Tim stayed beside him, holding the wet towel and the basin. The "emesis basin" it was called—such a euphemistic name for such a practical and prosaic article. The boys agreed on "pukette" as a name far more descriptive and less innocuous. This was pretty strong stuff for boys who a few months before had sing-songed:

> Jason, Jason, get the basin.
> Too late, Pop, get the mop.

Sunday morning, right after breakfast, everybody started to play a game called "Risk." I did not play but sat nearby and knitted. That particular game had always seemed ruthless and aggressive to me, but that day I exulted in every rowdy remark, every loud put-down, every rude rejoinder.

Clearly these are not people on the brink of disaster.
See how they laugh and play?

The very normalcy of the noisy, raucous game seemed to hold the dark at bay.

At midmorning, Steve decided he did not want to finish the game. Kathy carefully marked each person's play so they could continue when the operation was over and Steve was back in his room again.

Shortly after lunch, other young people began to arrive. Surely few hospital rooms have held such a throng as that host who rallied around Steve that Sunday, December 16. Many drove from Carbondale, to tell him in their own clumsy way that they loved him. Many were unable to come—like his friend, Eric, who walked four miles only to find his ride had left without him. When the day was over, forty people had been there—sixteen in the room at one time!

There had also been a steady trickle of visitors from Bill's former pastorates—dear friends who came to pay in kind for the years we'd shared their lives—for the anxious hours Bill had spent with them.

As the nurses made frequent trips to bring pain medication, they appeared oblivious to the visitors and even seemed apologetic about disrupting the fun. They, so much more than we, knew what was in store for Steve.

Late in the afternoon, Dave drove Tim to the airport, and as he reached for Steve's coat, Steve called, "Keep your mitts off my new coat." But he grinned and Dave looked quite jaunty as he walked out the door wearing it.

All night long a string of nurses checked on Steve. Dr. Ryan also made frequent visits. Bill and I scrunched into our chairs in the corner, trying to be unobtrusive, but there was no way I could sleep. It was not the hard and unyielding chair that kept me awake; it was the dark foreboding—it would not go away.

A little before midnight, I slipped into the bathroom with paper and pen; I sat on the floor and wrote, "Sunday, December 16," at the top of a blank sheet.

Kathy, our first-born was christened twenty-three years ago on that date; Bill's father had died twenty years before on that date; and now it was another December 16.

My fingers raced over page after page as my heart overflowed with love for Steve—with the yearning that he be made well again. It was the first of many love letters I wrote to my very ill son during the next months.

In the morning, with as much light-heartedness as I could muster, I said, "I'd like to read you a letter I wrote last night."

"I don't want you to read it to me," Steve said.

"Honey, it's not a sad letter. It's just a love letter that I'd truly meant to write to you before you got sick—I think it was the night you had two flat tires and I was so worried. It's not sad—it's just a letter telling you how much I love you."

"Then sit with me and hold my hand instead," he insisted.

And so I did. The television was on and, although his eyes were on the screen, my eyes were on him. Occasionally I saw his eyes brim full and a big tear slide down his tawny cheek. We did not talk—just felt the nearness and the clasped hands. Now that he could have enough medicine to quell the pain, Steve seemed almost well—what lay ahead was unthinkable.

I kept that letter, and weeks later, I slipped into the intensive care unit and read potions of it to him. Perhaps he heard. Perhaps he already knew what I'd written that day when he said, "Sit beside me, Mama, and hold my hand."

By late afternoon, Steve did not seem so well. No amount of medication could quell his nausea. One nurse explained that it might be the mounting tension, with the surgery so near. But I was afraid it was more likely the effect of the tumor.

I didn't know which theory was worse. I knew so little.

One day that past summer, Eric had come home with Steve for lunch. I fixed them pizza and corn on the cob.

Just as I set the food on the table, Steve, who'd been as hungry as Eric, said, "I don't think I can eat after all, Mom; I'm kind of sick all of a sudden."

That's all there was to it.

After Eric finished his half pizza and two ears of corn, he laughed and said, "Well, I've eaten my dinner, I guess now I'll eat Steve's." And he did, while Steve sat at the table and talked to him.

It was such a little thing, and it happened only once—only once. But why didn't I suspect something?

My nurse friend, Marti, told me later that had been a warning, if I'd known to pick up on it. As I ran that summer back through my mind, I remembered my antacid tablets. Occasionally Steve asked for a couple. Surely, it could not have been more than two or three times; I remember he asked for aspirin about that often, too.

How could I have been so casual about that? How could I have passed off nausea as an effect of late working hours?

How could the doctors have probed and measured and checked him for two months and not have seen the tumor that the sinus infection only masked?

Late in the afternoon, a nurse and an aide came in to explain to Steve that his head was to be shaved. Of course he knew it would happen, but it was a little shocking to hear them explain it. Kathy and I tried to cheer him up with our Yul Brynner jokes.

Then I said, "When Grandma was a little girl, one of her friends had typhoid fever and lost all her hair. It grew back blonde and curly. Instead of black hair, she had blonde curly ringlets all over her head."

Steve groaned. "That's all I need—blonde curly ringlets."

I turned to the nurse and asked, "How do you think it will come back? Black like his eyebrows, or in blonde curly ringlets?"

She chuckled. "Oh, I *know* how it will come back. It'll come back in a bag."

Her joke seemed funnier to her than to us.

The hospital chaplain was a man named Bob Davis. I spent some time with him and was disappointed that he didn't pass out rabbit's feet, sugar pills, or a sure certainty of God's healing power. Bob Davis had not talked with Steve at any length because visitors or medical staff had been in Steve's room every time the chaplain came to visit. However, he seemed to be touched by Steve's illness—to be grieved by it personally—and he listened, really listened, as I told him about our family and what a special person Steve was.

I liked Bob Davis for many reasons. For one, he didn't fall apart at the sight of a woman broken and in despair, with her nose running and snot and tears falling down in her lap.

When visiting hours were over, none of us could bear to leave. Steve wanted us, and the nurses looked the other way.

Once I asked Steve if he'd like to talk to the chaplain, and he replied, "No, Mom. I've made my peace with God."

As evening dragged into night, there was no one Steve had to act brave for. There was just our little family—and he could be genuine with us. We were so scared that we were exceedingly gentle with each other.

We had discussed life and death—and our faith and our doubts about eternal life—many times.

But now Steve said to me, as he put a card back in its envelope, "One thing I've learned—never send a serious card to someone who's seriously ill."

Perhaps that's why he didn't talk of serious things to me. We had talked about deep things since he'd been four, but it was to Kathy that he said, "If I die, I guess I'll know Aunt Earle. She'll love me. And there's Uncle Ralph, too."

Sometime in the night I heard Steve say, "I wish they'd put Mom to sleep tomorrow, just as they put me under. She'll never be able to make it. It'll be harder on her than it is on me."

Soon it would be tomorrow. Tomorrow. As a child, when I could hardly stand the anticipation of a birthday or Christmas, I learned that once I could say, "tomorrow," the event was almost upon me.

But, now, tomorrow no longer held a golden promise.

By the light from the hall I see it is past midnight. It is no longer tomorrow, but today. It is officially Tuesday, December 18, 1973. I wonder if any of us will live through it.

REMEMBER NOW, HANG ON!

"Remember now. Hang on!" The words caught in my throat as I bent over the bed of my son.

It was 5:45 a.m., Tuesday, December 18. I did not know that operations were ever scheduled so early. Dr. Racheson had told us this one would be long and difficult.

"You've always been the kid who could hang on the longest and fight the hardest," I told Steve. "You can struggle and fight your way out of any kind of stranglehold, remember? There was only one time David ever tied you up so that you couldn't get loose. Remember that?"

"Yeah, I remember." He turned to Dave, who was hovering close by. "You bound me tight and trussed me up like a steer and then tied the rope to the ceiling beam, you Dilbert! I could have gotten untied, but I'd have fallen twenty feet to the floor and landed on my head."

David laughed and squeezed his brother's shoulder. "Hang in there, buddy. You're the one who never says 'give,' remember? Well, just keep it up. Today's no time to stop being scrappy!"

"Remember now . . . Hang on."

Our words, somewhere between plea and command, must go with you into the operating room. They must be so imprinted that you will not lose them in the long dark hours ahead.

"I know. I'll remember. I'll fight with all I've got."

Despite the pain, the nausea, the fear, and all the dangling tubes, wires, and other monitoring paraphernalia, Steve managed somehow to look almost jaunty and optimistic as he said this.

Half laughing, half crying, Bill, Kathy, Russ, David, and I kept murmuring little endearments and words of encouragement to Steve as we leaned over the stretcher while the orderlies wheeled him away. As long as we could reach him, there had been much patting, many little pressed kisses, squeezes of his hands. Three quick squeezes always meant "I love you." Now, they moved him quickly away—too quickly.

They are trundling Steve away so swiftly. One wheel wobbles and makes a noise. We follow them down the hall of Barnes Hospital, St. Louis, Missouri, U.S.A., World, Universe, Mind of God.

We are nearing the elevator. Oh, I cannot bear for them to take him out of our sight. We are trailing along behind, still waving. There is his long, thin hand waving back from the white gown.

Steve had always hated the stops on other floors. So many times in the last two months, he had endured interminable waits for this test or that. There were no books or magazines to read in the elevators or halls; no letters to write; no windows; no TV. There were no roommate's laughs or groans to take his mind off his own great problems.

Oh, my son, lying on a gurney in a hallway, there is nothing to divert your thinking from the terrible danger that has gathered like a cloud about you—a dark cloud that can not be scattered. What must you be feeling now?

A few times Bill had slipped down and waited with Steve, although these narrower corridors had been off limits to all but patients and hospital personnel. Once I glimpsed a big room off one of these hallways. It was like a vast concrete barn. Did the floor slant? Surely not, and yet I remember it as having about a five degree tilt. I wondered what would happen if the brakes gave way on all those tables. Would the patients go careening around in some macabre soap box derby?

"I am going mad," I thought.

The elevator gates clang. The whine tells us Steve is on his way down to the operating room. We turn. Catching hold of one anothers' hands, we make our way back up the long corridor to the waiting room.

We wait. We are stick people now—wooden sticks of hope and endurance. Bill carries a book he does not read. I look at my crossword puzzle book but do not open it. Kathy has a piece of knitting, but never starts to knit. David seeks no distraction, but every time I look at him, his knuckles are white.

Occasionally David and Russ make the rounds to look out another window. Every hour or so, the three young people drain off some tension by walking up a few flights of stairs. There is little conversation. If someone tries to make a little joke or pleasantry, it meets such meager response that it hangs in the atmosphere like a voice balloon—naked and apologetic. We are all geared for one thing today —endurance.

We had always been a touching family but hadn't thought much about it, until the month before. Bill and Steve and I had been to St. Louis for Steve's checkup. A couple of friends were waiting with David when we got home. When we came in, each of us crossed the room and touched David in greeting—cuffed his knee, clapped his shoulder, ruffled his hair.

We were not conscious of doing this until we heard one friend say, "Gee, I wish somebody'd be that glad to see me."

That morning our need to touch was evident. We sat in a close huddle. It was not yet dawn, and as I looked from the window, car lights streaming along the highways below us looked like arteries—arteries and veins flowing with blood.

Nobody had slept much the night before, for the dark had been filled with endless, nightmarish procedures. A nurse came to insert a long tube into the large blood vessels in Steve's arm; it seemed like she was trying to push and thread a great length of it into his body. Once, Steve had winced and asked the nurse to stop, for it was no longer going the right way. She pooh-poohed that idea and probed further; finally she had to call for the doctor's help. He told her Steve had been right. Steve felt a little smug that he could be that much aware of his body. After they left, he explained to us that the tube was going to his heart, to monitor his cardiac response during surgery.

By three in the morning, a bevy of pre-op nurses moved in and began to ready Steve for the morning. They were efficient, but they couldn't agree on whether the hole in the toe of the long white elastic surgical stocking went on the top or the bottom of his foot. One said the opening must be on top so his toes could be drawn out during the operation to appraise the color of his nails; the other was just as sure that the slit must be on the bottom of his foot so a blood sample could be drawn if necessary. I don't remember how they finally put those stockings on.

I hope someone is looking at Steve's toenails now, checking their color. I've seen them almost navy blue a time or two when he's stayed in swimming until he was shriveled and pruney, with blue nails and chattering teeth.

The nurses had had to send the stockings back and get the next bigger size. No one was prepared for the size twelve feet on that slender young man! How long and thin, and yet so graceful, Steve's legs looked. We all laughed as he twisted them this way and that, mimicking a tall, wiry ballet dancer in white leotards.

God, how desperate we were to have something to laugh about.

It is with a sense of unreality that I remember the awful carefulness with which we treated each other. As things got worse and worse, we became kinder and kinder to one another. The little bits of crossness and irritability, the little bits of griping and bickering stand out as blessedly normal.

The drama being played out on the brilliantly lit, stark white stage had a bizarre and foreign feeling. I felt foreign and strange myself. It seemed almost as if our family had become disconnected from our former lives in Carbondale. Only that moment had meaning—the *now* was always in pin-point sharp focus, and everything else was hazy.

Six weeks or so later, when I went into a grocery store, I was bewildered. The conversation, the shelf items, the carts—everything seemed strange. I had become acclimated to the hospital and to crisis. So singular was my concern that I hardly recognized the person I'd become. I was no longer concerned for authority, if it seemed counter to what seemed best for Steve.

I remember the nurse who patiently explained that we must not spend the night with Steve again.

"Only one family member is allowed to stay with a patient, and the hospital frowns on even that."

I said, "Yes Ma'am," but my thoughts were hard and uncompromising. Did she really think I cared a whit about her frowns? About the rules so soberly and carefully drawn up to ease the running of this hospital?

Against my son's straightforward and unblinking look as he said, "I don't want to be left alone again," frowns and rules paled to nothing.

In that single, simple request, Steve revealed his fear at what he knew was in store for him. He was a little boy again, unashamedly asking to sleep in our room after a scary dream; asking that his family not abandon him to this snow-white sterility on the eve of his great ordeal. For him—for that child—his mealy mouthed Mama could be a lioness.

No, Steve had not been alone. We stayed with him—and not just because he asked, but because we yearned to be together for whatever loomed ahead.

Dr. Racheson had told us that Steve would be in intensive care for about five days, and then he would have his own room again. Until then, there was no place to put anything, so other patients kept part of his stuff—eight bold poinsettias and Kathy's black Santa boot filled with real holly. Kathy stuck a red German mushroom in it for good luck.

Somehow Steve had managed to talk and laugh and plan with us those last five days—rising to our efforts at gaiety. I planted a pretty little cactus garden in a piece of pottery from a yard sale. Steve had always made indulgent fun of my yen for yard sales. Once, when he went to the giant craft show and flea market in Brown County, Indiana, Steve remarked, "Mom would go crazy here!"

Where is that cactus garden now? I remember that we labeled it "Stephen Warner. Please save." We left it at the nurses' station, where the label seemed a constant prayer.

Bill and Dave put tape on all Steve's valuables—the radio, the binoculars, the terrarium, the other paraphernalia. While he was home in November, he'd gone out in the woods and found a big hickory nut to put in the terrarium beside a tiny chipmunk he'd bought in the gift shop in St. Luke's. This touch of whimsy underneath the miniature forest caused him to smile.

He had given away some of the fancy baskets of fruit. He had so many. He ate the grapes; he sent the pears home to Kathy, who never in her life had had enough; and he and Dave ate all the fresh pineapple. "M-m-m," they said as they tasted the thin, sweet juice sliding over their tongues.

Why didn't I buy more pineapples while they were growing up? Were they that much more expensive than the things I did buy? People get odd ideas about how money should be spent—moral if I want it, questionable if you want it; wise if I do it, spend-thrift if you do it—such subtle duplicity.

Like Steve's water bed. Right after Kathy's marriage, Steve used his own money to buy a water bed. Grandpa helped him make a sturdy frame for it from heavy oak two-by-twelves, and Steve took great pride in learning to fit the corners neatly and to countersink the screws. One afternoon, I saw Grandpa's little red pick-up truck coming down the lane with Steve in back, proudly steadying the big frame. They carefully maneuvered it down the walk and settled it into his room.

Waterbeds were just becoming popular in Illinois in 1973, and everyone who visited us, old and young, had to try it out. It seemed odd, but Kathy, still so young herself, was a little shocked by Steve's waterbed. I think she felt she'd been out of the house only a month and we had already let him slip into moral degradation! I couldn't understand why feathers were more moral than water, but why did I insist on canned peaches when more fresh pineapples would have been so nice?

Once I heard Steve boast, "I'll bet there aren't many boys whose seventy-two-year-old grandfathers would help them make a water bed."

He painted the frame black, to match the red and black carpet he had chosen for his room. He helped me choose the black plush fake fur to make the huge bedspread. His music medals, the natural driftwood cross he'd found at the lake the summer before, the crossed fencing swords a friend brought from Spain, the Tibetan masks another friend had brought from Nepal—a striking room—uniquely his. He made sporadic attempts to keep the clutter straight.

Two nights before, Russ had teased him. "Boy, you'd better come home and clean up your room! It's a mess."

Steve flashed, "It'd better not be a mess. I cleaned it up just before I came here—the day before Thanksgiving."

His brother-in-law laughed. "I know, man, but the stack fell down!"

The thought of his room pulled at my heart. It was nothing without him.

It is difficult to tidy a room when there are so many projects waiting to be tackled. On the window seat were the arrows waiting to be refeathered. In one corner were the football helmets. Early in the fall Steve had been enthusiastic about organizing football scrimmages and tackle games on Saturday and Sunday afternoons, and so the school coach had given him eight or ten helmets that were being discarded. Steve was delighted to get them for "his team." Months later, someone sent me a note he had written on one of the attendance records at church. It read:

> From now on, except special occasions, I would like to have a football game on Sunday afternoon. Everyone is welcome to come and play. We will play at McAndrew Stadium, or at the practice field. If you can play, sign the sheet under this note. If you need transportation, call me at 549-8328. Game will start around 2:00 and we will be through in time for choir.
>
> Steve Warner
>
> P.S. Persons weighing more than 612 lbs. or less than 23 lbs. are not welcome.

Seven high school boys had signed the sheet.

After his diving course, scuba gear, complete with flippers and breathing tank were added to his room. It was a beautiful room—but no, it was not very tidy.

Someone has put a cup of coffee in my hand and I drink it. It is black and bitter and not very hot. I note that our family is now sitting on the floor of this waiting room that serves the families of patients who are in surgery and in the ICU. When did we get down here on the rug? Its bold pattern is of giant green leaves intertwined with grotesque dark vines. I will forever be able to see it when I close my eyes—it adds to my constant state of near nausea.

I realized that the room was crowded, that other families were sitting huddled in their own little islands of fear—some on the floor, some on the red furniture. I began to sort out the family groups.

Someone passed a bag of bagels, and I realized they came from a cluster of three sisters, all in the nebulous range of middle age. When they learned that the taste was new to us, they passed us a package of cream cheese and a little knife, insisting that we try them first in "the only way they should ever be eaten." The sisters made little clucking noises and motherly gestures towards a little old, gray man in the corner. He wore a gray suit and a gray hat; his eyes were gray, and this morning his skin also looked gray. Later, I would learn that he wore gray overshoes and carried a gray cane in the deep snow that was to follow. Now, he sat quietly, oblivious to everyone, his thoughts on "Mama" in some operating room below.

What time is it? I ask no one in particular, so several people answer. Some discrepancy as to the exact minute creates a relieved bustle as people synchronize their watches. This diversion causes another sixty seconds to pass.

Into the tension strode Hilda, a buxom, red-haired nurse who had come "to clear out this waiting room."

But when she commanded, "Go," we just looked at her. When she said, "There are too many people in here; you all cannot stay," we looked at her some more. When she said, "Only two members of each family will be allowed to remain here," none of us stirred from our seats.

Who of any of us would leave?

She said, "You cannot sit on the floor, you people. How does it look? Barnes Hospital cannot have you sitting on the floor."

We all just sat and stared. Everyone, that is, except Maureen, the youngest of the three sisters.

She leaped up and exclaimed, "You're right! It's shameful that we have to sit on the floor. How dare such a big hospital not have adequate waiting facilities for the families of patients being operated on? Who's in charge here?"

"I'm in charge here," Hilda countered, still huffy and officious.

"Well, who's your superior then?" Maureen was gaining momentum. "There's not one of us who's here because we want to be, and furthermore, I'm complaining about your attitude!"

I never knew whether she did complain or not, but no one—Hilda included—ever again challenged our right to stay. It was an infinitesimal victory in relation to the battles we were all fighting, yet it gave us a kind of satisfaction.

It is now past lunch time, but no one goes to lunch. No one dares leave. The doctor might come during that time.

When do surgeons eat? How? Does someone stick a sandwich in their mouths and they chew as they tie, being careful of the crumbs? These men I see at the hospital cafeteria and those I glimpse drinking coffee at the doctor's lounge—have they left a patient to wait, bound and gagged on an operating table, while they slip out for barbecued ribs or chicken cacciatore?

Does an anesthesiologist stand by? Who monitors the monitor that monitors all the vital signs? Even Rosie the Riveter had to rest—had to take coffee breaks. Doctors might even have to grab a nap. No one could stand the rigors of a twelve-hour surgery! No one. I wonder if even the patients can stand it!

Oh, please Lord, there is one patient. . . . What time is it? Someone tells me and I cannot believe it has been only ten minutes since the last time I asked.

Time is such a relative thing, and it does not pass at all when the only word is "wait." When prayer is the constant and one scarcely dare hope, the hands seem never to move.

This scene is not real! We are not real people. We are some kind of stage prop, or if we are real, we are frozen—immobilized. This is some moment caught in time and cast in wax or chiseled in stone. It will never pass!

There was a stir, and the heart of the room leaped. A doctor was striding down the hall, and the people to whom he "belonged" jumped up as one and ran to meet him. "Mama" was in the recovery room. The sisters started to talk and laugh and cry all at once—released from the fearsome tension of waiting. They gathered their purses and their bagels and their little gray Papa and went away.

Oh, my darling. The shift has changed and the sun is low in the west and still no news of you. Surely you are still hanging on or we would have been told.

I thought that afternoon about how America has sat and gawked with horrible fascination at hospital scenes portrayed in gory detail on TV. We have peered with boredom or microscopic scrutiny as the entire gamut of human emotion was strewn about our living rooms. But surely not even a blood-lusty public could stand for long the stark realism and horror that takes place in a large hospital.

A detached part of me noted that, unlike in a well-produced TV show, there was a minimum of staging, a paucity of props. Sometimes a family was summoned to take a few steps away from the door. You tried not to listen, but the words sounded so loud and distinct in all that silence that you could still hear; and so you watched and you listened. And when your turn came, you knew other people would watch and listen. No one turned the dial.

What time is it? Who has Steve's watch? His billfold? "STEPHEN WARNER, PLEASE SAVE." This plea is in every heartbeat.

Supper trays trundled down the hall. We were the only family left. I jumped as the carts collided. I did not realize how tense I had been—like a tightly coiled vine—a honeysuckle vine or the corkscrew tendrils of the wild grapes in our woods. A coiled and clinging vine, clinging in my supplication—utter weakness dependent upon strength from outside for support.

God, be with him. Let thy Shekinah light flood his being.
May thy health and strength flow through him. Oh God, let
my baby live.

I remained poised. I dared not uncoil.

At last a doctor came down the corridor. We recognized him as
Dr. Sessions, Steve's surgeon for his sinus operations. He had
looked in on Steve several times during the day, and he came by to
tell us that the operation was over. The tumor had been removed,
and Steve would soon be in the recovery room. Steve's doctor
would be in to talk to us.

Oh joy, Oh blessed joy. He is alive! He has lived through it.
Oh, thank you, Jesus.

Whatever I have been that is good, I will double it.
Whatever in me that is bad, I will weed it out relentlessly.
Whatever he needs from now on, I will strive to give. God,
I am so glad he is alive, I will spend my life filling the gaps
that now may be in him. So patient I can be. And strong. My
strength will never flag if it is spent for him!

Hang on, darling. We're over one more hurdle.

SURROGATE FOR ALL MANKIND

It had been almost an hour since we talked to Dr. Sessions. I grabbed a pen and scribbled these words on the back of my crossword puzzle book:

> Would that I could nourish him from my breast.
> O that I could scoop from my crop and give to him
> as pigeons to their helpless young.
> I would dip into my vitality—
> the very vitality of my veins,
> and feed myself to him teaspoon by teaspoonful,
> but I cannot. I cannot do it for him.
> I cannot, but oh, that I could!

It would be three years before I would read *Eric,* the beautiful tribute Doris Lund wrote to her boy who was dying of leukemia.

In his teen-age independence, Eric had said, "Mother, you can't do it for me."

She had replied, "Of course not, Dear. I don't want to do it for you."

Eric countered, "Of course you do. You'd like to do it for me. What kind of a mother would you be if you wouldn't?"

What time is it now? Almost six o'clock . . . and still no word. Surely it is not possible for the human body to stand so much—not even Stephen.

Occasionally I saw other doctors making their rounds, but no Dr. Racheson to tell us that Steve was in Recovery.

Will I still recognize Steve's doctor? It has been a lifetime since morning.

I commanded my mind to recall earlier days—happy
events—anything to remove the metallic taste of fear from my
mouth.

I remembered one night when Steve was barely six, just
beginning second grade. I'd brought home a beautifully illustrated
set of sixth-grade readers, and for several nights the boys had been
looking at them after they went to bed. As I bustled about, busy
with day-end pleasantries, I realized Steve had been looking at one
page for a long time.

"What's so interesting about that picture, Steve?" I asked.
"You've been looking at it for a long time."

"I'm not looking at the pictures, Mama. I'm reading the story.
Please don't make me turn out the light. I'll be through soon."

He became an avid reader. As he grew older, I've known him to
have five or six books in the hopper at the same time. Once I asked,
"Why don't you finish one book before you start another?"

He answered patiently, with his own perfect logic, "I don't want
to read the last chapter. When I read that, I will be finished with the
whole book. This way, don't you see, I've still got the story in my
mind and I can think about it and plan and wonder how it's going to
end."

*Oh, Steve, your story must have a great ending. It has read
so wonderfully well for seventeen years.*

Still no Dr. Racheson.

A nurse, passing through, told us snow flurries were forecast for
the next day. There had been a light snow the week before—on the
day Steve had been given so many tests. In some ways Steve was
still the inquisitive little boy who wanted to know everything. He
learned about every test he was given, and he told us about them in
detail. One series of tests made it absolutely necessary for him to lie
prone for the next twelve hours. Sometime during that time it
started to snow—our first real snow of the year. Bill and I moved
Steve's bed over near the window and cranked it up as high as it
would go, so that he could see the flakes without moving his head.

We must have stood there by his bed for an hour, just appreciating the snow—just appreciating each other.

"If you look straight up into the sky, those downy white flakes look just like specks of black soot," Steve said.

Many times during past years, we had all watched "the old witch shake her feather bed," as we crouched in doorways or huddled together in the cold, sheltering each other from the wind, scarce daring to breathe for fear of melting the wondrous stars falling on little sweater sleeves and woolly mittens. Sometimes we took the Dracula cape, made from an old velvet skirt, to catch those fleeting marvels.

One day, the week before, Steve had slipped his new corduroy coat over his pajamas and rode down in the elevator with Kathy and Russ. Kathy told us that Steve walked out in the snow and put money in the meter, then he threw back his head and let the snow fall on his face and tongue, tasting the snowflakes. They made a few snowballs and tossed them at each other. Finally, before they came back in, Steve did an impromptu dance in the swirling whiteness. He'd always been great at impromptu dances.

Dr. Racheson has just rounded the corner.

We draw closer together, as if to gain courage from each other. I feel completely alone—yet also a part of something. I am a separate cell, yet a cell within a battery. I cannot explain the strange tangibility of that supportive fellowship. My family is standing here, too. I feel their mass, their bulk, their essence, though I cannot see them.

In these brief seconds there is a rush of feeling—a sense that we are standing in for humanity tonight—surrogates for all mankind. Today I may have to pay for my fifty years of sunshine.

We all saw Dr. Racheson and stood up, as one body, to face what must be faced. He walked straight toward us, as if he were a mannequin pulled on a track. ". . . in the Recovery Room . . . Doing quite well, really. All his vital signs are good. It was deep within the cerebellum. It was in a little deeper than I had expected."

I can still hear him as he continued." It was a little larger than I had thought it would be." He paused. "Quite large, really. About the size of a tennis ball. It was encapsulated. That means it was contained within the shell, as a whole."

As I tried to absorb all he was saying, I worried that he did not look at any of us directly. He seemed to be looking about eight inches over my left shoulder. Only occasionally, and then only as if in weariness and with great reluctance, did he drag his eyes around to meet ours. There was a depth of sorrow in them.

"It was fairly well calcified; that is, it was quite old. It's been there a long time. . . . I think I was able to get it all. It was *fairly* well encapsulated." He hesitated.

I braced myself for his next statement.

"There *was* one rather long tongue." His gaze wavered and settled once more over my left shoulder.

Anxious questions burst to the surface. Will there be any lasting effects? How long will he have to be in ICU? Has it affected his thinking? Will he be paralyzed?

Dr. Racheson did tell us that the intelligence was not located in the cerebellum, but he answered most of the other questions by saying, "Only time will tell. We'll see tomorrow."

He told us Steve would be brought to the intensive care unit soon, where we would see him. He left then, and we began to breathe again.

"Mr. and Mrs. Warner may come in now." We don the white robes and masks for this first of a thousand visits to the ICU of the tenth floor of Barnes Hospital in St. Louis, Missouri.

The strings of the mask were confusing. My hands shook so that I could not get the knot tied tight. We never got over this extreme agitation as we prepared to go in to see Steve. Sometimes the knotted strings were so tedious we jerked them out of the masks entirely.

As we walked in, I saw a large open ward with many narrow white beds. Curtains were drawn about some. They were all so white. They were all so still.

I thought, "It is like groping through a morgue to find a body you can identify."

I hated myself for this traitorous, morbid thought. I looked with pity, amazement, and sometimes horror at the forms lying on their narrow beds.

Finally we saw Steve. A sheet was pulled up to his middle. He was naked from the waist up, and his dark summer tan had an odd pallor. He was shaking with cold and shock. The nurse said it was normal for post-op patients to shake like this.

He was so thin. He had lost a great deal of weight during the two previous months. The little bony knobs on the tops of his shoulders—angel sprouts, we called them—stood out like drawer pulls. He had developed his back muscles until he could almost flap his shoulder blades like wings. He did that sometimes to gross his sister out.

The shuddering and shaking were frightening. I was almost afraid to touch him, but I hugged him and clasped him to me. I had not expected him to be so wide awake and functioning so well. The chill made his teeth chatter, but he greeted us all, that dear son who looked then so much like a closely shaven Tibetan lama. His head was not bandaged, though we were told it would be later. Since he was lying on his back, we did not see the incision, a cut about six inches long on the back of his head.

His eyes would not stay in focus. As he tried to look at things, his eyes drifted downward. We learned later that this was called nystagmus, and it usually subsided in a day or two.

Bill laughed through tears of joy as he asked, "What's the matter with your eyes, son?"

"I . . . think . . . my . . . vertical . . . control's . . . out of . . . whack." Steve chuckled at the little joke. His speech was thick and the words came slowly.

We were allowed to be with him only five minutes each hour. We slipped in one more time before we left for the night.

Steve looked at us and asked haltingly, "What is this thing with the robes? I look up and think I see a robed choir coming in. Are you trying to confuse me or something?"

We gripped his large, beautiful hands, smoothed his long thin arms, slid our palms over the thin hardness of his legs. We pinched his toe a little—brushed his cheeks with our lips. Anything to prolong the leave-taking. Anything to impart more sensual, more tactile strength.

Once more we whispered into his ear, "Remember, hang on now. You've always been the one who could hang on the longest and fight the hardest!"

We said this so often. We believed it so deeply.

SHUT IN BY THE STORM

How jubilantly we had clung to each other in the first few hours after that interminable surgery on December 18. How confident we were of Steve's recovery. We felt the worst of the vigil was over. This stage was called recuperation. Beautiful, beautiful word, recuperation . . . Beautiful, beautiful stage, recuperation . . . Beautiful, beautiful child.

God, but he is beautiful. Even shorn of all his hair—that shiny hair he was so proud of—he is beautiful. His head is well-shaped, and he has a handsome brow line.

In one of his early school pictures, his ears looked like little pink lollipops glued on at right angles. Yet now, even with no hair to cover them, they cling sedately to his temples. I look at his thick, finely arched brows—already the scar from the hateful obliteration has faded until it is barely noticeable. As I sit and watch him, he is truly beautiful in repose.

In kindergarten some boys had told Steve that his head was too big. He worried about this until our pediatrician asked him, "Do you think your daddy is handsome?"

"Yes."

"Well, you're going to grow up to look just like him some day. Your head is just the right size. If those boys tease you anymore, tell them it has to be that big to hold all your brains, because you're a smart boy!"

I noticed his eyelashes. They looked like curves of black chenille resting on his cheek bones. Black, woolly worms, one nurse called them—glossy, oiled black woolly worms. They always shimmered so about his merry eyes that I thought of them more like butterfly wings—black velvet butterfly wings, fluttering. With those lashes,

Steve was the one who could give the longest, most ticklish caresses to cheek or brow—we called them butterfly kisses.

Once, when we wheeled him, bed and all, from ICU to another place for some tests, a lady whispered to me, "Oh my, she is so lovely!"

When we got back to ICU, I ribbed him about it.

His comment was a laborious, "Oh—great! That's—just —great!"

The surgery, drastic as it had been, brought hope. At first, it seemed miracle enough that he was alive and bright and inquisitive—fretting to get out. We realized he was far from recovered, but what progress we felt he'd made when, on the third day we found him sitting up in his chair between the beds.

Then, the shock of how he really looked hit us. It seemed somehow obscene to see his beautiful, brown body strapped to a chair. The lack of muscle control was more obvious as he tried to hold himself erect, and somehow he looked even more pitiful sitting up. He seemed ill at ease and did not say much. So, as always, arm in arm with elation came dismay. How long and steep lay the road ahead.

We were never told what to expect or when, so each minute bit of progress, like sitting in the chair, surprised and pleased us. From the time we'd first seen him as they trundled him into ICU from the recovery room, he had been hooked up to tubes and bottles and monitoring devices, yet the third night after surgery, I heard Pat, the marvelous male nurse, mention almost casually, "Steve ate most of his custard at noon."

"Custard? You mean he's able to swallow?"

It had not been a good day. In one of the brief moments we were allowed to see each other, allowed to touch again, Steve had focused his great eyes on mine and pleaded in that desperate, halting voice, "Get—me—out—of—here. Please. Please!"

It broke my heart. I pleaded, just as desperately, "Please, hang on just a little longer. Dr. Racheson told us you would be in your own room by Christmas, and it's already December 21. Oh, please try to hang on a little longer. We can't take you out until Dr. Racheson orders it."

He never asked again.

Steve liked Pat, the only male nurse in ICU. The ratio of patients to nurses was never more than two to one, so Pat, who was young, too, spent quite a bit of time with Steve. I was always glad when he was on duty, for he would tell me little things that Steve had been able to do that day. Soon after surgery, Steve wanted his watch, so Pat went to Steve's puny pile of "valuables" and got it for him. Afterwards, he always went to Steve to check the time.

Dr. Racheson told us that the isolation of the ICU seemed hardest on young boys and old men, so Steve's awareness of date and time and place was watched closely for signs that he might have become disoriented. It was so good to be reassured each morning that Steve knew all these details. Even in the alien and restricted environment of the intensive care unit, he still showed the same inquisitiveness—the same unflagging interest in medical techniques and the hospital milieu—that he'd shown for the last ten weeks, and, indeed, all his life.

He seemed to be doing so well. Thus, it was with shock that, the morning of December 22, I saw Willis and his wife walking down the hall. Willis was walking with just the aid of a cane! His wife's hand on his arm seemed little more than a caress—almost like holding hands as they strolled.

Willis had had brain surgery after Steve! I knew he had. I remembered because it was *after* the freakish snow storm of December 19 and 20 when the city was brought virtually to a standstill. I remembered because of the kindness of a patient named Vernon. Many of us slept on benches in the halls, or curled up in chairs in the lounge because we dared not leave. It might be days before we could return. Bill lay on a bench in a corridor, and sometime after midnight he woke from a troubled sleep to see Vernon standing above him, offering his pillow.

We'd met Vernon the day before, walking up and down the corridor. He looked like the Duke of Windsor out for a stroll, except that on his head he wore a long, glamorous wig—borrowed from another patient. Everyone had laughed at Vernon's performance—everyone except his wife. Another patient whispered, "She knows, poor thing. She knows they didn't get it all." That night, Vernon stood beside Bill, sans bravado, sans any of his clownish tricks, sans his optimism, just reaching out to do what little he could do—to offer a pillow.

That was the day before a pretty young black woman came to sit with us in the ICU lounge while her husband—Willis—was having surgery.

How could Willis be so much better than Steve? Willis had expression in his face already; Steve's face was still immobile. If Steve tried to smile, it was a voluntary turning up of the corners of his mouth—a pitiful caricature of a smile. Willis could walk without listing; Steve could not remain upright in a chair without support. How could Willis seem so well when Steve was still so undone, so maimed?

I sensed that Dr. Racheson had expected Steve's progress to be faster, but family and friends, and especially the hospital staff, all assured me that he was "doing as well as could be expected." It was just a matter of time. Until I compared Willis's progress with Steve's, I assumed they were correct.

The sudden realization that Steve wasn't doing well at all came as such a shock that I grabbed my pen and pad and wrote the following words.

It is 8:30 a.m., December 22. In ten hours people will be telling me to have faith and keep cheerful because then it will have been only ninety-six hours since surgery. I could buy that for twelve hours and twenty-four and even forty-eight. By seventy-two, it had lost its impact and at ninety-six it will be utterly meaningless and wild. Steve is not improving. At least, he does not seem better to me. Yesterday morning I could tell that Dr. Racheson was also dissatisfied with his progress. He kept saying, "Steve is not doing as well as I had expected," or "I'm surprised that Stephen is not responding quicker."

Only his Daddy and I are in the waiting room this morning, and we are glad for a surcease of conversation. Sometimes I think I cannot bear to hear another patient's story told again in stark, unrelieved detail, nor can I stand to tell, or hear Bill tell, one more time about the horrifying circumstances that have fallen on our Steve. I do not attempt to keep a diary, but today when the waiting and the impotency are overpowering, I search for pen and paper. This demand on my attention is both bane and blessing, for in all this descent into our personal maelstrom the most stabilizing thing I've felt is the touch of human hands—that, and the bare fact that we quickly find that we have (or *are*) a common denominator.

Staring us all in the face is the human predicament, and none of us has an answer. We all feel cheated by our churches and temples, and maybe even by our culture, because nothing is here to support us when we are at rock bottom. During the last few days, I've sat with Jews and gentiles, Southern Baptists, free-thinkers who lost their faith years ago, and another minister's family—United Church of Christ—and we all felt bereft. Worse, tricked. Suddenly, "The Lord giveth and the Lord taketh away" seems a cruel cat and mouse game.

Food is some tasteless mass I push down to please others, hoping that somehow the salivary glands and peristalsis will take it out of my throat. The Kosher bagels were somehow a comfort—because they were shared by another family in distress. Also, because they are so tough, they require you to chew, and that relieves a little tension. Whatever the pain, the agony for Bill and me, it is so much worse in that tiny corner cubicle where our little Tibetan Lama struggles with it alone.

The day of Steve's day-long brain surgery, I thought I had found a little stability. I thought then that I had hit rock bottom—and that there *was* a steadying bottom there, a foundation—which I seized on as The Foundation—and felt sustained. Now, I don't know; maybe the only steadying factor was that having reached nadir I could go no further. Now I have gone further. "Stephen is about the same," the nurses tell me. "Not responding quite so readily," the doctor said. "He should be coming around," he continues. My foundations tremble.

Pray? My every heartbeat is a prayer for Stephen. Occasionally some shred of memory, some remnant of faith makes the need for audible prayer overwhelming and I run to the chapel—or to the bathroom—to pray, but all I can do is beg. I've been taught that one doesn't beg from a good and loving God, so I try to enumerate the things I can legitimately pray for, and the list is long—strength for the day, light for the way, the ability to get through whatever comes without becoming bitter and shriveled, the strength, if Steve lives, to be able to give him the supportive kind of mothering he might need, eyes that will still be able to see my other children and my husband and not hate the fun and life that continues, despite our heartsickness.

I hear familiar carols on the P.A. system and I cannot remember their names.

As my list of petitions lengthens, doubt gnaws at me again and I plead, "O God, if you can do all these *hard* things, then why can't you do what should be infinitely easier for the finger of God—just pluck out the hated tumor and let health flow into him?" My belief has always been that God is love and he wills good to all.

When Alan Dale, my twelve-year-old brother, died I learned that the Scriptures were not specific promises or talismans that we could mumble or fondle in order to bring about some miracle. Perhaps because of this I have not frantically searched the Scriptures for promises, nor have I agonized in prostrate form, though I have taken some comfort from our friends who have. I have appreciated when candles have been lit and prayer vigils kept, but my prayers

are more like the lines I scribbled on the back of a get well
card this morning:

> Rage and fury my sad heart rend.
> My doubts, I sob the long night's end.
> But in the chapel
> I kneel to pray.
> "Thank you, God . . .
> Steve swallowed custard
> Today!"

In retrospect I wonder when the clammy grip of fear first settled
on us again. At forty-eight hours after surgery when we saw how
Steve had to be tied in his chair? At seventy-two hours when I
sensed the doctor was worried? But there had not been a time since
October 11 when we were without fear—not a time since the
December 13 diagnosis of a tumor that we were not dry-mouthed,
pleadingly scared.

The next time I could catch Dr. Racheson, I asked him point
blank how Steve was doing.

Once again fixing his gaze somewhere over my left shoulder, he
said, "Steve's not doing as well as I'd hoped. He ought to be coming
around more quickly; I don't like the slow responses in his arm and
leg."

On December 23 we were not allowed to see Steve until late
afternoon. Finally, Kathy and I went in together, and when we could
not get him to talk as much as he had the day before, we were
worried. He seemed sleepy—listless.

The nurse was glib and bright, and in a reassuring voice she told
us, "Well, you just caught him at a sleepy time. He was talking up
a storm to me a little while ago."

Greatly relieved, we went back down the hall to the lounge to
wait until the next hour's visit. To eyes untrained in everything but
love, he had appeared worse.

When next we got in, around 5:00 p.m., Steve seemed more
alert, not talking much, but responding when we asked a question

and initiating a remark or two. In only five minutes there is not much to say.

We could hardly believe it, but just before we left he said, "I want Pop Tarts. Pop Tarts and Coco Crispies!"

"Oh, and you shall have them, my pet. You shall have them as soon as the doctor says you can."

One more "I love you," and we tiptoed out, giving his big toe a gentle tweak as we went. He gave us a feeble wave.

Steve's eyes had shown a little eagerness when he asked for the Pop Tarts and Coco Crispies. The nystagmis was subsiding, and his eyes no longer drifted down, like a rolling TV screen. His vertical control was not so completely "out of whack," but neither were his eyes normal. He could bring them into focus, but slowly they would drift downward. Both Dr. Racheson and Dr. Drews, the ophthalmologist who came by every day, told us this, too, would subside.

Every little bit of good news was seized upon so eagerly—the rest of the family waiting in the lounge couldn't believe he had actually asked for food! What a good note to tell the grandparents when we made our nightly phone call.

Our exultation was not long-lived. During the nine o'clock visit, Steve was again withdrawn and far away. We had to get him out of that ICU! That must be what was wrong. The doctor had warned us that isolation was especially hard on teen-age boys.

Only one thing gave us encouragement—even a chuckle. In a desperate attempt to communicate I had grasped at our earlier conversation, saying, as I started to leave, "And tomorrow, maybe even tonight, Daddy will get your Pop Tarts and Coco Puffs."

As if pulling closer to us from a long distance, Steve corrected me with just a touch of his old asperity, "Coco—*Crisp*—ies," he said.

I laughed at my mistake, and with another tweak of his big toe, we left him for the night.

Bill had not seen much difference in his responses, but I could not be lulled into thinking he was just tired. I had seen him this way twice. Something was wrong. We stopped by the nurses's station again. This nurse was not so glib.

"Yes, I did notice a difference in his responses, Mrs. Warner. If I were you, I'd ask the doctor about it tomorrow."

Tomorrow.

It would be twelve or eighteen hours before I'd see the doctor again. How dared anyone be so casual about my child! We left, filled with apprehension and sick with fear.

The next morning I took up my place in the lounge near the door. I did not write or knit, but watched unblinkingly for Dr. Racheson to come down the hall.

"What's happening? Why can't Stephen talk any more?"

I asked my questions urgently, frantically, again and again, but I never received an answer. Dr. Racheson seemed angry that I would ask—and angrier still that Steve didn't talk.

"He can talk whenever he wants to. For some reason or other he's just decided not to talk," he said.

I knew that was not so. It was outrageous for him to say such a thing.

Steve never spoke again—not really.

Oh, perhaps for a week he could interject a word or two a day—a few jarring monosyllables—and then never anymore.

GRACE NOTES

After we had been in the hospital a few days, I was surprised to find a soft stubble when I kissed Steve's cheek. When Steve was little, he admired his Uncle Bob's hairy legs and hoped he'd be hairy, too. As he got older, he thought he might like to grow a beard, but he worried about how his whiskers would grow around three parallel hairline scars just left of the cleft in his chin.

When he was a fat, heavy baby, he leaned so far over to see what Kathy and David were measuring on the floor that he toppled his high chair and sliced his soft chin to the bone on the metal rule. The next summer he bounced out of a speeding wagon pulled by Kathy and David and again landed on his chin. The third cut came when he was four years old and he fell on some boulders during a vacation in Maine. The scars barely showed, but he worried about whether he could have a nice beard or not.

Years later, we learned that David and Kathy made him believe that when he was born, his mouth had been too big and the doctor had to staple out some slack! Adults can only guess at the little things that worry children.

It is early in the day and there are not many people in the lounge. I am knitting a sweater, clean, broad stripes of brown and blue and white. I don't know who will wear it most. I'll put "Warner Bros." on the package and slip it under the tree. Under the tree? Surely Steve can be in his own room by Christmas and we can have a tiny tree.

Sometimes I felt we had been in that hospital forever—but it had been only ten weeks. Only ten weeks? When we first went to St. Luke's in October, the leaves were just beginning to turn. Both Kathy and David brought Steve small scarlet branches of dogwood and sourgum from home. After we moved to Barnes, someone sent him a great, lurid paper jack-o-lantern.

Jack-o-lanterns. As the yarn sped through my fingers, punctuated by the flash and click of the needles, rich memories flashed through my head like slides from some hidden projector. Jack-o-lanterns . . . Hallowe'en. Steve loved to masquerade for Hallowe'en. I remembered once when he dressed up as John the Baptist—beheaded, of course. I don't know where he got the idea for such a ghastly disguise, but it was fun to fix him up once the idea got rolling.

We made a "table" from a big cardboard box covered with a very elegant red cloth with a white crocheted edge; I had let a candle burn a big hole in the center—a hole just big enough for an eleven-year-old boy's head. We sewed paper plates and plastic "silverware" on the cloth and then fashioned the silver platter from cardboard and aluminum paint. Steve doused a stocking with mercurochrome, pulled it over his head and poked it up through the hole. He snuggled himself into the silver platter, and "voila," the decapitated saint. He could carry his table on his shoulders.

Such innocent but audacious hi-jinks the kids have pulled! Much later, friends who had taken pictures of him as he appeared at their doors sent them to us. Somehow, the whole ludicrous tastelessness and mirth were good to remember. Memories flooded my mind—so many memories—so many incidents.

From the tenth floor window one night, we saw some people shooting Roman candles and other sparkly things in Forest Park. We never celebrated Christmas with fireworks, even though Bill and the boys loved them.

As we watched, I remembered a summer a couple of years before. Dave and Steve had experimented for days with lengths of pipe and the gunpowder from firecrackers, trying to get a really terrific explosion. They assured me they were careful and never used anything for wadding in the pipe that could be dangerous. They sorted out and removed all the little sticks and twigs, and inserted quantities of poke berries, for they had concocted a devilish scheme. Their friend Tim, who always looked like an ad for Mr. Clean, was coming to spend the day, and Steve and Dave had planned the perfect welcome. Steve was to hide behind a stack of firewood and light the fuse, while Dave was to leap forward, brandishing the pipe, just as Tim rounded the corner of the house.

The scheme worked perfectly. There was an explosion and a dark red stain quickly soaked through Tim's white tee shirt. He jumped back, clutched his chest, and yelled, "Hey, you guys shot me!" He was stunned, then puzzled, and finally a little chagrined as he realized the stain on his fingers was poke berry juice. The three of them rolled on the ground and howled with laughter, and then they went to work to make a bomb even bigger and better.

But despite their hard play, their fascination with fireworks, rappelling, and the other daring things they did, Dave and Steve were both gentle young men.

Oh, sweet, goofy, funny lads. You did know how to enjoy the sunshine, but how can you endure this awful shadow? "Into each life some rain must fall," we had foolishly sing-songed so long ago when we filmed "A Day in the Life of William Stephen." Now, only seventeen fantastic years later, not a shower, but a deluge, is threatening to drown us all.

Those funny, wild, impetuous years. Such a mixture of slap-dash, free-wheeling creativity and great, intuitive sensitivity. His Aunt Virginia reminded me of a time when Steve was eight or nine years old. "Do you remember the stoning of Stephen?" she asked. "You were having an open house and Stephen had set up a little worship center on his bedside table. He'd opened his Bible to "The Stoning of Stephen" and had set pieces of gravel up in a ring around the story." I had forgotten it completely, but I could see it then, after Virginia reminded me.

Bill and I had often laughed, "Steve will be the one who's a bishop—that is, if we can keep him out of the pen!"

From the time he was five years old, he would occasionally be found at the altar on Sunday nights—asking questions, wanting to grow closer to God. It's difficult for a minister's children to separate the call of God from the filial awe and love they have for their father. But Steve always seemed to be listening intently, and until he was about eight, if we sat near the aisle, he would often slip from my side and walk out with his father to greet the people as they filed out. In high school he wanted to be a veterinarian—and maybe a preacher, too. I remember him asking, "Mom, do you think I could be both?"

A vet, a preacher. . . . There were other long-range plans. He had plenty of time to decide.

Knit one, purl two, repeat the pattern to the end. The pattern is lovely, but it is not finished. It is a long, long way from being finished.

When Kathy was little, she had a cookbook with a recipe for cinnamon toast. It was called "Ronnie Rooster's Sugar Toast." As they grew up, the kids still jokingly called it that, and every month or so when I would come home to no bread, no butter, and the feel of gritty sugar on the counter, I knew that the boys and Ronnie Rooster had done it again!

Though memories crowded on top of memories, I remembered only a fraction. As an adolescent I was thrilled to get an envelope marked S.W.A.K.—sealed with a kiss—or to read a note signed XXXOO—kisses and hugs. How ridiculously short of warm, loving flesh and blood kisses were those paper kisses. Yet the incidents by themselves were like paper kisses—and that's how those scattered events in Steve's life compared to Steve himself. But the years were winged things—not flat paper kisses.

God, Oh, God! So much to invest. A young man of seventeen must be ninety percent potential. . . .

The doctors made their rounds in masks and long white coats, striding through the halls, going boldly into the inner sanctum of the ICU. They became witch doctors with voodoo masks, supernatural men, wielding the power of life and death over common mortals. I jotted down notes lest I forget what I wanted to ask in the precious moments of my audience with them.

Once, I was especially reluctant to leave Dr. Racheson. We had waited from 9:00 a.m. until late afternoon, and it had taken such a short time for him to say, "About the same. No change."

I turned quickly and said, "Oh Doctor, if only you knew what you're fighting to save. Steve is such a special boy."

The doctor looked down patiently and said, "They all are."

"But not like Stephen, not—not like Steve," David murmured brokenly.

We understood what the doctor meant, but our hearts echoed, "Not like Steve."

HAVING DONE ALL, TO STAND

The calendar in the nurse's station said December 24. That meant it was Christmas Eve. The corridors were quiet. Patients who could had gone home for Christmas.

My mouth twisted toward a smile as I remembered Steve's cocky words. "They sure can't keep me here, you know. I'm past sixteen now and any time I want to leave, I can get dressed and just walk out of here, legally."

He'd whistled this graveyard tune a day or two before his surgery.

My darling, would that you could just throw off that sheet as you did when Tim was here, get on your clothes, and walk out. Give us another impromptu dance in the snow.

It was strangely quiet in the lounge with so many of the patients gone. We felt peculiarly alone. In one sense we felt kin to all the families we'd met on this floor. We were all of a piece—a piece of the same worry, the same fear, the same family of man. In another sense, each family and each family member was separate—alone. Although we yearned to give him strength, to share his fear, and to go through the agony with him, Stephen fought his desperate battle by himself.

Signs of Christmas were all about us. Red-cheeked visitors walked through the halls, arms piled high with wrapped gifts and bright poinsettias. The indefatigable voices of the electronic carolers echoed from every nurses' station. The gaiety contrasted sharply with our leaden hearts. I forced my mind to recall other happy holidays. False faces, turkeys, and Christmas stockings.

Christmas was the apex of our year. One night, long ago, we found everyone's schedule miraculously free, and in a moment of sheer exuberance we decided to sing carols for friends, neighbors, relatives—anyone who would listen. It was so good that a tradition was born on the spot; by tacit approval, schedules were kept free for that important night each year. Once, we took Lumpi the basset, and at every house, as the tenors soared on the finale of "The First Noel," he joined in the chorus. Forgetting all about frequency and pitch and sensitive canine ears, we chose to believe Lumpi was lending his voice to ours. He tried to master speech all his life.

Music had always been an important part of our lives, and after a great flurry of transposing and rewriting music for sax and clarinet, the children nearly always presented a special instrumental number at a worship service during Advent. I treasured those gifts; they took hours of practice and could never have been bought!

Selecting the Christmas tree was always a family affair; each babe in turn had been added to the entourage. All opinions were considered as soon as the least could lisp. I remembered one year in particular. We had all admired the graceful lines of the tree we'd lugged home, but Bill just had time to fasten it to the stand before he and I had to go to the church Christmas party. Hoping the kids could be happy with their own affairs for three hours or so, we left them alone.

I wanted to be a perfect mother. I hoped that in the final reckoning, or more importantly in my children's minds, the "wanting" would count. But I felt betrayed by Kate Wiggins and the saintly mother in *The Bird's Christmas Carol* and by Louisa Mae Alcott in her gentle portrayal of Marmie in *Little Women*. Those women ran their households so smoothly and so gently—always on time, always soft voiced, always sensitive to every need of children, husband, and community. Those incredible women, with their sparkling houses, were my heroes, my idols. Each day I truly tried to scale their Everests, and each evening I discovered my joys and contentment on much lower slopes.

But that night—the night of the Christmas tree—had been a truly beautiful event. It was a real Louisa Mae Alcott night—a page straight from *Little Women*. Stephen was seven, David ten, and Kathy thirteen—just the right ages for sparks to fly from a somewhat bossy and precise older sister and two younger brothers who often banded together to resist and annoy her. I become dewy-eyed as I recall the sight that awaited us when we turned into our driveway late that night.

In the middle of our big picture window stood the most beautiful tree I've ever seen. It was resplendent in all the array of a traditional tree—everything from pipecleaner candy canes made by kindergarten fingers, to exquisite crocheted snowflakes wrought by Grandmother's skillful hands. The shimmering icicles seemed to have been hung according to some blueprint. Tiny lights encircled the dark branches of the evergreen, and one green bulb blinked in perfect time to the music of a carol from the stereo. As we looked closer, we saw fat, lush strings of popcorn and cranberries, heretofore seen only in storybooks but reproduced in our living room this night by the miracle of love and three pairs of busy little hands.

Then we saw the loveliest sight of all—three beautiful children sitting proper and sedate upon the sofa, so full of themselves and their surprise they could stand it no longer. Amidst much hugging and dancing and exclaiming, they explained just who had gotten the idea, who'd done this, how no one had fought, how the boys had "minded," how Kathy had been "nice," how they had scurried to get it all finished and the mess cleaned up before we got back.

I remembered their shining faces. Christmas had come for us that year. A gift had been given, a gift received. It was enough.

Steve loved *The Messiah,* and though it was always a part of our Christmas, he had never sung in a performance of it—not even "The Hallelujah Chorus." The year before, our Chancel Choir was to sing that work as a part of the Christmas Eve midnight communion service. As we drove into town, Steve said wistfully, "You know, it's funny, but in all the choirs I've been in at church and school, I've never been in a performance of this; every year we practice it, and I know it, but at the last minute the schedule is changed.

I'm sorry about that, my son, for everyone ought to get one chance to sing "The Hallelujah."

Some time in the afternoon the family of Stephen Warner was summoned to ICU. We went in, trembling, not knowing what to expect. We almost bumped into Hilda, standing there with a big box in her arms—the same Hilda who had been so formidable the day of the surgery.

Now she beamed as she said, "It's Christmas Eve and this young man's got to have some Christmas presents. Look what his Youth Fellowship sent him."

The box she carried held about a bushel of gifts, all beautifully wrapped and carrying warm and witty greetings. Atop them all sat a funny, wispy Santa's face, with a red felt cap and a white rabbit's tail beard. We each selected a gift to give Steve, but, Hilda, in a beautiful, grand gesture, dumped the entire unsanitized, unsterilized, unrobed, and unmasked array onto his bed. She strewed gifts from his head to his feet on both sides.

We all laughed. How good of the kids to remember! We felt a little lighter. Maybe tomorrow would be Christmas after all.

But Steve would not let us open any of the gifts. By gesturing he made it clear we were to save them—every one of them—until he got into a room of his own. Then, and only then, would he celebrate Christmas! I put the funny, furry Santa, which was from his friend Karen, into his hand, and his fingers closed hungrily about it.

Had his hand been that inert immediately after surgery? I think not. Is this what Dr. Racheson calls slow responses? His thumb cannot close around the little Santa. Only his fingers curl.

They let us stay a little longer because it was Christmas Eve. At about 9:30 they called on the intercom to say Steve's family could now come in, two at a time, for their goodnight visit.

Kathy and Russ were the last to go in. When they came out, Kathy was tremulous with a mixture of fear and hope. She was weeping—a statue would have been moved by the poignancy of Steve's condition.

But as Kathy put her arms about me, she said, "Oh, Mama, Stephen is still *there*."

Yes, he was. He was wrapped and gagged by the muteness, almost smothered in the encroaching paralysis, but he was alive, and he was still Stephen. As they had bent low over his bed and caroled "Silent Night," he had looked at them and soundlessly mouthed every word!

Holy infant so tender and mild. How many hundreds of times we have sung this beloved carol. It was always our closing song at each house as we caroled. "Stille Nacht, Heilige Nacht." Will we ever sing it again, mother and child?

We left the hospital and went to a nearby restaurant. Again, the image of a broken plate hung heavy in the air. The never-ceasing sound system ground out yet another verse of "Silent Night." The laughter and holiday revelry seemed far removed and slightly blasphemous. I slipped through the celebrating crowd to a pay phone to call the grandparents. I could not say "Merry Christmas."

Oh, my darling, may the Christ child come to you in your little cubicle, this Holy Eve. May he dazzle you with the wonders of his Advent and hold you close.

HOPE AND DESPAIR—CHEEK TO JOWL

Church bells pealed throughout the city, proclaiming Jesus' birth. The air was crisp and cold. Bill and Dave and I were in a hurry to get to the hospital, for the doctor's schedule might be different on Christmas Day; we did not want to miss him.

We settled ourselves on the edges of chairs in the lounge. We had seen Dr. Racheson going down the corridor of the other wing. In a little while he swung into view, seeming glad to see us for a change.

His greeting was cheerful. "Steve's better today. I think he's going to be all right."

We were so overcome with joy that our tears and laughter mingled freely. The doctor shook our hands (I think he smiled), and I heard him say several times more, "I think he's going to be all right."

What a morning! Christmas had come with all the gifts I'd ever wanted—and all I'd ever want in the future—wrapped up in this single package!

Stephen was going to be all right! Hallelujah! Hallelujah!

Steve, you say you've never sung "The Hallelujah Chorus."
I'm sorry, but you've sung many hallelujahs just as true and
acceptable, and now you'll have another chance at Mr.
Handel! Praise God! You're going to be all right. With that
news we can sing Hallelujah, even if we should all be mute.

We telephoned the grandparents and told them the good news. We called other friends. And each time we could say "Merry Christmas."

"Merry, *Merry* Christmas!"

Reassured by the doctor's report, Bill left for home on Christmas night to catch up on some of his work that had piled up at the church.

The day after Christmas I took up my morning vigil in the lounge. There was no regular time for families to meet their doctors, so we gathered early and waited late. Usually once before noon and again between 4:00 and 7:00 p.m. we could spot our private doctor making rounds and could grab a word with him. Occasionally Dr. Racheson would give us a curt nod, indicating that he would come to the lounge and speak to us later.

I did not have long to wait that day. Dr. Racheson motioned for me to come out of the lounge to talk to him in the corridor. His manner of speaking was always abrupt, so I suspected nothing.

"Mrs. Warner, Stephen isn't so well this morning. I'm having him prepared for surgery. The paralysis on his right side is more pronounced. And I don't know why he isn't talking. There may be a clot that's causing the trouble. I'm going in again to see."

I could only stammer, "But yesterday . . . I thought . . . If you think . . . My husband. . . ."

"I need you to sign these papers if your husband isn't here. It may be afternoon before the surgery is over, but I'll report to you before I leave the hospital."

Once I signed the papers, action was swift. Almost immediately orderlies pushed Steve's bed out of the unit. I ran beside the gurney until it was trundled into the elevator. As soon as Steve was taken away for surgery I called Bill, only to find he had already left for St. Louis. I breathed a little easier. In two hours he should be with us.

There is something in the human psyche that makes us think that misery shared is somehow misery diminished. For some strange reason, the bleakness lessens when there is a hand to hold—especially the hand of my husband who loved that son as much as I did.

In a little while I looked up to see two couples, long-time friends, standing in the doorway. They had come to St. Louis for the after-Christmas sales and had decided to check on Steve first. Then David and Kathy came. We all waited. Silent—grim with apprehension.

What could have happened since yesterday's, "I think Steve's going to be all right?"

How could we go so quickly from recovery to deterioration? From jubilation to despair?

Why was Bill taking so long to get to St. Louis from Carbondale?

It is hard to explain how I could spend so many hours in the hospital and yet know so little. I was always there, but I was told nothing—nothing at all—unless I pried and prodded. And even then I realized I'd still been told nothing.

John Gunther expressed this same thought in *Death Be Not Proud*. Although his son's struggle was years ago, the situation had not changed. All too often families are regarded as necessary evils that come with the cases. That is unfortunate, for although we were not medically learned, we were not ignorant people either. We could have been talked to with much more candor.

In retrospect, I wonder at the rules that kept me away from Steve. I sat there, twelve hours a day, week after week, wanting nothing so much as to be with him—just to watch his chest rise and fall, if nothing else. Yet I was kept out of the ICU. We were allowed to be together for only a few moments each day.

Steve waited, yearning to see us, and we waited, yearning to see him. But we were on opposite sides of a closed door.

That day, December 26, after five hours of tense waiting we saw the doctor, but the news was disappointing. He had found no clot, no reason for the paralysis, no explanation for Steve's cruel muteness.

Still, we were a little encouraged when Dr. Racheson told us everything looked all right and that, perhaps, the paralysis was a little less pronounced on the right side. But when we were allowed into the ICU, we could see no difference—only that Steve was once more hooked up to respirators, heart monitors and the other machines that are a ghastly part of post-operative care.

Again, the weather added to the bizarre atmosphere. The entire south end of the state was a sheet of ice. Bill finally arrived—worried and wan—knowing nothing about the new surgery. After two time-consuming, though minor, accidents, he had continued over the ice at a snail's pace. It had taken him eight hours.

Records were being broken. Never had the snows been so deep. Never had the ice storms been so widespread. Never. . . .

At another time, the storm would have been exciting—the fierceness of the winter exhilarating. Now, the blanketing whiteness only added to an already eerie scene—a scene in which we were unwilling actors—where our son was forced to play the tragic role. Steve 's countenance seemed perpetually sad, like the masks worn by ancient tragedians.

Once I asked Dr. Racheson, "Why is Steve's expression always so sad?"

The doctor answered crisply, "I imagine, because he *is* sad."

Later, another doctor explained that the inability of Steve's facial muscles to express emotion was the aftermath of brain surgery. The phenomenon was purely physiological and only temporary.

That night, like so many others, we left the hospital not knowing whether Steve would live until we were allowed in to see him the next afternoon.

FRAIL AND SLENDER REEDS

Thursday morning, December 27. Again I was alone at the hospital—waiting to see the doctor. I could not see Steve until afternoon, but the doctor would have seen him, and perhaps I could learn a little.

It had been a week since Steve had begged so piteously, "Get—me—out—of—here—please. Please."

It seemed like forever. The words echoed and re-echoed through my mind. Whenever he focused those great luminous eyes on my face and grasped my hands with his beautiful long fingers, I knew he was repeating this silent plea.

The doctor stood in the doorway. "Where is your husband, Mrs. Warner?"

Ominous words.

"He had to return to Carbondale for a meeting. He won't be back until late afternoon." Then I ventured, "Did you need to see him?"

"Yes. We have heard from the biopsy."

A thick, unrelenting grayness filled the room.

"You mean—you mean *that* wasn't good either? You can tell me, Doctor. I am strong."

"No, I'll wait until I can see Reverend Warner."

There could be only one thing horrible enough for Dr. Racheson not to tell me. There were only two answers—Yes or no. Benign or malignant.

God in heaven! No! How many staggering blows were going to be hurled at Steve?

That evening, hours after Bill and I had sat side by side on the hard sofa of the lounge, Dr. Racheson came. Frail and slender as a reed—hardly moored to reality, yet wooden, stolid, as if never to move again—I heard only scraps of conversation. Ugly words.

"We felt almost certain . . . unexpected report . . . an ependymoma . . . usually attacks teens or young adults . . . a certain percentage . . . some degree of longevity . . . however . . . the majority fatal. . . ."

"Doctor, I can't tell him. He's had too much. I can't tell him this—not on top of everything else."

"You won't have to. I'll tell him." The doctor spoke quietly.

"When? When will you tell him such a thing?"

"Whenever he asks."

I do not remember the rest of that evening.

So I had been right in my fears all along. The gods *were* jealous, and if we were too happy, they would strike us down—just when we least expected it.

Even the old Hebrew had written, "I, your God am a jealous god."

Perhaps this was what that passage meant. The pagans had believed it.

Old crones had whispered, "You mustn't love him too much, or. . . ."

Or what? Was I to find out?

I'd heard the old ones cluck, "He's too pretty. Too pretty to live."

Arachnida had been turned into a spider because she dared to challenge the gods in a weaving contest.

Was that the reason this onslaught swept over Steve? Was he too handsome, too merry, too brilliant?

Was Fate rubbing his nose in all the bitterness of life? Was every blithe and jaunty attitude, every gay and gladsome outlook to be erased? Was every bit of his sparkle to be ground away? His hilarity?

Rational thinking? Of course not! But was there anything rational about that whole rotten business?

My saner, restrained self knew we lived in a world of percentages, a world governed by cause and effect.

Or was it a world governed by accident and luck—and the other side of "luck," which was "unluck"?

How often had I heard Steve sing, "If it Weren't for Bad Luck, I'd Have No Luck at All"?

His eyes would twinkle with merriment as he improvised endless verses of that rollicking old tune—behind the lawnmower, in the shower, while paddling a canoe, or sitting around a campfire.

There had been no foreshadowing in that. Steve had always been the lucky one.

Only once, the night of his thirteenth birthday when he told me he never thought he'd live to be thirteen, did I ever hear him question his own luck. In every game of chance he seemed to have an edge. The roll of the dice, the cut of the deck, the flip of the coin seemed to be in his favor. Steve, the Lucky.

The mystical, trusting side of me besieged Almighty God without ceasing. Phrases and promises tumbled through my mind and my yearning heart like prayer beads in fumbling fingers.

"A thousand shall fall at thy side and ten thousand at thy right hand, but *it* shall not come near thee."

"There shall no evil befall thee, neither shall any plague come nigh thy dwelling" (Ps. 91).

"He healeth the broken-hearted" (Ps. 147:3).

"Come unto me all ye that labor and are heavy laden and I will give you rest" (Mt. 11:28).

"Him that cometh to me I will in no wise cast out" (John 6:37).

"The Lord hath sent me to heal the broken-hearted, to preach deliverance to the captive and recovery of sight to the blind, to set at liberty them that are bruised" (Lk. 4:18).

"Him that cometh to me I will in no wise cast out" (John 6:37).

Oh God, do not cast my man-child away. Oh that I could find the secret of the widow of Nain! You raised her son from the dead. Will you not also deliver mine? Deliver him from this loathsome evil that's cutting him down on the eve of his manhood. You raised the daughter of Jairus. My beautiful son can be no less worthy! Look. It's my own darling I lay at your door, Oh God. Do not turn us away.

"If I am not worthy, then hear and answer me because of my very persistence—my importunity" (Luke 11:8).

"God, I have never liked that parable of the woman you did not send away merely because she kept knocking. It does not speak well of you, God. I am so desperate, I am craven in my pleadings. I grovel, I prostrate myself—I continue to knock at your door."

I argued with God and then begged him not to hold it against Steve. I reminded Him that he said to come boldly to the throne of mercy and ask, believing that it would be done.

"Ask anything in my name" . . .

"Where two or three are gathered together."

People ached with prayer for Stephen. People of little faith, people of no faith, and people of differing faiths were all united in this. Surely by now, not two or three, but thousands were gathered together.

Reminder followed reminder, telling God what he had promised.

"The effectual fervent prayer of a righteous man availeth much."

Didn't any of us qualify? Weren't any of us righteous?

"If you have faith even as a grain of mustard seed. . . ."

I didn't *want* to move mountains. I just wanted to strengthen my faith until it could bring one young man to his feet triumphant!

I had always believed that every individual was unique and precious in God's sight.

The very hairs of our heads are numbered. Surely, God, you cannot be ignorant that Steve's hairs are all shorn and there is a hellish malignancy within that precious skull. Oh, Lord, we are in desperate need of thy healing touch.

"Never a sparrow falls," you said.

I longed to croon to him then as I did when he was little:

> Little dove, little darling,
> Little sparrow, little starling,
> Little light, little joy,
> Little treasure, little boy.

One day, the summer before, when Steve and I were home alone, we talked about my death. My family had long known that I rebelled at the thought of dying. I kept clawing at new doors, looking for understanding or acceptance. I had such an egotistical lust for life—for my existence to go on as *me*.

But as my son lay there, helpless, I knew there was something for which—without a moment's hesitation—I would lay down my life. Only no one could grant me the trade.

> Once before in some great lack,
> I said, "I'd walk to Hell and back."
> But if Stephen were made whole today,
> I know I'd walk to Hell and stay.

Oh how I bargained. But even as I bargained, a still small voice said, "God doesn't work like that!"

I wish a still small voice could have told me how God *does* work.

I could understand then why parents would take their children from one end of the globe to the other, seeking healing waters or some dark Rasputin with mystic powers. How wonderful it would have been to believe in anointed handkerchiefs and the laying on of some special person's hands. I did not know anything to do except wait and hope.

I questioned many things that gave other people comfort. I had heard them say they could leave a loved one in the Lord's hands. But the Lord had them over a barrel. When they could do no more, what else *could* they do except say they were committed to the Lord? All I believed of God told me that God would not be with my child in any special way just because I *said* I'd committed Steve to his care. But I knew that God *was* with us. I could not love a God who would sort souls like a deck of cards and deal one pile to be healed, another maimed, and the other left to die.

I was bedeviled by the problems of partiality and selectivity. One night I was so near exhaustion that, knowing I could not help Steve, I prayed to be freed of the awful burden long enough to get a little rest. I slept peacefully from 11:00 p.m. to 4:00 a.m.

Other times I was driven by the feeling that Steve was slipping into a deep abyss and only by some mother-type extra sensory perception could he be pulled out. Sometimes I believed in this power so firmly that it seemed I would go days without sleep. At those times I lay, tense, pleading with him to hang on—to fight a little harder—to please not be afraid. It was a terrible responsibility, and it was blessed when I could be relieved of it.

Bill and I stand in the hall, clinging to each other as Dr. Racheson paces down the corridor. Stephen, the doctor says he will tell you that the tumor is malignant—whenever you ask. That's a laugh. I was not conscious of the irony of that remark at first, but since you can neither voice nor write that awful question, the possibility of the doctor ever having to answer is remote.

But oh, Steve, you must have wondered. You must have guessed.

Steve was still in the intensive care unit. Each day we were told, "Not yet. He's still too unstable to be outside. Maybe tomorrow."

Our days, like the doctor's words, were distressingly the same. My body was an automaton that went through the motions, but the core of my being prayed without ceasing—without surcease or respite. I had no rosary, no ivory beads, but the faint click of my knitting needles moved the procession of my thoughts and prayers along.

Juxtaposed against the rational and the mystical was the superstitious. "Hubris." Such a funny archaic word. Could I have committed the sin of hubris? I had always been proud of my children. I had always gloried in their logic, their vocabularies, their intelligence. Was God debasing Stephen to punish me for that? I had never thought that was inordinate pride, nor that my exultation was sinful.

Usually I could toss those thoughts away as sick and irrational. But on bad days—and there were so many bad days—it was hard not to see a spiteful, vindictive personification in the savageness of the things that mutilated Steve. It seemed I saw every grace, every attribute flayed from his body—every nuance of his buoyant personality stripped away.

Steve's loss of speech was especially hard. When he was on the eighth floor, he had seen so many men with laryngectomies using magic slates to communicate that, when he lost his ability to speak, we took one into ICU. Alas for Steve, the magic slate held no magic. He grabbed it eagerly, then bewilderment spread across his face. He did not know what to do with it.

Yet, his quicksilver mind remained lucid and aware. My friend, Dr. Jack Barrow, explained weeks later that everything was still there—Steve's intellect, his understanding. Everything was intact except the relay station. That was where the damage had been done. The tumor and the surgery had destroyed the relay station. Steve could not communicate.

Occasionally I would feed him lunch or dinner. That was a joy, for not only could I be with him longer, I could also feel a little useful by tending to him.

Another welcome diversion came when I was called for a consultation with the dietitian. She asked many questions as we planned his menus for the next two weeks.

"Yes, he likes milk. Sometimes he likes hot sweet tea but he hates the smell of coffee. He loves his Grandma's lemonade, but milk or tea is a safe bet here," I explained.

Steve was being graduated from pureed meats to ground beef, and that meant hamburgers. They were called Barnesburgers by the staff, "soybean burgers" by the patients. Steve had always been a hamburger hound; even his work at McDonald's where he handled them all the time hadn't killed his appetite for them.

Steve, you are always so funny when I go to McDonald's, standing brisk and businesslike behind the counter. Knowing that I am waiting there next in line, you work hard to keep your eyes from meeting mine until you take my order.

Did I look at you? I thought I did. I thought I saw.

The dietitian's question broke my reverie.

"How about meat loaf on Sunday or a little baked fish?" Her voice was kind.

My mind spun off again. Sunday dinners. Sunday evening December 16, just two days before Steve's big surgery, Bill who always loved to treat us to little surprises, had taken us to Queeny Towers, the fine restaurant within the hospital complex. He thought it would give Steve a change from hospital fare and a little touch of festiveness. Stephen had looked well and quite smart in his blue robe as he maneuvered his wheelchair swiftly down the corridors. We could hardly keep up with him.

However, we were met with disappointment at the entrance. The maitre d' told us that no one could be admitted without a coat. We were turning away when a smartly dressed woman at the cash register quickly came from behind the counter, took off her own brown blazer, and put it around Steve's shoulders.

"Now," she said pertly, "Just let them tell you that you don't have a coat on."

I don't remember what Steve ate, if anything, but I do remember that woman's kindness. So many people were so good to him. For a moment I'd forgotten the dietitian. "I'm sorry. What did you ask? Desserts? He likes fruit—and almost any kind of ice cream—especially fruit flavors."

Remember when you had your heart set on making blueberry ice cream for the church social this summer? You went to Blueberry Hill that morning to pick the berries yourself. The ice cream was really good, but that awful blue-gray color!

"Yes. Ice cream would be fine," I told the dietitian. I asked if they had blueberry. I bustled with efficiency and energy. I was doing something for my child. He was going to live! Of course he was.

Look! We have ordered hamburger on whole wheat bread, whole kernel corn, French fries, celery and carrot sticks, milk, and hot tea. We have made practical, solid plans for two weeks hence! Here is exactly what Steve will eat for dinner on January 12! Good, solid, dependable food. It says so right here. Good, solid dependable printing on good, solid dependable paper.

The year was drawing to an end. Would Steve live to see another? Those menus helped me believe he might make it into 1974. They were the best I could do.

The last day of any year had always seemed depressing to me. December 31, 1973, was no exception. When Dr. Racheson made his rounds about 10:30, he told us that Steve was about the same. His arm and leg movements, and even his eye control, might be a little better.

I fed Steve lunch—ground beef. He liked to hold the bread, but he got too much crammed in his mouth and I had to gouge it out. Oh, my agile, quicksilver son. Everything else he managed well. Every day we tried to find one good thing. That day it was the coloring book from a boy back home. Steve seemed alert and he *smiled*—a genuine smile, not a grimace on command, and four or five times, maybe more, he chuckled and laughed out loud at the book's funny cartoons about hospital life. The sound was almost normal. It seemed to surprise and please him, too.

But Kathy and I both noticed a lessening of control of his lips. His "kisser" was not as firm or controlled as it had been. Stephen had always been a kissing bug.

Kathy had never liked to be kissed, and she would squeal and run away when her juicy baby brother headed her way. When they were older, although they were clearly fond of each other, there was a tacit understanding that there would be no kissing. Once, when Steve was in sixth grade, in a sudden burst of tenderness, Kathy leaned over and kissed him.

Steve jumped up, whirled around in mock surprise, and exclaimed, "She kissed me! My sister kissed me!" He dashed outside and ran up and down our block shouting, "She kissed me! My sister kissed me! Do you hear? My sister kissed me!"

We were weak with laughter, but between her laughter and tears (for she recognized some truth in his implications), Kathy begged, "Mother, get that kid in here or I'm going to go out and kill him right on our lawn!"

Ah, Steve, the kissing bug.

He seemed to be doing better when we left for the night. His mouth seemed less flaccid. Maybe we had imagined the change.

New Year's Day. I wrote just the date, "January 1, 1974," in my tablet. I could not go on. I was so afraid. I could not chronicle Steve's dying.

New Year's Day was also Bill's birthday. We thought it might cheer Steve if we could have a little celebration. Everybody's birthday was special. David's birthday would come next. He would be twenty-one the next month. Surely Steve would be home by then to help his brother celebrate that special birthday.

The more I thought about birthdays, the more I decided we needed to celebrate Bill's in some way—for Stephen's sake. An unnatural, forced intimacy occurs among those who wait long hours together in the waiting room, provided for the families of ICU patients. Perhaps Ron, who had become a friend over the previous two months, could help. The first time I had seen his wife, her broken face, injured in a car wreck, had looked like the Mona Lisa—a portrait of the Mona Lisa done in mosaic. Shortly after dinner, Ron came swinging down the corridor, carrying a brown bag with a little supermarket loaf cake and a big red candle. On our goodnight visit with Steve we carried in the cake with its oversized but jaunty candle. Steve shared the celebration (if it could be called that), and we each held a hand as he mouthed, "Happy Birthday, Dear Daddy."

Bill asked Steve, "How about you blowing out the candle, Stephen?"

He meant to make Steve feel a little more involved, and Steve nodded eagerly. But when he started to blow out the candle, it was pitiful to see his bewilderment. He was unable to purse his lips or push the air out with sufficient force to cause the flame even to flicker.

Our time was up. On that sad and scary note, the "party" ended and we slipped away. When I got to my room, I added the following line to my morning's entry.

January 1, 1974

Never have I been so aware of the joy that has been ours, so tremulous with the joy that could be ours again. Never have I been so afraid.

JANUARY—OUT AT LAST

The new year felt just like the old. The next day held the same worries, the same tensions, as the endless days before. That is, it did until late afternoon when we saw Dr. Racheson come out of ICU and head our way. He always spoke abruptly, as if he had just made a decision on the spot, although I knew this was not so.

He said, "I'm taking Steve out of ICU tomorrow."

Joy! Joy!

We could hardly wait to see Steve—to tell him the good news.

He raised his eyebrows, his sole means of facial expression, and lifted the corners of his mouth in a pathetic caricature of his old grin. A lovely hint of the old gleam shone in his tortured eyes!

This was a real milestone! We were making headway at last.

We were surprised to learn that Steve was to be moved in with another patient, but Dr. Racheson explained that he did not want Steve to be alone. He would be with a responsible patient, in the room nearest the nurses' station. Those precautions made us apprehensive, but we were jubilant nonetheless.

Steve's roommate, a middle-aged man, was deeply touched by Steve. He accepted the rather frightening responsibility of watching him and calling the nurses if he got into trouble.

Steve seemed pitifully grateful to be out of the ICU and once again in a world of color and texture and family. He took great interest in the placement of his possessions.

It had been a long, long time since Christmas Eve when Hilda had strewn the bushel of gifts on his bed. Steve had not let us open any of those gifts, though his fingers always clung tenaciously to the little fur Santa. Each night in the ICU, as I put the Santa in Steve's hand, I'd breathe a little prayer.

"Oh Stevie, hang on, darling. There *is* a world outside this hellish, sterile isolation. There *is* still a world of form and shape and softness waiting to welcome you back. Please don't feel you've been abandoned to some place in outer space—a place run to the incessant beep of the heart monitors."

When I am a thousand years old the hair will still rise on the nape of my neck at any repetitive sound of a certain frequency. All the heart monitors will come rushing back, all the sinister implications, all the ghastly fears. And beneath them all, I will hear him plead.

"Get— me—out—of—here—please! Please!"

At last he was out. Here was our son! Here was our personal Advent.

Now it was Christmas! It was time to open the presents. Bring on the gifts!

Steve enjoyed the crazy notes the kids had sent him. Their free and easy nonchalance belied their real love and concern.

Mary Beth had written a letter. He chuckled as we read it, a staccato sound, far different from his old throaty laugh. His voice had always reminded me of corduroy—thick brown corduroy—rich and deep, yet soft and thickly textured at the same time. Still any sound at all from him was welcome.

The first gift was a puzzle. An intricate labyrinth, far beyond his present capabilities. We laid it aside "for later" and opened another—a miniature paint-by-number set with a delicate sable brush and many, many tiny jars of pigment.

Steve's face was stricken. He motioned, "No more, no more."

Those gifts—gifts that had seemed to the kids to be perfect for whiling away hours in a hospital—merely pointed up Steve's great diminishment in dexterity and ability. He never let us open any more.

But never mind the presents! There was much that we could do. He was out of the ICU, and he was still our Stephen! He had somehow hung on to himself. For seventeen days and nights he had endured the twilight zone of the ICU. He had clung to Stephen and to sanity, despite that suffocating world of white and chrome whose sounds were the beeping of the monitors and the raspy breathing of the respirators. That "No Man's Land" was hardest on boys and old men, and he'd come through it.

The rational part of me recognizes the efficiency of intensive care units. No doubt they have saved many lives, but another part of me bewails the unspeakable anguish that is borne by the patients.

The first day out was sheer joy—sheer joy and blessed hope. We could hardly keep our hands off Steve. We could hardly talk without cooing.

We had been told Steve couldn't speak because fluid, caused by swelling from the surgery, was not draining properly. The pressure from that was responsible for his muteness as well as his paralysis. Any day, the doctor had assured us, he would just start talking.

That very day he said a word! Someone had sent him a Jim Croce record, but the "e" on the end of "Croce" was lost in the album embellishment.

Bill and I, deplorably ignorant of contemporary musicians, said, "Oh, here's a record by Jim Crock."

Steve looked rather pityingly at us and sort of snorted— "Crock."

That night when Kathy called, he repeated "Crock" for her. He seemed to enjoy phone calls from Kathy and Grandma those first few days.

We were so fearful we could hardly stand to leave him overnight without the constant supervision of the ICU nurses. I found large safety pins and carefully rigged the cord that summoned the nurse. His hands could not fail to feel it if he needed to turn on his signal light. We made several dry runs to see if he could maneuver it, and I left feeling confident he could manage.

On the way out, I stopped at the nurse's station, as I did every night, to make sure the nurse on duty had the Gordon's phone number where I could be reached. I was only seven minutes away.

One day, in the gift shop, I found a little magnetic board with numbers and the alphabet and bought it for Steve. He picked out his initials and put them on the board. Then he put up all the numbers from 1 through 10. He couldn't get them in a straight line, but he picked them all up in the right order.

The next time I called Bill, I told him, "When you come back Tuesday bring one of those. And pick a good one. That's a way he can talk to us! I know it will work!"

I continued. "And Bill, he can read! I picked up a magazine and held up an ad to him this morning. It was in big print and without hesitating he mouthed, 'Our new menthol is a lemon.' If they can just get that pressure regulated, maybe he's going to be all right."

I rejoiced each time Steve mouthed a word. I did not try him often, but I remember how encouraged I felt a week later when I held up an ad for Stix's big January book clearance and he immediately mouthed the words, "Book Bonanza." He formed the words unerringly, though soundlessly.

The days were terrible with many frustrations, but also happy because we felt we were seeing progress. Our lives fell into a tightly circumscribed routine where little things, little accomplishments loomed large.

One of Steve's many cards pictured a huge, happy-go-lucky Snoopy. Each night, as I left, I put that card and a tiny wooden zebra Kathy brought him on the table at the foot of his bed. Steve liked to manipulate the zebra whose antics were controlled by a spring at the bottom of the stand. The zebra seemed to give direction to the restless, ceaseless movement of his fingers.

I would put those two little fragments of nonsense and normalcy alongside the little magnetic board on which I spelled out, "I love you, Steve," and then I would leave. That little ritual seemed to please him.

We were incredibly optimistic during Steve's first week out of ICU. The busyness of the hospital routine, the little rash of treatment and testing activities, the cautious assurance of the doctors that they saw improvement, Steve's bull-dog persistence and his great will to live—all these helped quell the dark forebodings of Dr. Racheson's diagnosis.

Steve's loss of speech continued to baffle Dr. Racheson. He told us Steve was just so despondent that he was sulking; he did not want to talk.

Stephen? I never believed that for a moment.

Then Dr. Racheson told us the problem resulted from intercranial pressure, caused by improper drainage of the spinal fluid. Innumerable spinal taps followed—each one duly signed for. Bill told me the most excruciating pain he had ever experienced was from the spinal taps he'd had in the army. Yet, from my post outside the door, I never heard Steve scream or shout. No matter how frightened, nor in how much pain he was, my mute child took what came with silence.

During the first week after he left the ICU, Steve might utter a word a day. Usually it was when he was not trying—as if it sneaked in when the debility wasn't looking. Those occasional words would always fit the conversation, but sometimes the syllables would be reversed. No one knew what caused the disruption of the normal speech pattern. But then no one really understands the miracle of speech at all.

Much later I was to read something John Gunther had written as his own son battled brain tumor.

All that goes into a brain—the goodness, the wit, the sum total of enchantment in a personality, the very will, indeed the ego itself—being killed inexorably, remorselessly, by an evil growth! Everything that makes a human being what he is, the inordinately subtle and exquisite combination of memory, desire, impulse, reflective capacity, power of association, even consciousness—to say nothing of sight and hearing, muscular movement and voice and something so taken for granted as the ability to chew—is encased delicately in the skull, so marvelously interlocked as to be beyond belief. All this—volition, imagination, the ability to have even the simplest emotion, anticipation, understanding—is held poised and balanced in the normal brain, with silent exquisite efficiency. And all this was what was being destroyed. It was, we felt, as if reason itself were being ravaged away by unreason, as if the pattern of Johnny's illness were symbolic—a primitive to-the-death struggle of reason against violence, reason against disruption, reason against brute unthinking force—this was what went on in Johnny's head"(*Death Be Not Proud.* New York: Random House, 1953, 107–9).

In Stephen's head, too. We might have written those words. We had lived them.

In retrospect it seems an unnecessary burden that we were continually kept in the dark, almost as if Steve's condition was none of our business. One morning, after Steve had endured two brain surgeries and we knew he had a malignant tumor, Bill and David and I met Dr. Racheson with a few admittedly heart-rending questions. They were questions surely any family would ask.

"What can we expect? What will he be able to do? Will he ever walk? Talk? How? When?"

Dr. Racheson seemed to fly mad, and he retorted angrily, "I call these morbid questions. I have not buried the boy yet, and I certainly did not expect his family to. I think Steve still has a good chance."

In some strange way this made us feel better at the time. But as I look back on that morning, I believe the questions were valid and we had a right to honest answers—if not then, certainly during the next tragic months.

I never understood the doctor's attitude. Surely our thoughts and fears were as bleak as any truth the doctors could have told us. But maybe not.

Sometime that same week Dr. Racheson came into Steve's room on evening rounds and announced, "Steve, we're going to walk tonight!"

Oh joy! Somehow just by the movement of brows and eyes Steve showed his jubilation!

Dr. Racheson lifted him from his wheelchair and maneuvered him across the room. Steve had on those funny red and white checked tablecloth pajamas, and I can see him yet, as his long legs once more tried to function.

"Not so high—not so high, Steve," Dr. Racheson cautioned, for he goose-stepped at first. "Slower now, that's good. Not so high. Much better. Fine. Good. You'll get the hang of it again."

Steve had to be supported heavily, for he still listed far to one side. The portion of his cerebellum that controlled such things as balance had been affected. Steve had worried about water skiing, but this was what it meant.

"That's *good,* Steve," the doctor said again as he eased him, excited and flushed with accomplishment, back into the chair.

"That *really* is very good," the doctor assured me as I walked him to the door.

Stephen seemed so pleased and hopeful.

Steve's paralysis was no longer so pronounced. It was just a matter of slowed and less refined reactions and a loss of fine motor movement. He had learned to pivot himself from his bed to his wheelchair and back again. His long arms—Neanderthals he had always called them—and his hands were still beautiful and strong. Though his thumbs had lost some of their dexterity he could still handle things and could propel his wheelchair down the halls. That seemed to please him, and he'd stop at the door of each friend and throw up his hand in greeting.

Because Steve was so tall and his balance so impaired, it took two people to support him, but at least three or four times a day he walked the circuit of the entire East Pavilion. Was he getting steadier? Surer on his feet? We thought so.

We *willed* it to be so.

He dutifully stopped and looked out each window at whatever sight we showed him. St. Louis's Planetarium is shaped somewhat like a lady's bonnet, and at Christmas time, in some spirit of civic frivolity, the city encircles the entire building with a great red ribbon tied in a gigantic bow. The decoration made the building look even more like the Sunday hat of some missing giantess. At first it seemed whimsical and lent a bit of levity to our walk, but as we looked at it day after day, week after week, it became misshapen, swollen, and slightly grotesque.

But the sunsets were beautiful that winter, and at a certain hour they bathed the city in molten gold. Once we'd seen Colorado's Royal Gorge awash in gold just like that. Nearly every afternoon the rays of the setting sun turned our limited view from the hospital

room into a fabled city, a fairy tale city such as those that decorate
the frontispieces of special books—or even Mt. Olympus itself.

*Or the City of God set on a hill. "I will lift up mine eyes
unto the hills. From whence cometh my help? My help
cometh from the Lord." Oh, Lord, don't you think it's about
time we were getting some help?*

One morning we discovered an out-of-the-way corner—a place
from which we could see the heliport. Once we saw the helicopter
land, but usually we just watched the busy little sparrows flitting
down below—little sparrows that had somehow made the
evolutionary adaptations necessary to succeed in an environment
filled with the swing of cranes and the constant flow of traffic. Their
chirps, though muffled by the din of the jack hammers and the noise
of engines, persisted. Sometimes we would sit there for half an hour
watching. Watching the sparrows.

*Sparrows. Not a sparrow falls but you see it, God. Did you
see the one in the driveway crushed by the workman's
truck? Sparrows are bought and sold for a farthing. What
does anyone want with a sparrow, even for a farthing? But
here is a Sparrow, Lord, of infinite worth, whose everyday
has been surrounded by love. Look on Him, Lord, I beseech
you.*

Steve put his whole trust in Dr. Racheson. We believe he did his
best. But I'll never forget the night after he'd helped Stephen walk
for the first time. When Dr. Racheson came into the room, Steve
reached up those long skinny arms to be walked again.

But Dr. Racheson said, "No, not tonight Steve. You'll have to
get an orderly to help you. Last night you gripped me so hard my
arm is still sore."

Steve just looked with those sad, sad eyes in that otherwise
expressionless face.

But I thought, "Doc, if the situation were reversed, I'd walk your boy if I had to do it on bloody stubs."

That was one of the saddest nights I have in my memory. Instead of helping him walk, Dr. Racheson scolded and berated Steve—told him he was tired of him sulking and feeling sorry for himself.

"You're worrying your mother to death!" He repeated this inanity several times. Yet, all during the tirade, the same words kept coming through. "You are going to get better. You *are* going to walk again. You *are* going to talk again. Now I just want you to straighten up and quit acting like a big baby. We're tired of it. You're looking good. You *are* going to get better. Do you hear?"

As he stood up to leave, Dr. Racheson ran an experienced hand over Steve's precious skull. He frowned and felt here and there. Then he strode to the door and beckoned me.

"It doesn't look good," he said. "The fluid is not draining at all. I'm going to have to put a shunt in."

Within minutes a crew was there for another dreaded spinal tap. Then they wrapped Steve's head in a tight, Swami-type turban, called a pressure bandage.

Later that night Steve made a little strangled sound. Then, to our astonishment, he said, "How much—how much—how much, t'geth'r—ba-room?"

We laughed and cried at the same time. But we got him to the bathroom—on time.

That was the most he'd said in weeks, and we were sure he would continue. But he did not. A year later I had an appointment with Dr. Racheson and I questioned him about that night.

"Why were you so mean? Why did you do that?"

He answered wearily. "I've known it to work sometimes. You know, we don't know why the speech is lost."

We could have stood this cruelty if it had worked. But oh, how immeasurably sad it was to bear the apparent cruelty without the cure.

Somewhere I'd read that after surgery or an accident, other portions of the brain could be taught to take over the damaged section. In fact, Dr. Racheson himself, prior to Steve's surgery to remove the tumor, had explained this ability of the brain to compensate for loss.

Could that be possible with Steve's loss of muscle control? If the tendons and muscles went through the old familiar motions, would the brain regain its refinement, its subtleties?

Could that same principle work even with the speech? If we fed data into that great computer could those infinitesimal impulses be retrained, retracked so that once again they could go through the right processes?

Delacotti's method of patterning brain-damaged children sometimes brought astounding results. Would it work there?

No task seemed too hard if it would help—no commitment too long.

But no staff person would talk to us about the process. They acted as if they had never even heard of the theory. Still, we played with a ball and manipulated modeling clay. We spent so much time chasing the ball under beds and dressers that we had a friend bring us a bean bag.

Steve liked to throw the ball and, later, the bean bag. It gave him happy involvement with his dad, too. He could not throw underhanded, but he would throw awkwardly, using his whole arm in a wide overhand swing.

Steve's motor control was abysmally impaired. But even though so many seemingly unrelated skills were missing—like throwing underhanded—miraculously, his mentality was still intact. We were able to have close and meaningful times. He listened to adult conversation, paid close attention, and joined in with gestures.

One morning excitement was pretty high in the old ball game. Bill and Steve had kept the ball going back and forth, across the play area, for a long time. Steve had the ball and Bill called out, "Wind it up now. Let's see a good one." To our shocked dismay, Steve brought the ball down from throwing position and very deliberately started to wind it up like an alarm clock!

Once again there were prickles on the back of my neck. It was so innocently done that Bill still thinks Steve may have been clowning. Communication was so restricted, I cannot be sure, but I don't think so.

Later when I described the incident to Dr. Racheson, he said, "Ah, the idiom. . . . We do not understand."

Right then, I didn't understand anything—life, death, disease, God.

Not anything.

Damn the Pale Horseman

When did I get scared—really cold, clammy scared?

I can no longer remember a time when I was not scared, yet something had changed.

Steve no longer cared whether the nurse call was secured to his pillow at night. He had not said a word in days.

He would become restless and uneasy and make little whimpering noises—little staccato sounds that were neither laughing nor crying.

That agitated state was frightening to see, and I felt as if a menacing Rumpelstiltskin danced in a nimbus about his shoulders, threatening to carry him away. Somewhere near my beloved son, a leering chimera lurked.

Tuesday, January 8, was a bad day—all day. Mama and Daddy had driven up to see Steve, bringing him a new pair of pajamas. He had seemed pleased to see them and wanted to wear the pajamas. Mama was feeding him a tangerine when the glittering look came into his eyes, and almost immediately he wet the new pajamas, causing him to become greatly agitated. Before I could calm Steve down, it began to sleet and Bill made rapid plans to take the grandparents home.

Harsh winds hurled the ice pellets against the windows. I was parked in a limited parking area. If I did not move the car, it would be towed away before night. But by the time I reached the car, it was encased in a half inch of ice. The doors were frozen shut. It took a long time to get inside and then a longer time to hack enough ice from the windshield so I could see to drive. When I tried to back out, the wheels spun on the ice, and the car would not budge. Luckily I had a shovel in my trunk, and while I hacked away at the icy curb, I wept in utter frustration and fear. Tears froze on my cheeks. It took nearly two hours to move the car. That afternoon was one of the few times I remember crying.

Damn the weather! Damn the Pale Horseman who dares to blow his foul breath on my child—who dares to besmirch him with his fetid stench! Damn my impotence, my helplessness!

Steve's behavior pattern began to change. By the time Bill had brought a magnetic board with those letters that were to unlock Steve's prison, he had lost the ability to manipulate them. Each night, as I fixed "I love you, Steve" on his bedside table, I wondered if he saw it. But one day as we sat "playing" with the board, I purposely put up "Steev." He clumsily shoved the "v" aside and tried to put it in the right position.

Steve knew! He still knew.

For a couple of weeks the hand signals we had adopted when he lost his voice in ICU had been clear. One squeeze meant "yes," two squeezes "no," three squeezes "I love you!" But now the signals were not dependable. He might give the same signal for opposite things, or he might make no signal at all.

Sometimes he seemed distressed that he could not make us understand. Other times he seemed remote, his hands flaccid as we tried to get a response.

His behavior was erratic. That was the phrase I used when I called home. That was one of the most frightening phases in that entire time of terror. I knew something was happening, but I did not know what. Frantic, I cornered anybody in a white uniform—from orderlies to nurses to Dr. Schwartz, the head of neurosurgery, himself. But I got no answers.

I had not been home for more than a month, and family and friends thought I needed a rest. Finally, I agreed to go home on Saturday, January 12th—but only if Kathy and David would come and stay with Steve.

To my dismay, they brought Bob Morgan with them. Bob had been a close companion to both boys, but I did not want him there then! Those boys had swum and canoed and worshipped and hiked together. They'd tasted each other's thoughts and opinions, but I did not want Bob there that weekend.

When Steve got out of the ICU, his friends had asked to come see him. I had always put them off.

"Wait a little while. Just one more week. Just 'til he's a little stronger."

I hadn't wanted them to see him then. I didn't want them to be frightened. I didn't want them to feel strange around Steve when he came home. The longer they waited, the fewer horrors they would have to forget.

I hadn't realized this at first. Steve looked so beautiful to us—so "normal"—that when he first came out of ICU I thought it would be good for Kay and Nina Cogswell to slip in and see him. It would be good for him to see some young faces. Their mother, Barbara, who had visited us three times a day since October 12 agreed.

Nina, a high school sophomore, and Kay, a senior, knew what Steve had been through. They had listened as we wept and talked the nights away in their living room. Two years later Kay wrote me the following words.

Steve was found to have a tumor. From that point on school didn't matter. I went . . . but I had an inner pain that colored everything. . . . I talked to friends who had known Steve. I was forced to try to explain what was happening and I had to face their (to me) meaningless statements that they would pray for him and think of him. They might. But they wouldn't think of him as I did, because they just didn't *know*. Every morning I would wake up happy, but that happiness would immediately be replaced with the worry that nagged at my mind. I would lie in bed thinking of the Warners and how all the time you would be thinking of your son.

I would get home from school and piddle around waiting for my mom to get home and bring us news. Every night at dinner she would tell us of her latest visit with you, her lunch hour spent worrying with you. I was envious that she could be there, that she had a chance to speak with you and your uncertainty. . . . One day my mother brought the news that the tumor was malignant and I am ashamed to admit that, at 17 years old, I didn't know what that meant. I was sitting in the living room when my mother told me. I remember it, because that was the first time I considered the possibility that Steve might not live. Till then I concentrated on my own optimism, based on the idea that people I know don't die. . . .

Then I went to the hospital. It seemed so great, to be able to finally visit my friend who was having such trouble. My optimism returned and I was convinced that having seen Steve, everything would be all right. He would get better, he'd know how much I cared. . . . It didn't work. Nina and I tried to give you a break. We tried to fend for ourselves and found we didn't have any idea what to say or do. There was Steve, unrecognizable to our invulnerable hearts, only he was unable to communicate to us. We found nothing of the person we had known. We were both afraid. Nina went to find you, to ask you to free us, and I was alone with Steve for a little bit. For that little bit I tried to read his mail to him, and I know I treated him as a complete idiot. He couldn't answer me, so I acted like he couldn't understand me. I was appalled at my . . . reaction.

I left the hospital that day more upset than I had been, ever before, and halfway to the car my stomach cramped up and I doubled over in tears. My father tried to comfort me, but I cried, quietly out the window all the way home. . . .

One night I was listening to Jim Croce's album, *I Got a Name*, which I had recorded for Steve because he got it for his birthday but couldn't listen to a record [in the room]. Do you remember when he told you how to pronounce it? I do, and I will, every time I hear the name "Croce.". . . Then I put on *John Denver's Greatest Hits*. . . . 'For though my life's been good to me, there's still so much to do—so many things my mind has never known. . . .' I cried, truly cried, sobs and all, that night. Nothing could help me return to my optimism. . . .

Maybe you thought I felt nothing; I felt a lot, I feel a lot, present tense . . . my heart is torn, with a big hole in it where satisfaction should be, because I know that life isn't satisfying.

Did you know I had a crush on him in sixth grade when we were in Sunday School together? I like to think of him informing the world, "YOU, are a dead frog." He used to tell me that.

I had known how badly the visit went. After that I tried to keep everybody else away. Now there was Bob. I did not want him to look at Steve. I wanted no one to see him. I felt like an animal who must drag her maimed and mutilated offspring deep into the woods; deep into a burrow, where perhaps his wounds would heal.

My twenty-four hours at home were horrible, far worse than sitting by Steve's bedside. I had never known such heaviness and sorrow as I felt when I walked into our house. Artifical pine roping dangled forlornly from a beam in the living room. A few tiny ornaments had been tied to the branches of the Norfolk Island pine —mute evidence of Kathy and David's pitiable attempts at decorating in early December. The contrast of this great, empty house—a house that I once thought I loved—with anything that was valuable or really important was so poignant. As I walked through its emptiness, I heard a strange keening sound. With shock, I realized it was me!

When I returned to the hospital on Sunday, Steve seemed a little better. It was perhaps an hour before Dave had to leave—Kathy and Bob had left the day before. I remember this as being one of our easier times together. As Dave bent to hug Steve and tell him goodbye, Steve reached out with his maimed but still beautiful hand, plucked the navy sock cap from Dave's head, and put it on his own. There it sat, atop the big white bandage, until bedtime.

Steve listened carefully and intently, and he seemed calm as I told him about all the things I'd done, all the people I'd seen. I told about going over to Grandma's through the woods.

*Steve, I wish you could see the woods. They're just
beautiful. Do you remember that day last year when we
were out of school because of a snow day, and you and I
walked the path to Grandma's? That was the day we
discovered the tight little dogwood buds already formed on
the branches. Remember how they were magnified by their
coating of ice? We had the camera and you took my picture
gingerly crawling over the stile and I took yours down at
the end of the long rows of ice-covered barbed wire. I
remember the sun came out and there we stood in acres of
diamonds, beside a forest changed to a fairyland. Well, now
it's just like. . . .*

I could go no further. I threw my arms around his bony
shoulders. He put his long arms around me and hugged me as hard
as he could. We rocked back and forth and crooned to each other on
that hospital bed, and I cried for both of us.

"Oh, Steve. It's not pretty at all. The ice is just cold and hard and
ugly without you. I hated it. It was not beautiful. Nothing will ever
be beautiful again until you can get well and come home."

I don't remember all that I said—just a few moments of shared
rage and anguish and fear. Just a breakthrough of honest emotion.

Did he make little sorrowing sounds as he clung to me? I don't
really remember.

Of all our hospital hours, I treasure that time of honest sharing
most. It was infinitely better than the thousands of times I'd said,
"My, you're looking good this morning. We're all fine. Now!
Wonder what we're going to have for lunch?"

It was difficult for our family to be completely honest, despite all
our resolve and the straightforward manner we had always shared.
I thought I had come to grips with death, but it was *my* death I'd
wrestled with—maybe even the deaths of parents or spouse—but
not my child.

The staff encouraged us to adopt an optimistic bedside manner,
probably because all their training and their zeal and devotion were

dedicated to healing, and they became ill at ease with despair—angry with dying.

I remembered the note Steve had written back in November, when he said he had accepted the fact he would probably be blind—"but after a great deal of thought and MUCH PRAYER, I'm sure I can handle it." Could he also handle the deluge that was now sweeping over him? And so we kept up a brave front for his benefit. Would it have benefitted him more if we had honestly shared our anguish?

When he was unhappy and frightened in kindergarten, he seemed to be genuinely helped when he discovered he didn't have to pretend he liked it all the time. Charles Schulz had Charlie Brown say, "There is no burden like a great potential."

I also had the feeling that there was no burden like eternal optimism—like false gaiety.

"Treat him normally" was always the answer we received when we begged to know how we should treat him.

"Normal?"

What an ambiguous word at best. It was completely meaningless in our situation. So we chatted casually about the news, about TV programs, about happenings at home, about friends, about the weather, the mail, school. About the coming summer.

And then there was the malignancy. Dr. Racheson had still not told Steve.

Why?

Steve had never asked, of course.

His condition was still so unstable that the doctor was unable to start cobalt treatments—treatments we were told had the greatest degree of success in Steve's kind of tumor.

But that would come soon. That horrible bridge was still to be crossed.

How Long, Is a Chinaman

Bill and I were frantic to get "something" started. We were at a standstill. Our days fell into a pathetic pattern—a grim routine where every option was odious. Nothing was common or ordinary. Friends, were supportive in every way possible, but there was just nothing anyone could do for Steve.

In the midst of our sorrow, we were aware that our family was more fortunate than others. Some families knew no one in the city and had only a lonely rented room to creep back to each night. Many had additional worries about such things as bus schedules to cope with. But our host friends, the Gordons, were superb—always waiting when I got "home," with a warm fire, a cup of tea, a compassionate heart.

Once, after I had been there nearly two months, I said, "Bob, I never dreamed when you invited me to stay, it would come to this."

He replied, "Normagene, none of us ever dreamed it would come to this."

Another time he gently said, "When you came you were friends. You have become family."

The Gordons had a beautiful and spacious parsonage, and they said, "So seldom are we in the right place at the right time, please accept our hospitality. We count having you here a privilege."

They made us feel as if they were the privileged ones—not us. I will always remember them with love and gratitude.

At last we were told that Steve would begin speech therapy on Wednesday. We were delighted. Something was going to be done! Steve was scheduled to begin physical therapy, too, but the starting date kept receding.

We were ignorant about so many things and no one tried to explain. Although the staff didn't know everything, often just a word could have quelled our darkest fears. To our untrained eyes, the remoteness into which Steve seemed to be sinking appeared to be psychological in nature.

We'd say to the doctor, "We're afraid if speech therapy isn't started soon it will be too late."

We thought that surely he could interpret the dark forebodings that were in our anxious faces and our scared pleas.

I felt that Steve's fear and agony would be somewhat assuaged if he could talk.

Talk—talk—talk.

We had always referred to Steve as the kid who never found a period once he learned to talk. Whenever he'd been to camp—even a weekend retreat—he'd come back hoarse as a frog, and we'd greet him by saying disparagingly, "Well, I can see he's had a good time—he's talked until he's hoarse!"

The spring before, Steve had gone with Dave and Russ to help sandbag Kaskaskia Island, trying to save it from the flooding Mississippi River. The next day Dave told us how hard Steve had worked, how he had done a man's work all night.

But then he added, "Mama, he never shut his mouth the whole time. I heard two or three people ask, 'Who is that kid that talks and sings all the time?'"

Dave laughed. "Russ and I pretended not to know, but we could hear him too, and he was easily an eighth of a mile away."

As Dave told us that, I could sense the pride and love he had for his wacky brother.

Even though it had been weeks since I had heard Steve's voice, its rich throaty tones rang in my ears.

One night I told Steve that Grandpa had known a man who stuttered badly when he talked, but when he sang in a quartet he didn't stutter at all. Immediately, Steve's mouth opened, and I knew he was trying to sing. Alas, there was no sound. Even his sneezes were soundless. Only the staccato sound of his laugh remained.

Every day I tried to bring little bits of the real world into Steve's room—a pine cone, a smooth stone, a piece of rough bark, a bit of pungent juniper. Once I brought a pigeon feather I found in the parking lot—anything to help him in that desperate pull from the hard white sterile world of the hospital. Nearly every visit David brought a sprig of heals-all and tossed it on Steve's bed or laid it almost prayerfully on his pillow. When the snows hid that little wild flower with the magic name, he brought other things.

Kathy, too, brought him tactile things—things she hoped would give him pleasure and help him hang on to reality—grim as that might be. One week she brought him a great box of rosettes that she and Russ and Dave had made. Steve had never gotten enough of those little delicacies and kept them in the stand beside his bed. Later, as his condition deteriorated, he lost so much dexterity, he either could not grasp them or his fingers closed too tightly and he shattered the star and snowflake pastries.

But when Kathy came, there was always a little circle of joy around her—joy and optimism.

The words "erratic behavior" were evasive and euphemistic, but I could find no better way to describe what was happening to Steve.

When he could not do on one day what he was able to do the day before, we despaired. Then, perhaps a week later, when he was able to do them again, our hopes would soar. He seemed constantly to be on a yo-yo. Up and down. Erratic. We would see something that made us think he was better—that he had arrived at a milestone in his recuperation. Then, too often, we'd never see that skill again.

The ability to perform came and went without apparent reason. Steve could not write a scribble on the "magic" slate, yet about the middle of January I found a sheet of yellow paper from a legal pad someone had left on his bed. He had printed "D A D" in large shaky letters. We found the numerals one through twenty-two scattered at random about the page. Other times the mere sight of paper or pen threw him into a state of agitation, and if he got a pencil in his hand, he seemed even more confused and bewildered.

Walking was usually a rather pleasant part of his schedule, though it never became easy for us. Steve always had to be supported heavily on both sides, but walking helped pass the morning, and it helped ease away the long afternoons. It might even have helped him. He was stripped of almost every avenue of response. Of his great physical dexterity, all was gone except gross motor movements. He had learned even in his diminishment to pivot himself from his bed to his wheelchair and back again, but he always had to depend on others to help him walk.

New words that go beyond "courage" and "bravery" and "pluck"—beyond "stamina," "tenacity," "endurance," "determination"—would have to be invented to describe Steve's tragic battle. Locked in though he was, there were little evidences every day that he had not lost his sense of humor. One day, as friends were walking him down the hall, Bill said, "Son, I believe the surgery has taken away your pigeon toe." Immediately, without pausing, Steve began an exaggerated imitation of Charlie's Chaplin's famous walk. Somewhere, somehow, Stephen was still there.

I wrestled constantly with the idea of God's omnipotence and the poignant needs of everyone on this floor.

Stephen had usually accepted his position docilely, but one particular morning he did not want to go out—did not want to join the promenade. Did his wants matter? Did they carry any weight at all? Did anyone care? He raised those long arms and pressed his hands against the door facing. In the only protest he could make—since by now he was stripped of almost every means of communication, every vestige of free choice—he simply braced himself and refused to be taken out. He was still pretty strong, but he was no match for two nurses. They laughed at him. Teased. Cajoled. Patronized. God, how agonizing it must have been to listen, listen, listen for sixty days with never a comment, never a pithy remark, never an expressed opinion, never an appropriate rejoinder.

We never knew why that particular day he didn't want to walk up and down the corridor, up and down the hall, up and down. But I suspect he *never* wanted to go out there and expose his maimed and broken body for everyone to see.

There was another time, perhaps a week later, that was even more poignant. David and I had pushed his wheelchair to the end of a long hall where there was little traffic. It was from here that we had watched the sparrows earlier in his illness. David had pivoted him from his chair to a bench near a sunny window, where we stayed for perhaps half an hour. When the time came to return to the room, Steve cringed, and sort of hunkered into the window-well, refusing to get back in the wheelchair. David and I cajoled, then wheedled, then scolded, then forced, as David picked him up and placed him in his chair.

Oh, my dearest. Forgive us. We love you so, but we do not know how to help you.

Would it have been easier on Steve if he had not been so lucid, so aware of his condition? Every option was equally repugnant, every alternative carried its own agony, but sometimes I thought it would have been easier. He had charged into life so expectantly, embracing each day with verve and optimism. I think he must have been incredulous at the hand life had dealt him.

What did he think those last months when all his thoughts were locked tight within?

That thinking is still more than I can bear.

> When I was one I had just begun.
> When I was two I was nearly new.
> When I was three I was barely me.
> When I was four I was not much more.
> When I was five. . . .
> A. A. Milne

Perhaps all of life is an unfolding, and there is never a sense of having arrived. But surely no age is more poignantly poised on the brink of "becoming" than seventeen. Seventeen.

A boy of seventeen must view himself as ninety percent potential—one hundred percent becoming. Though undecided about the details of his future, Steve had just begun to realize the dizzying possibilities that lay ahead. The contrast of Steve's Before and his Then must have loomed spectral before him.

His visage never changed. Yet once, when a letter came from home saying the kids were going to dedicate their talent show to him, I saw his shoulders sag, as if he were saying, "Am I really that serious—really that bad?"

Until mid-January, mail call was one of the highlights of the day. Then, the mail became so unsettling that when anyone read it to Steve, the chimera gloated nearby and the pitiful whimpering sounds began. Finally we did not read it to him anymore. We could only guess why the letters and greetings were so disturbing. Perhaps the constantly diminishing control he experienced was too great. Maybe his longing to be with his friends swept over him in unbearable waves. Maybe just the words "Get Well" emblazoned across a gaily decorated card were too much of a mockery.

To carry on a twelve hour monologue without becoming utterly inane and patronizing was not easy. Often we just sat in silence. Sometimes we held hands. One of his most genuine-sounding laughs followed my wry defense as I turned to him with, "Well, this conversation wouldn't be so boring if you'd hold up your end of it!"

Kathy brought anything that she thought might cheer Steve in any way—any treasure to see or hear or taste.

One night she phoned and asked, "Mama, what can I bring him tomorrow? Or you? Is there anything you need or want?"

"Yes, Sweetheart. Bring us the blue bird of happiness."

I did not mean my answer to be bleak. There was just nothing that could be done. Nobody could help Steve.

When Kathy came, she spread out on the bed all the things she'd brought from home. Then she flashed a smile as she set a candle in the middle of the pile—a candle in the shape of a tiny exquisite bluebird.

How long does a vigil last?

How long can a family stare death in the face?

How long can anyone, however strong and courageous, remain at the literal point of death?

How long can a truly beautiful human being be suspended on a hook, dangling somewhere between living and dying?

Nobody knows. Nobody knows.

How Long, is a Chinaman.

A CHANGE OF VENUE

"Why didn't you tell me your insurance had run out?" Dr. Racheson spoke with his usual abruptness as we met in the hall one morning. Wretched as our days were, and as uncertain and frightening as Steve's progress seemed, still there was a consoling familiarity about East Pavilion, Barnes Hospital. We had been there since the middle of October. We knew the whereabouts of the vending machines, the elevators, the nurses' stations, the telephones. We knew the nurses by name. These were little islands of comfort in a sea of discomfort. So Dr. Racheson dropped a minor bombshell when he asked, "Why didn't you tell me your insurance had run out?"

No one had ever mentioned money or anything connected with it. I was aware that our insurance maximum had been exceeded weeks before, but I assumed our finances were a matter of record. When an occasional thought of money flitted through my mind, I dismissed it. It made no more dent on my real worry than a sea-gull makes, lightly skimming the surface of the deep, dark Atlantic. Sometimes I thought dully, "Well, I guess now I'll learn how people get along who cannot pay and know they are not going to be able to. I'll find out what happens."

"Worth a farm in Texas." That southern Illinois country expression, one that denotes fabulous worth, often came to my mind as I cradled my broken Steve. Worth a farm in Texas, that boy! Worth a million farms in Texas, that child! It was an accepted part of the entire rotten parcel that every penny we could scrape up anywhere was for his recovery. We never discussed it. It was never a conscious decision. It was an assumption. Love's right of assumption. The state of our finances truly was of little importance to us. We just assumed the house and what land we owned might be used. Once Bill and I remarked that we didn't think we should let Grandpa and Grandma sacrifice the farm they had owned for over fifty years—surely we could find other means. But we never doubted for a minute that it would immediately be plucked from its dear surroundings and plunked into the coffer if it could mean his recovery!

Do you hear that, Steve? Did you realize that about your doughty old Grandpa? That crotchety old dear who is far quicker to criticize than to tell you how much he loves you? Did you realize he would gladly do that for you? "Worth a farm in Texas." Oh my, yes!

Yet, standing before Dr. Racheson, I felt stupid and dumb. I felt contrite for having been so naive about money. I mumbled, "I guess I just assumed you knew our money was gone. It is a matter of record that we had only $20,000 worth of insurance. You know my husband is a minister. I supposed it was obvious that we are not people of means." I remember gaining a little strength as I floundered for the words. "Surely no one has enough money to pay for such long and dreadful hospital stays. What do other people do?"

"I will see if I can get Steve a bed in Barnard," he said.

"You mean you're going to *move* him? I don't understand. Where is this Barnard?"

"Barnard is the public cancer hospital right next door. Occasionally I send patients there, if there is a free room. If you had told me, I would have done it two weeks ago. Steve is going to need weeks of hospitalization yet, and probably months of therapy. I don't understand why you didn't tell me," he continued. "I've seen them take a family's home and all their property to pay a debt. I'll see if I can find an available bed."

"Doctor!"

He stopped and turned back, for he had already started down the hall. "What about the care? That's the important thing—not us, not our home, but Stephen. Will he receive the same treatment? The same medications and therapy?"

He assured me that the care would be the same. "In fact," he said, "you may find the nursing staff is even a little more personal because of the smaller patient load. The head nurse there is one of the best you'll ever meet."

Dr. Racheson explained that if Steve was transferred to Barnard, he would have a different doctor—Dr. Worth. We had met him. He had been in on all consultations about Steve, from the very beginning. Dr. Racheson assured me that he would remain in contact.

He continued, "Let me assure you again that everything that's being done for Steve here will be done there."

I thought dry, bitter thoughts.

Yes, Doctor. That's right. Nothing can be done for him here and nothing can be done for him there. Zero equals zero. Things equal to the same thing are equal to each other. Theorem No. 365. Three-hundred-sixty-five days it is so.

Aloud I said, "I'll talk to Bill. We'll have to think about it, and I will let you know when I meet you on rounds this evening."

That was Saturday, January 19. For the first time, I made my way to the hospital's finance office. There, seated before a quiet, gray man in a gray suit, I spilled out our miserable story, ending with, "What do you think I should do? I have to make a decision today."

He asked his secretary to bring Steve's file. After he read it, he said softly, "Mrs. Warner, if Dr. Racheson can get you a room at Barnard, please be assured your son's care will be comparable. I think you should take the room."

Bill and I agreed that if the care was the same, we should move Steve. That evening Dr. Racheson told me he had reserved a bed at Barnard. We had to be there by 4:00 p.m. the next day. I hadn't realized there would be such a rush.

Would we feel guilty if we let Stephen be moved to another hospital, albeit a part of the same complex? It was the sensible thing to do in this bizarre nonsensical affair—we all agreed. I remembered conversations we had had with several friends. We hadn't understood when they referred to the guilt people often feel when a family member is seriously ill. I did not think we would feel guilty. Sorrowful, but not guilty.

The next morning, the Sunday of the move, David and Bill and I were in Steve's room before breakfast. Somehow he let us know he'd like French toast, so I slipped down to the little cafe and got it. It was a good morning. "Treat him normally," I'd been told. "Make him use his fork." I will always remember the sight of him, naked from the waist up, sitting erectly in his hospital bed, holding his fork awkwardly, but oh so carefully, maneuvering each bite of that French toast to his mouth. Some mealtimes were ordeals, but that morning he handled everything well.

I was always depressed when the family had to leave us. But that afternoon, when Bill and David, and Kathy and Russ left for Carbondale, I felt especially alone. Bill came at least twice a week and the children at least every weekend, but sometimes it seemed that most of the responsibility was on my shoulders. I dreaded the move.

With the family gone, it was up to Stephen and me, so the two of us began our exodus through the corridors of that great hospital complex. We were making a change—at least a change of venue. It would be the same obscene crime against body and spirit, just a different setting—a different arena for the gladiators. My puzzle dictionary defined gladiators: "From the Latin *Gladi* meaning 'sword': a combatant in deadly combat; one who fights to the death another person or beast."

I prayed that Steve's eyes would not see the name as I wheeled him onto the elevator: Barnard Free Cancer Clinic.

But I had seen it. Here *it* was. Cancer. Ugly, menacing, threatening, bestial. Here, spelled out in concrete, was the beast my own dear gladiator must wrestle in deadly combat. The word—the disease—became personified, as I trundled my broken child into the arena.

Grimacing, loathsome beast, we are not done with you yet!
We are not finished. Our Steve can lick you if anyone can!
Don't you know I see him lying in bed touching each finger
in turn to his nose—touching fingertip to fingertip—he's
practicing. Practicing all the little exercises Dr. Ryan had

him do. Filthy beast, do you hear me? You have met a winner this time, so shuffle your grisly bloody bones off to do your deadly combat with some lesser adversary. Stephen has never tucked tail and run from anything. He will do you in!

I will never know, but I suspect Steve did see the name of the hospital. Every time I showed him letters of any size he let me know he comprehended them. Even after he could no longer mouth the words, he would show some glimmer of recognition. Then there were the snapshots Dave had brought him of their long and satisfying back pack trip the spring before. Steve seemed to enjoy having them around. Sometimes, to be sure he was still with me, seeing and knowing, I would slip one of the pictures upside down. Without fail, he would stretch out his long hands—hands still lovely though greatly diminished in dexterity—and laboriously turn the picture right side up. He consistently did an odd thing with one photo in that pack of snapshots. It was a picture of David, standing on Inspiration Rock, in the LaRue Forest, overlooking the broad valley. It was an excellent picture, but each time, Steve would take it from the stack and drop it onto his bed. Once he flicked it to the floor. What did he want to do with it? I will never know. There are so many things I will never know. Oh, what an agony not to be able to communicate.

The rooms in Barnard were just hospital rooms and would not have seemed so bleak and hopeless if we had not grown accustomed to the poshness of the East Pavilion. At Barnard there were four patients in each room. One of the patients, a lad younger than Steve, was surly and unfriendly. I disliked him immediately—not because he was surly but because he looked so healthy and well. He was plump and pink-cheeked. I am ashamed to say that I liked him better when I heard him on the telephone late that night.

"Please, Daddy, come and get me. I don't even think I have 'it' anyway."

I never knew what his particular "it" was, but the next day his father came and got him. I never saw him again. A nurse told me later that in two or three days "it" caused them to rush him back. Another of Steve's roommates was Mr. Rader, a beautiful, snow-haired old gentleman who looked remarkably like Mark Twain.

Each patient had only one drawer at Barnard, so we took most of Steve's belongings, including the box of still unopened Christmas gifts and a thousand get-well cards, to the Gordons. But we did bring along a little gadget Uncle Bob had made for him. It was a set of wooden gears—made from polished walnut—whose only purpose seemed to be to wind itself. Bob called it a smoke grinder. We also brought along a novelty one of Bob's workmen had carved for "the nephew." It was a snake concealed in a wooden box. The snake would pop out at you if a certain section of the box were pressed.

That first night in Barnard, Dr. Worth stopped at Steve's bed and asked, "Aren't you the young man with the snake in the box and the smoke grinder? Show me how they work." Steve laboriously turned the handle . . . pushed the magic spot. Although he could no longer manipulate the devices easily, he seemed pleased that Dr. Worth asked to see them.

Steve's withdrawal and agitation seemed to worsen at Barnard. There was little room and little privacy. I was not comfortable there; I was self-conscious about talking to him and trying to draw him out. There was only one TV for two beds, and the other boy did not seem willing to have it turned so Steve could see it. In fact, he seemed afraid of this strange, silent young man who'd been moved in with him. Afraid of my Stephen! I could not bear it.

Perhaps all this added to his distress. Increasingly, he seemed to be teetering on the edge of some frightening, undefinable abyss. Later in the week, I voiced some of my fears to Dr. Worth.

He answered me gently. "You've known all along, haven't you, that all Steve's problems are physiological? They are the result of the pressures on the brain caused by the fluid that will not drain off. Steve's not losing his mind. What you're seeing are physiological effects."

This was not much—it surely took less than a minute of his time—but horrible as it was, it laid to rest some of the more frightening words—"schizophrenic," "autistic," "withdrawn," "neurotic," "psychotic"— that had lodged in my mind.

A few nights earlier Joanne Gordon and I had watched Tennessee Williams's *The Glass Menagerie*. The hour was late, the play was eerie, and I was chilled to my marrow with fear—suddenly overwhelmed with despair. Turning to my friend, I sobbed, "Oh, Joanne, if I ever get to take him home at all, it'll be either in a box or a cage. I am so afraid—so scared!"

To have been reassured all along that Steve's behavior was physical and not psychological would have relieved some of those fears.

I think there were not more than two or three nights after December 18—Steve's initial brain surgery—that I felt any assurance he would live until I could come back the next morning.

Hear me, O God, I beseech you. Be with him all the time. Be with him when I must leave. He that keepeth Israel shall neither slumber nor sleep, so please God, keep my child tonight and do not let him be afraid.

Often, late at night, when I walked away from the hospital, my consciousness eroded by grief and worry, I felt that the tether that held me to reality was wearing thin. I felt detached. On the worst of those nights I had the eerie feeling that I was no longer on the earth but had been whisked to another planet where every face and every emotion was weird and alien. The heavy snow that concealed the contours of the spiral parking garage added to the surrealistic feel. Either this was all happening to someone else or I was wading through a heavy dream, unable to wake up.

Each night I talked and wept about the day to Bob and Joanne if they were home. If they weren't, I wrote. One night, sometime after midnight, I closed my bedroom door and reached for my tablet.

My Dearest Stephen, My Beloved Son—-
I smile as I think how you would chafe and scoff at all my terms of endearment. . . . Although you're not his private

patient anymore, Dr. Racheson comes to see you. This morning he told me he still sees you making progress every day. Hang in there. Today you shook his hand and stuck out your tongue! Here, that's considered good! Once he seemed delighted that you'd been able to pick your nose. For shame! (Just keep it up!)

. . . I suspect I may often try to keep up a meaningful conversation when you may be so drearily tired of my voice! You've always been . . . understanding. Please look beyond my babble to the yearning intent of my heart.

. . . I want you to understand, son, that I love *you*, because you're you. Not because you are musical or athletic or handsome or brilliant or even good. It is *you*, William Stephen Warner, I love.

If you were to lose an arm or a leg, I would not love you less. Shakespeare said this best: "Love is not love, which alters when it alteration finds." No matter how long it takes for you to do the things you used to do, or if you *never* can do them again, always remember, it's not the things you do, but *you* I love.

Good night, sleep tight, don't let the bedbugs bite.

C.Y.K. Steverino

Mama

When Stephen was young, I decided it might embarrass the kids to have their mother kiss them good-bye when I dropped them off at school, or choir, or Cub Scouts, or whatever, so we decided instead to say "CYK,"—"Consider Yourself Kissed." We used it all those years. Stephen might not have been embarrassed, for even that past summer, as I headed for the sanctuary on Sunday mornings, I would see the youth flocking down the hall, hear a "Hi, Mom," and feel a peck on my cheek.

Grandma said he did the same with her. She said, "I treasure every one, for I know he's growing up so fast I just wonder how much longer he'll keep on doing it."

Keep on doing it a long, long time, Steverino. It gladdens old ladies' hearts! Probably it's not too bad for the young ladies either!

C.Y.K., STEVERINO

Each day I awoke grateful that the hospital had not called during the night. Each day dawned like every other day that winter. I had no feeling of dawn, yet I knew it must be morning because it was getting lighter. Each day, I was aware that for Steve there had been no respite, no retreat. He could not escape his battle—a battle that raged twenty-four hours a day.

I looked forward eagerly to the days that Bill came to visit. But then, after he arrived, I often felt resentful because he spent so much time with people other than Steve and me. Sometimes Bill acted as if he couldn't get away from us fast enough—by reading or by actually leaving.

I could not absent myself from the tragedy of Steve, either physically or emotionally, and I resented the fact that Bill seemed to. I *wanted* to stay there. As long as Steve was in agony, I did not want to be relieved. While Bill welcomed company and relaxed in others' presence, I was ill at ease. I did not want to be dissuaded from my full-time concentration on Steve. How dare I find relief when my child could find no respite? I felt it was unseemly for Bill to laugh with anyone when our son might be dying. Bill was a great boost to everyone's morale but mine.

But Tuesday, January 22, was going to be different. That day we would begin a new family schedule. January's weather had been unusually bad, and Bill's long trips on Tuesdays and Thursdays had not been satisfying for any of us. He seemed to be on the road twice as long as he was at the hospital. He decided to come on Tuesday afternoons and stay until after visiting hours on Thursdays. He would still be away from the church only two days, but the time would be parceled out in a fashion more satisfactory to everyone.

Steve was to begin speech therapy that day. Therapy. Mr. Webster defines it as a "remedial or curative process." Therapy was what we'd been waiting for.

Steve seemed eager, but when the therapist brought him back to his room, half an hour later, he was dejected.

The therapist explained that the morning had been only an evaluation—to see if Steve could profit from therapy. She said, "Frankly, I could get no response whatever out of him, but we'll try again Thursday."

Evaluation? To see if he could profit from therapy? Again, a million fears clogged our throats.

Before David left that afternoon, he went through the little games we played with Steve every day—games that let us know his reasoning was intact despite the havoc wrought on his "relay station." Admittedly our instruments for testing were crude. We'd write "Alaska, Mississippi, Illinois" in big letters on the slate; then we would ask questions. "Which state do you live in?" "Which state is the coldest?" Kathy had made large cards with sketches of Zanzibar the Siamese and Lumpi the basset. "Point to the cat." "Which animal barks?"

Such infantile questions! I have no idea what Steve thought, but his responses were accurate. What did that therapist mean when she said she got no response? Maybe on Thursday she'd let David go along.

That day, the first day in our new schedule, there had been several tense and anxious times. Beautiful Mr. Rader—our own Mark Twain of the ward—had died with dignity that morning. Had Steve been aware of it? I was not always sure how much he saw, but I suspect he knew.

Nothing had gone well all day. The change in the hospitals required many adjustments. Bill arrived late. Then, while I fed Steve his supper, Bill went to visit a friend in an adjoining hospital. He stayed and stayed. Supper did not go well that evening, either.

The supper trays had been collected, and still Bill had not returned. How could he stay away so long when Steve and I both needed him so much. I knew where he was. He was visiting one of his church members in a hospital nearby. Surely she did not need him as much as we did.

A nurse came to take Steve's temperature and check his blood pressure. As she stuck the thermometer in Steve's mouth, he clamped his teeth down hard on it.

Quickly the nurse said, "Oh, I thought he was able to hold it in his mouth. Never mind, I'll go get a rectal one."

"You don't have to," I retorted, a little angry and a whole lot scared.

"Oh, Steve," I pleaded silently, "you can't be going in the direction I see and dread. My darling, you can't get worse every day. You've held this stupid thermometer in your mouth dozens of times a day for a hundred days! You can't stop now! I won't let them treat you like a baby! These nurses over here just don't know all the neat things you're able to do. You even take your own medicine. You've handled your Gelusil glasses every single time. And you can use your fork."

I sobbed inwardly and watched fearfully as Steve's eyes glittered and his jaws clamped down on the thermometer. In a tight voice, I said, "Now stop that." I popped his cheek. He looked surprised and shocked.

My heart will break each time I remember that incident.

Twice in his life I had slapped Steve—maybe three times. He cut his teeth early, and by six months he had four little pearly incisors. I was still breast feeding him, and although he usually nursed placidly and contentedly, occasionally, at the end of a full meal, when the milk was gone, he'd pull back and literally strip my nipple through his clenched teeth. Once—maybe twice—I popped his fat little jaws, almost instinctively, in self defense. Oh, the tears! He was so shocked and surprised. It broke his heart to have his mother inflict pain on him. The wails would bring Bill, who would scold me for slapping an innocent child—a baby yet. I would start to cry and the baby and I would console each other. It was a long time ago, and we can laugh about it now, but it always made me sad to think about it.

There will never be anything but sorrow connected with the last time I slapped him.

"Treat him normally," the staff people said. "Treat him like you always would." But what was normal? What did they mean? Nothing was normal. We had lived so long in the realm of the bizarre and obscene that I didn't know how to treat Steve.

He was quiet as the nurse removed the thermometer from his mouth.

Wednesday, January 23, seemed filled with promise. Again, we were to *do* something. Steve was excited, too. The whole morning was to be spent in physical therapy.

I was always sorry when I failed to interpret his motions correctly, but one of our to-be-laughed-at-later incidents centered around my obtuseness. Before we took him to therapy, Bill and I thought he should go to the bathroom; Steve was always distressed if he had an accident. After waiting some time, I reached over and turned on the faucet, thinking the running water might speed things up. The water ran three or four minutes with no results except that Steve became more and more agitated.

Finally, since it was obviously doing no good, I turned off the tap. Steve looked up and clapped his poor hands together several times in exaggerated praise. His gesture said, so eloquently, "Finally! *Finally* she understands." A year before, he would have added in raucous adolescent jargon, "Good! Throw her a fish." We were delighted to see that funny little spark of Steve.

That day his eagerness was easy to perceive. He was pitifully eager to be doing something! Finally, his name was called, and Bill and I took him down to therapy.

We were disappointed when, again, he did not do the things he could do in his room. "Sit up." "Lie down." "Pivot into the chair." "Up on your knees." It was the young therapist's first day on the job, and he felt responsible for the session having fallen short of our expectations.

Later that day we went to another center, and when we saw how that therapist handled Steve, we knew we were watching a pro. She had two teen-age boys of her own, and as she talked to Steve about them and about his school and his life, she watched his responses and evaluated every motion. She had him wheel himself to a table where there was a confusion of blocks.

"Make me a building, Steve. How many can you put on top of this one?"

At first Steve wouldn't touch the blocks, and when at last he took one, he just moved it from one hand to the other. The therapist didn't seem upset. She just said, "Never mind. Here's a paper and pencil. See what you can do with them."

Steve grabbed the paper, wadded it up, and tore it in two before it fell to the floor. Seeing our dismay, the therapist tried to assure us. "Don't be upset by this outburst. It happens many times. You see, the paper and pencil signify to him all the skills he has lost. His sense of frustration is just too great at this point for him to handle. Don't worry. It will disappear as he gains control again."

We turned to look at Steve. While we had been talking, he'd wheeled himself back to the blocks and had built a tower of five. That was a truly hopeful sign. We thought so—and so did the therapist.

The therapist showed Steve one more thing—an immense, red, white, and blue ball, partially inflated. Something like a medicine ball, it was six to eight feet in diameter and almost filled the small exercise room. Steve took one look at it and just dove! He leaped from his chair and landed on the soft surface of the ball! God, how he wanted to get well.

"I hope I'll still be able to water ski."

Those words he had uttered—so long ago it seemed—sprang to mind. I remembered again his body jack-knifed in the great high dive off the bluffs of the Current River. Only he and his sweet summer love, Niki, would dive from that highest spot. When we planned our itinerary for Christmas in Mexico, he had insisted on Acapulco. "Man, I can't wait to dive off those cliffs," he'd said.

More optimistic and light-hearted than we'd been for weeks, we left the therapy floor. That impromptu plunge onto the ball! Was it because he thought this was the type of therapy he could do? Or was it an irresistible urge to play? So often we had said, "He'll never be middle-aged, not even when he's seventy."

Not even when he's seventy. . . .

"THE FLOOR OF THE DEEP SHIT"

"And behind this door the soldier saw another dog with even bigger fiercer eyes. They were as big as towers, and they went round and round."

—*Tinderbox,* Hans Christian Anderson

Wednesday, January 23, we faced yet another door that must be shoved open. It was a door we had tried to forget . . . a door yet to be unlocked. It was the door to a room that housed all the trolls that live under the bridge. It was the door that hid all the splay-footed demons of the world. It was the door to the arena where Steve would do personal combat with old Split-Hoof himself. A battle where life fights against death . . . reason against non-reason . . . sense against nonsense . . . chaos against order and purpose . . . design against gross violation.

In the hall, the day before, Dr. Worth had said, "I think we must get started with the cobalt treatments. I'll schedule him for Wednesday afternoon."

We hesitated to voice our fears and hopes. "Doctor, if there is no hope for Stephen, we want to take him home. We've talked it over. If he doesn't have a chance, we think he deserves to come home and spend his last months with us, in the surroundings he loves—with his cat and dog by the fireplace. Please be honest with us. Do you think he has a chance?"

Dr. Worth always seemed concerned. He took time to reassure us that Steve had a chance with the cobalt—and once again he warned us that there was no chance without it. But, tacked on to the end of that encouraging speech was a remark that stunned us, almost turning us to inanimate beings. As dumb, driven cattle, we heard him say, "Why, with the cobalt, he may have one to three good years."

Good God! Is that what they call longevity? We had assumed that once Steve got through it, he'd be through it forever.

Oh, that there was some place of refuge where we could fly with him!

I could not bear to follow Steve to this new place. Before, I'd gone hand in hand, willing to stay with him forever. But at this door I could not go on. Whimpering cowardice took over, and I begged Bill to accompany Steve. As we sat in the waiting room together, I wanted to grab Steve and hide his face against me so that he would not see the waiting death beside us.

Some patients were sitting in wheelchairs, some were lying on the narrow gurneys. Some had only stubs sticking out of sleeves or poking out from the gown tails. The poignancy of their quiet passivity was almost more than the spirit could bear. Here the stillness of meek resignation, the silence, became thunder that reverberated and bounced off the walls until it lodged as a mortal blow in my breast, a great weight solid with aching.

That day Steve was the only young person in the room, the only person who appeared to be under fifty. But age was hard to determine here. The ravages of the disease could age one ten years in a single week. At first glance they looked as if they had just returned from a pleasure cruise in the Bahamas—bronzed from their romp in the sun. Then I become aware that the suntans looked unnatural—a little too yellow, the skin stretched abnormally taut. And then I saw their sunken eyes. It was not the sun that had burned those bodies.

Eric, the tragic hero of Doris Lund's *Eric,* expresses the despair and hopelessness I felt in that waiting room. Seeing one after another of his friends die, despite their courage and all the skill of the medical staff, he said, "Mom, that's the deep shit. The deep shit. That was the floor of the deep shit." I agree. That was where our rage spun like a Dervish, only to dissipate in helplessness. That was where we sagged with the realization of our impotence.

We could do nothing to help him. Nothing at all. We had been unable to do anything from the very beginning. I had felt such anger once, when one well-meaning woman rattled on in a cheerful, loud voice, "Don't you worry, young man. Your mother won't let anyone hurt you."

I made no audible retort, but inside I was screaming. "Lady, Mama can't do a single thing about it. They can pummel and pull and punch and scrape all day long and I can do nothing. He can be put through excruciating agony and I cannot help him. Now, in our hour of trial, I—who could kiss away his tears and kiss away the pain of his bruised knees, and nibble at his little baby toes burning up with fever—I can do nothing. Now, when he may be dying, I cannot ease his pain one iota. How dare you tell us that it is otherwise?"

A nurse appeared and called Steve's name.

And so, without ever having been told the tumor was malignant—because he hadn't asked—Steve was wheeled in for his first cobalt treatment. Later I found this note I'd scribbled to him.

My Dear, My Darling, My lovely Lad,

Even as I use the word "Lad" I can hear you snort. It was always so hokey when the father of Lumpy in "Leave It To Beaver" kept referring to him as my lad, Clarence." Yet, you are my lad, my Laddy-Buck, and it doesn't seem hokey at all to call you that tonight. Allow me.

I'm sure it is not so, but it seems like the pain connected with removing tape is a funny, laughable pain, like breaking your little toe or having the mumps when you are an adult, and even the doctors and nurses seem to get a grim thrill out of inflicting it. Never before have I said, "If man can go to the moon, why can't he do this or that," but now I, too, say that if man can go to the moon and back already he ought to be smart enough to devise some kind of dressing as good as adhesive tape without the drawbacks. I'm sure if I live a hundred years I'll always cry when I think of the removal of the pressure bandage for your one and only cobalt treatment.

Oh God—we knew so little and the doctors, who know so much, knew so little also! I had seen the doctors strip the tape from your head, and I know the speed is intended to be merciful, but they ripped this same area so often you and I were afraid you'd never be able to grow sideburns. Do you know I never knew you shaved until the peach fuzz started growing in the hospital?

As you know, I chickened out on the radiation therapy. Son, I could not go in, so Papa took you himself, and I sat out in the lobby. When you came out, of course the bandage was off and I said, "Surely a woman was more gentle with the tape." Daddy said, "Oh no, she wasn't!" And he cried as he told me how she'd ripped it off and he showed me on the back of your head where every hair had been ripped out by the roots even though they'd only grown a quarter of an inch. We had not heard your voice in so long that I asked fearfully, "And did he scream?" and your Papa sobbed and said, "No, but there was an examining table covered with paper near his wheelchair and he just reached out with those yard-long arms and ripped off about two yards of paper and wadded it—but no sound ever came."

Oh my darling, I've kissed away so many little aches and pains and now when you are mortally wounded I cannot help you though our flesh aches with the desire to take your pain and agony for you.

Oh Chulalongkorn, how can I ever live without you?

Adoringly,
Mama

That day, after a month of waiting, it suddenly seemed as if activity and change were coming from every direction. The day before, Tuesday, Dr. Racheson had decided it was time to put a shunt in Steve's skull. A shunt is a refined valve (designed by the father of a hydrocephalic infant) to drain excess fluid from the brain.

We had been waiting for this for so long. "This is the thing that will make the difference. Oh, I'm glad. I wish he'd done it two weeks ago before we lost so much ground."

We had a silly expression we used when a ray of hope broke through the darkness: "Who could have believed that rocks can fly?" We'd ask each other that in disbelief as our hearts soared at some minor ecstasy. Little victories assumed such great importance. We eagerly grasped every crumb of hope and quickly made of it a whole loaf, only to be bitterly disappointed to find that it had been but a crumb after all. How many times, hearing a speck of good news, have I laughed through tears of relief and said, "Rocks *can* fly. They really can." Nothing else seemed to express my soaring hope—the release from heavy soddenness to joyous flight.

Just as, ages ago, Steve had been eager to undergo the obliteration, so I looked forward to this surgery to implant a shunt. The procedure would not be particularly dangerous, as Dr. Racheson described it. Steve had lived through infinitely worse. And oh! What promise it held—to free Steve's speech, to rid him of his frightful disorientation.

Surgery was scheduled for sometime Thursday, January 24. The first week of our new schedule with Bill had to be set aside.

That day had been such a full day—a good day, really. The first hurdle over the sinister cobalt treatment had been made. The responses Steve had made for the therapist—and her hopefulness—were heartening. Thursday's surgery might bring a real turning point.

Bill was to stay until nine o'clock and then go back to Carbondale. He would return Thursday night. We had fried chicken for supper, and Steve seemed to enjoy it. He held the drumstick in his right hand and chewed quite normally. He had no trouble swallowing that night. When he was finished he gave the bedside table such a push that it rolled three or four feet away. Then, we took him into a patients' lounge where there was a big color T.V. When we finally left for the night, he was lying in bed, propped up on his pillows and wearing his checked pajamas.

"See you in the morning, Love!"

A kiss, a squeeze, a toe tweak, and we slipped out.
That night I picked up my pen and wrote:

January 23, 1974
"It will happen to thee and to thee, but never to me" is the way Dr. Elizabeth Kubler-Ross says each of us thinks about his own death, and the words have echoed and re-echoed in my brain for the last five weeks and more when my son's life has hung by a thread. I have felt my body absorb like physical blows, one horrific announcement after another—and would feel the words eventually get to my brain where they play themselves like a stuck record over and over again until they soak into my consciousness . . . "the majority are fatal."
I learned one thing—that the human being has great dignity. Mr. Rader—the aged Mark Twain—died nobly yesterday morning and only occasionally asked for a sip of water or called a name from his past.
But closeness, or size, or concern of family is no safeguard. Steve has been surrounded by adoring family and friends, but the ravages on his body are just as relentless. I would feed myself to him teaspoonful by teaspoonful but I cannot lend him one ounce of strength.
The beauty and elasticity of the human spirit! It bears the unbearable because there is no alternative.
"To thee and to thee, but never to me." Yesterday's "with the cobalt he may have one to three years." *That is longevity?* Yet after these last two weeks I would be glad to know we would have even one good month with him.
If it were Kathy or David I would have had equally poignant thoughts, but Steve, my baby—he'd talked so often about his future, his marriage, and his plans for the future. Mostly kid stuff. "Mamma, I want you to be sure and give this spaghetti recipe to my wife." There's an old spice rack in his bottom dresser drawer that I was going to give to the Thrift Shop, until he said he wanted it.

He and Tim were such pretty boys that sometimes it flitted through my mind that they might be molested. Once Betty and I become "rather upset" when each thought the other had picked them up after a late show. After an hour, Bill and I started out to look for them. About midnight, still three miles from our house we saw them bouncing along the blacktop, singing at the top of their lungs. It was such a lovely night with a full moon they'd decided they'd like to walk the five miles home. They'd walked Eric home first. Boy-fashion, they'd figured we were already asleep and didn't want to wake us to tell us of this night-time lark! I was weak with sweet relief as we swept them into the car and brought them home.

All the things he's done that could have hurt him! The bike hikes and swimming parties and canoe trips and back packs, the caving adventures and now this last summer this new thing of rappelling. The first time I saw them looking like spiders as they dangled and bounced down the face of Stonefort, playing out their rope like webbing from some hidden spinnerets, I told the boys I thought it should be called "repelling" from a mother's point of view. Secretly, I thought it looked like fun and wondered then if I could ever be brave enough to take that first step backward off the cliff, trusting my weight to that tiny spider web of nylon rope. Dare I try it? Oh if he ever could be well enough to do it again, I believe I could do it too, just in celebration.

They've pooled their money and have purchased a lot of expensive equipment which they assure me is safe. What else would boys tell their Mama? I've become conversant with new terms such as brake bars, carabiniers, seat harness and pitons. As in other sports I find I worry less as their knowledge and equipment are improved. Before they got this new equipment, Steve tried to come down the face of a steep cliff just by body rappelling. Your own body weight serves as a brake, slowing your descent, but something was wrong with his wrapping, for he descended at such a speed that he got a bad rope burn on his right side and the inner part of his upper arm. The boys didn't tell me about this and it must have been a week before I caught sight of the great thick scab, still red and angry looking, that crossed his rib cage and ran also from armpit to elbow. They laughingly assured me it was all right now but told me I should have seen it when it was bad! The other day, Peggy, one of his favorite nurses caught sight of the still livid scars for the first time and said, "Oh my, what did they do to him here?"

By now his poor body is such a mass of scabs and cuts and bruises that she thought it was just one more. It began near where the subclavian incision had been made. He liked to roll that phrase off his tongue. We were quick to tell Peggy that those scars had been gotten in a much neater, cleaner way. It was good to remember that there had been a life, a full and exciting life before we took up our existence here.

Oh, will we ever return? I am so afraid.

In September (it is impossible that it was only September and not a hundred years ago), Bill and I went to watch the boys scale and descend the cliffs with increased cunning. While we waited, an Army Reserve group came to do maneuvers there so we stood back and watched. So slowly and carefully did the men climb the steep path. We could hear a few derisive remarks from our boys, and when finally the men were gone, just to prove to themselves what strong young bucks they were, David and Stephen started running up the same steep cut that slashes obliquely across the face of Stonefort and did not pause until they reached the top! "How was that?" they yelled down to us.

How could he have appeared so well when this insidious thing was already destroying his vitals? Why did I worry about all the rough-and-tumble things he did and never listen to the warning, "Cancer, No. 1 killer of children and teenagers!"

I never once thought of my children—not really. Of *me*,
yes, of my family in general, yes. An aunt died of cancer this
summer. There was an uncle—another uncle—and each
time, forgive me, God, but there was a little subconscious
sense of relief. The grimness of the statistics was a little less.
A little of the monkey's weight was off my back.

I have ceased to be shocked by what I see within. I
remember Frost's "Desert Places."

> They cannot scare me with their empty spaces
> Between stars—on stars where no human race is
> I have it in me so much nearer home
> To scare myself with my own desert places.

This week I've remembered my mother's honest wail,
wrenched from her by my young brother's death. "I would
have sent death to any door but mine." So would I. So
would you. I believe all other theorizing is untried,
sophomoric conjecture, and a great deal of posturing. I am
amazed at the singularity of my desire—I think never before
have I understood the phrase, "If thine eye be single."

Months ago I knew I would drain my veins for Steve.
There was not even a decision to be made. It was just a fact.
Now I know something else about myself—I would slit
throats for Stephen. This does surprise me a little. There was
no struggle of conscience, no melodramatic gesture; it is a
calm, resolute decision attended by no emotion and almost
no discrimination. I could not choose between my own
children—not sacrifice Kathy or David for Stephen—but
otherwise the only pertinent factor would be effectiveness.
I am a little surprised to see me as I am. I've always thought
of myself as a pacifist.

"If thine eye be single," and I have had a pin-point
singleness of desire and purpose for one-hundred days, one-
hundred nights.

"I have it in me so much nearer home
To scare myself with my own desert places."

But it does not even scare me.
Tonight is so long. It is so dark.

"It will happen to thee and to thee but never to me . . . ."

I am so afraid.

My son, my son, should it happen to thee, it has happened
to me.

It must have been past midnight when I put away my writing,
found my crossword and crawled wearily into bed.

TALITHA, CUM

The phone rang.

I sprang from my bed. Even in sleep I was a coiled spring. Each night I told the nurses, "I'm Stephen Warner's mother. Do you have the telephone number where I can be reached during the night?"

The nurse on duty always ran her finger down a list, smiled and said, "Yes, we have it, Mrs. Warner. We'll call you in case of an emergency.

The phone has stopped ringing.
Someone has picked up the receiver.

Listening at the door, I tried to swallow with a mouth that had no saliva. My heart jumped in my breast. Blood hammered in my ears. Bob Gordon's resonant voice went on and on. I was sure it was not for me. It was not about Stephen! As I turned from the door, I realized my limbs were shaking and my teeth were chattering.

The little clock on the bedside table showed a few minutes after five. I thought, "Someone, somewhere, must be in dire trouble or they would not call their pastor at this early hour."

Then, a knock at the door. I garnered my strength to open it.

Whatever has happened—whatever trouble you are in, Steve, if you are in the midst of it, then I can surely stand to hear about it.

"Normagene . . . Normagene, that was Bill."

"Bill? Why would he be calling? Bill's at Carbondale."

"No, he called from Barnes. He says that Steve started to convulse about 11:30 last night; they called him about 2:30 this morning and asked him to come. Steve is back in ICU."

"But why didn't they call me? Every night they tell me they'll call me if anything happens. Every night I've told them I'm only seven minutes away."

Bill met Bob and me at the door to the ICU unit.
"Come on in. They'll let us see him." Bill spoke in hushed tones.
We hurried to Steve's bed. Once again we kissed, we caressed,
we squeezed. But there was no response.
"He's heavily sedated," a nurse explained.
"How is he? What caused this? What happened to him?"
Unbelievably, we would go on asking those questions for weeks
to come, and no one could answer them. With all its consummate
skill and cunning, neurosurgery is *still* an inexact science.
Sophisticated paraphernalia filled the room. The sigh of the
respirator was like a rhythmic snore, the raspy breathing of some
leviathan of the deep.

We stumbled woodenly into the corridor, and for the only time
during Steve's whole hospitalization, we fell into each other's arms,
weeping, crying in dismay. "He's not going to make it. Stephen's not
going to make it."

As hopes were dashed and expectations dwindled, the victories
we fought for became smaller and smaller: three years, one year, one
good month. I had believed that our hope, our love, our
longing—Steve's indomitable spirit—would surely count for
something. I felt only flat hopelessness as we walked down the hall,
back to our old spot in the ICU Lounge.

Dr. Racheson talked to us a little later. He explained that Steve
had begun having seizures about 11:30. We had left him a little after
nine o'clock.

*Did he get to enjoy Kojak? Did the pink-cheeked boy ever
turn the screen or put the two-bed speaker any closer? Did
Steve fall asleep afterwards? Asleep in his checkered
pajamas?*

*They call it static epilepsy, this seizure that does not let up,
this storm that grabs and shakes the brain and body like a
terrier shakes a rat. Static epilepsy—fixed, stationary,
unchanging. They said it lasted for five hours. Five hours,
300 minutes, 1,800 Mississippis, 1,800 one-thousand ones.*

I should have been there. I could have helped hold him.
Maybe he could have heard my voice and felt less alone,
less terrified.

"Together," I'd told him back in Carbondale, on October 11.
"Whatever It is, we'll just have to walk through it together."
I had promised. He had a right to believe me. I had been only
seven minutes away. The leering chimera had moved in.
Rumpelstiltskin had stolen my baby.

They said a resident named Frank had stayed with Steve the
entire five hours. I didn't like Frank. He seemed rude and arrogant
to the patients and their families. But we are in debt to Frank. He
stayed with our son when we could not.

What fierce tempest could have continued to rage for five hours
against the strong narcotics available? For days afterward, Steve had
black and blue marks from his thrashing. Someone told me Frank
had held him down—fought with him all the night long—trying to
quiet him.

Later, I went back to Barnard to collect his snake-in-the-box,
his smoke grinder, and the rest of his pitiful pile of belongings. Mrs.
T., the head nurse, was on duty. I asked her whether Steve had
made any noise during those five hours he was convulsing.

I don't know why, but it seemed important to know.

Mrs. T. said, "Not really."

I picked up the pieces of his little wooden zebra. The night
before, when we were putting him to bed, he had squeezed the little
zebra too hard and the strings had snapped—the spring had flown
off at a tangent.

January 24 was supposed to have been a day of promise. The
shunt surgery might have worked a miracle. Maybe the physical
therapist could have unlocked doors long closed. Instead, Steve lay
in a feverish sleep. When David and Kathy came the next day, he
seemed to rouse only enough to recognize them.

Was it *that* day—or was it the day *before* or the day *after*—that
we first said to Dr. Racheson, "Doctor, if he is dead, let him die. Do

not keep his heart beating, his lungs expanding, if he is already dead."

Dr. Racheson seemed to be candid when he replied. "The respirator is not breathing for Stephen. He triggers it every time. Should the time ever come when his own breath no longer triggers the machine, it will not kick on."

That was how we all wanted it. That's how Stephen would have wanted it.

The respirator labors faithfully by Steve's side. The other big apparatus that has been wheeled in is a suctioning machine. I wish I hadn't asked. Endless tubes lead in and out of him, but he squeezes our hands in glad recognition each time they let us go in.

John 3:16 has always been a favorite scripture—"For God so loved the world that he gave his only son. . . ." But now, I feel angry whenever it filters into my mind.

Oh God, how can you know my anguish? You "gave" your son. That's why you're God and I'm just me. Mine is being wrenched from my arms by what? Evil incarnate? God omnipotent? By some cosmic casualness that merely lost him in the numbers shuffle? By some impersonal grinding evolutionary wheel that is interested only in the end and not the infinitely precious means?

In college I read *The Brothers Karamazov*. One incident haunted me for years after, and I recalled it as I pondered our place—Steve's place—in the framework of the world. A peasant child was shot because he accidentally let one of the czar's hunting dogs be killed. One of the brothers shouted, "Don't tell me that it is enough to realize that this is the beginning of the end of such inequalities. Surely it is not God's will that a child's life should be manure for future generations."

"For God so loved the world that he gave his only begotten
son that whosoever believeth in him should not perish. . . ."

Oh, God, can you not see that we perish? Every night as I
leave him alone, I want to say, "Now Jesus loves you. God
will be with you. Mama and Daddy have to leave now, but
don't forget, God loves you. God bless you, my Darling."
I am weak and dumb with despair.
Where are you, God, that we should feel so alone and
comfortless? Oh, Hound of Heaven, do you not seek us even
before we run to thee? Aren't you supposed to come part
way?
Please, Lord, forget I said that. I will not hold anything
against you. I forgive you. You can forsake me if you will;
I am of no consequence. Leave me to darkness, but, God, I
will never forgive you if you forsake him now. Cradle him
in your arms, lift up his wounded limbs. Cover his tortured
brow with your kisses. And please God, don't let him be
afraid.

I woke early Sunday morning, January 27, with the strong
feeling that Grandma and Grandpa must come to see Steve. He had
been taken off the respirator and did not look so frightening. He
looked beautiful to us. I didn't want them to come alone; they might
be saying "Good-bye." I called close friends from the church, and
they drove my parents to St. Louis.

The doctors said Steve was unconscious most of the time, but
that was not so. We could tell by the way his eyes followed us and
by the squeezes of his right hand.

I was glad we'd called my parents. Papa stood helplessly by,
acting self-conscious and out of place as he gazed down at this
youngest grandson of his, the most exuberant of the lot—the one
who least conformed to Grandpa's standards. Often Steve had
winced under his criticism, but once, after Steve went to the
hospital, he had said, "You know, Grandpa loves me just as much
as he does David. I'm just getting to where I understand him."

Now Papa stepped to his side and said, "Son, your squirrels are eating up all Grandpa's corn. Every day I lay two ears on that old stump south of the house and the next day they're gone. And do you know what I saw over in the soybean field next to your woods? Deer tracks! It looked like a whole lot of them had walked in the snow."

Deer had never been seen on our property or on Dad's. Steve's eyebrows went up to show surprise and pleasure.

Mama is a hoverer, a nurturer. She stayed close beside Steve, holding his hands, murmuring little lovings into his ears. Two or three more times, as they talked to him, he raised his brows in quick response to something particularly pleasing or surprising.

Papa told him spring would soon be coming to the woods—to the whole countryside—and he must hurry home so he could see it. Then Papa told Steve something that I've always hoped was a beautiful white lie.

He said, "Son, you know those May Apples that grow all over your woods? Well, I was walking over to your house the other day and right there, stickin' up through the dead leaves, was a green May Apple shoot about the size of my thumb. We're needin' you home to keep that path beat down between our house and yours."

It is important to me that in that tiny cubicle of space my righteous and Godly father loved that little morsel of humanity, my son, more than he loved strict, legalistic truth. I never knew for sure. I was afraid to ask. Had some freaky May Apple come up that early? Before January 27? I hoped not.

The woods were a constant delight to us all. One night before the seizing, when I could get no response from Steve, I sat close by his bed and said, "Let's take a pretend trip." I led us out the front door and up the flagstone path. We paused at the fishpond. We turned and went south through the blue bells and blood root he and Dave had helped me transplant. We paused at the old church bell that his great-grandfather had bought seventy years ago for their little country church, now abandoned. We walked down the path toward Grandma's. It was spring, and we saw fiddle head ferns, sweet Williams, and soft cushiony moss. We picked some spring beauties.

Steve came out of his lethargy, but with him came the growing agitation and the little whimpering noises. Was that better or worse than the remoteness? I never knew whether I should try to keep him oriented to his normal life or let him remain quiet. His glittering agitation and apparent withdrawal from all the world were equally frightening.

Grandma, always loving, always loved, was still holding Steve's hand. She bent to tell him she must go, and with his right hand, he brought her hand up to his mouth, to kiss it. He could not purse his lips to form a kiss but he laid her arm on his breast after brushing his lips in a tender kissing motion.

"Never mind, Stephen, Dear Heart, you've kissed me all your life and I've treasured every one."

That was our thinking, always.

We slipped away and the grandparents went home.

Sunday afternoon, at our five o'clock visit, Bill and I had a fairly satisfactory time with Steve. We talked over the visit from his grandparents—told Steve again who had sent cards, who had written letters. At the six o'clock visit Steve did not respond. But, after all, he'd had a pretty big day. He seemed about the same to the nurses.

When we called about the seven o'clock visit, we were told to come. But, no sooner had I turned to put down my yarn, than the lounge phone rang. The message was terse. "Tell the Warners not to come."

Panic raced through us. If Steve were any worse, he could not be alive. Two years ago, when David's draft number had been high and we were sure he would not be sent to war, an alarming thought struck me. Not Steve! Not my Bonnie Prince Charlie. Was it then to be my youngest son who would have his brains blown out on some foreign soil?

Some pagan fear had caught me in its net and made me think I must pay with one of my sons. One of my sons would be exacted from me, for the cost of our happiness—for the sin of hubris.

By now we knew the code numbers well. As the signals for the cardiac team and resuscitation therapy spread through the floor, we knew it was for Steve.

Our questions went unanswered.

"I'm sorry, Rev. Warner, I don't know."

"I'm sorry, Mrs. Warner, I don't know."

Finally, one nurse said, " I wish you wouldn't ask me." Then we knew. But, of course, we'd known all along.

I know what happened: The Warner boy was all right. They'd checked his vital signs at the proper time. He hadn't asked for anything. He hadn't bothered them, and they hadn't bothered to check. When we called to see if we could come and stand beside him for a few minutes, they turned to look. He had quit breathing.

At least an hour passed before we were told anything. That evening, once again, Frank was in charge. It was Frank who headed our way with yet another paper to sign. The three of us sat on a hard bench as he showed us where to sign the waiver for another operation.

The doctors thought Steve had suffered a brain hemorrhage. They must go in and remove a clot and repair the blood vessels. Does the brain itself have blood vessels? I didn't know. I just heard the words "hemorrhage," "surgery," "chance," and "no chance."

We turned to Frank with all the naked honesty we could muster and asked that dreadful question. "Does he have a chance? Does he have a ghost of a chance, even with this surgery? If he's dead, don't hurt him anymore. Just let him go. He's fought so hard—so long."

Frank was brusque, sharply impatient. I was weeping quietly, and as Bill prepared to sign, I murmured, "It seems to me, Doctor, that you get angry at the patients who do not do well, but. . . ."

He cut me off, abrupt and angry. "Why don't we cut all this crap and get on with the business before us."

I had never liked Frank. He was always so cold, so cold. I was glad Dr. Racheson would perform the surgery.

As they wheeled Steve toward the elevator, we walked beside his lifeless form. I wanted to cry out, "Please don't shave his head again—he'll make such a pretty corpse!"

Why would I even think such a thing? Steve's hair by then was like a dark close-fitting skull cap—quite neat and handsome, really. He had wondered how his hair would come back.

It's come back jet black, Son, just like your brows and lashes. No yellow ringlets. You'd like it. You always wanted to look like your dad.

We called Barb and Chuck Cogswell. Soon they and their daughters, Nina and Kay, came. They waited with us until Kathy and David arrived. I think that was the first time since the day-long surgery on December 18 that Kathy and Dave faced squarely the likelihood that Stephen would die. I had never seen David so distraught. They were both still in their hiking clothes, and David would not take off either his old navy pea jacket or his sock cap; he kept his fists tight-clenched.

Dr. Racheson came in around midnight to tell us that Steve was in the recovery room and we could see him soon. He had removed a big clot and had stopped the hemorrhage, but he didn't know how Steve would be.

As we were still talking, the nurses brought Steve and all his paraphernalia into ICU. In a few minutes, we slipped in. Steve was ghastly pale—gray and shaking horribly. Yes, they had shaved off all his hair again, and in their haste they had scraped and cut him in two or three places—long ugly gashes.

We huddled on benches in the lounge the rest of the night. We dared not leave.

The next day, Monday, January 28, Steve hung balanced between life and death. David was like a caged lion that could not sit still. He could not be reconciled. Kathy, our firstborn, our lovely daughter who saw life as an adventure, sat in stunned silence. Sometimes she could talk to David. He still wore his old navy pea jacket and sock cap.

From some inner wisdom, Kathy said, "Mama, if it eases David
a little to keep on those boots and those old clothes, well, leave him
alone."

Tuesday, January 29, was almost the same. Steve's condition
was "stabilized," whatever that meant. David and Kathy went
wearily home.

*It is now Wednesday, January 30. I walk back and forth
along the corridor beside the ICU. He's not three feet away
from me. If only I could walk through that wall! I've begged
them to let us sit beside him, just to watch to see that his
breast rises and falls.*

*Thursday, January 31. Can Steve last until February?
February, the month that has almost become synonymous
with dying in our family. My Grandpa, my uncle, my dear
young brother. Two years ago Uncle Ralph died on David's
birthday, February 15.*

Our family always seemed to breathe a sigh when February
limped over the edge of time, dragging its 28 days behind it. Surely
Steve could not hang on until February 4. Surely he would not die
on the anniversary of my brother Alan's death. There had been too
many parallels. Surely there could not be that much irony in the
world.

*Stephen is so sick tonight, so sick. I call home but I can
no longer find words to say. My parents are braver and
stronger than I realize. Tonight Mama says, "Now,
Normagene, you don't have to treat us like babies. We
watched our own darling die and we are strong enough to
stand whatever you have to tell us about Stephen, too, but
I'll tell you," and she cried, "it hurts almost as bad as Alan
Dale."*

*"Oh, Mama, he is so sick tonight. How can he be worse
and still be alive? He is burning up with fever and they
have him on an ice blanket with just a towel across his
loins. Oh, Mama, I'm so afraid."*

*"And Mama, tomorrow's going to be February whether
we turn our calendars or not."*

We did not dare leave the hospital that night. We slipped in to
see Steve two or three times, but we could not rouse him. As we left
we begged, "Please, if he rallies at all, we're just down the hall.
Please come after us. It's been so long since he's known we've been
with him."

They assured us they would call if there was the slightest
change, so we tried to get some rest. Later, when we were told we
could see Stephen, we found him as we had left him—lying still and
inert.

We could not believe it when the ICU nurse said, "I wish you
could have seen him early this morning. Sometime between three
and four he woke up and looked around. He seemed to recognize
us, too. I wish you could have seen him then."

Bitterly we left the room feeling we'd been cheated of a visit
with our boy.

With Stephen back in ICU I wrote more, mostly scribbles in the
margins of newspapers and crossword books and on the backs of
get-well envelopes. Occasionally, I wrote a letter to the
Mooreheads, friends so close it was like writing in a diary.

February 1974

Dear Mooreheads,

Our doctor told us yesterday that Steve's condition was
sufficiently stable for Bill to go home and work, so I'm
sitting alone. Alone—and not alone—for there develops a
real camaraderie among the anxious and heartbroken who
wait out crises in this room.

In this wry game of odds, there are few I've met whose odds for recovery I'd not trade for ours. But this is the old game of "If wishes were horses. . . ." Only two people have been on this floor longer than Steve, not counting the 35 days before we came to tenth floor.

I've crocheted a baby cape for Joanne Gordon's granddaughter and have already started on another one. I may give it to the first pregnant woman I see on the street. I feel like I'm knitting and purling myself together.

We get in to see Steve about six times a day for a total of about ten to twenty minutes. I don't know what fierce struggles were going on Thursday and Friday of last week, but he seems to have stabilized since then. He appears to be in a continuous torporous state. It seems such a genuine, innocent sleep that you cannot believe he would not snap out of it and come out yelling, if you dashed a glass of ice water in his face.

The only thing he moves of his own volition is his right hand and his eyes. I think they follow the sound of my voice now. It is hard to tell what is actually a movement in response to a command and what is just movement that coincides with the command. It is hard not to read too much into a hand squeeze.

If only we could talk to each other! I like to think God comforts him, but Stephen seems in his pitiful weakness to be forsaken.

He pulls out his catheter and the nose tube, through which he is fed. They tell us that is a good sign, for it means he is aware of these foreign objects in his body. However, now they bind his hand, the only portion of his body he can move. David and I try to imagine what it must be like to have only partial use of one extremity and then to have that either restrained or thickly mittened with thirty yards of gauze and tape.

He's always been a little claustrophobic; Dave could get the best of him in a wrestling match if he could pin his arms or hold his hands. I, too, use my fingers like gills—appendages for breathing—so I always understood when he'd cry, "Unfair, Unfair."

The binding is one thing I cannot bear, so each time I find his lovely hand clubbed and mittened I show the nurses how, if they will just tether the wrist to the side of his bed by two pieces of gauze like a "Y," he can't reach the tubes but can still move his hand six to eight inches and flex his fingers. I can feel him relax and "breathe easier" as I unwrap the strangling gauze.

The nurses humor me while I am there and fix his hand so it is free, but each time a shift changes, it is still done the same restrictive way.

I cannot think of a surer way to drive a young man completely mad than to have things befall him with the unrelenting savageness of this disease. It seems that he is being bound up in some poisonous spider's web, little by little, bit by bit.

Bill finds a wry solace from: It has happened to thee and to thee, so why not to me? I cannot reconcile myself to that thinking. I guess I always expected an edge.

I experience a curious longing to empty myself into him. When I was a little girl we had a whole litter of kittens to sicken and die. We suspect the mother had been poisoned. She had no milk, but I remember her dragging things she had killed to her little sick babies. Their eyes were not yet open, and they could not eat, but that did not stop her frantic prodding with frogs and birds. One morning she laid a young rabbit in their bed; frogs, birds, rabbits . . . I, too, would strew his bed with viands if I could find the magic for his healing. I long to dissolve that he might be nurtured, but alas, I cannot.

It is something like the travail of birth—a purposeful entering into the Valley of the Shadow, to wrest a manchild from the Deep. Except this time I am helpless.

However you know to pray, remember us.

The Warners

Occasionally I read—furiously racing through an entire text in a frantic search for answers to my questions about death and suffering. Most of the comfort of the familiar deserted me; much of it seemed a mockery in the wake of so great a betrayal! Perhaps that is why Martin Bell's *The Way of the Wolf* spoke to me. The unfamiliar imagery of his fables had a ring of truth. In every allegory however, the hero's name was Stephen. In every allegory the hero was walking toward a cross.

The hospital chaplain had become a friend by now. I cannot explain the manner of his help. He offered no sermons, no cliches. He never told us Steve's illness was God's will, or that "Sometime we'll understand," or "Somehow it'll work out for the best." He was just a very real person who grieved with us over our precious son. Sometimes we had coffee together. More often we shared only a few moments of humanity. He was able to help our family in the only way we were able to help Steve. As we had promised to "go through whatever comes, together," so Bob was just there—"To go through whatever comes, together."

When Kathryn Kuhlmann, a nationally known faith healer, held a crusade in St. Louis that winter, we discussed the Kuhlmanns, the Oral Roberts, and all others who believed, or at least convinced others to believe, that they could cause God to bestow his physical healing upon certain people—in a way the rest of us could not. Once I had burst into the chaplain's office and blurted out, "Is there anywhere we can go? To a quack, a charlatan, a magician, a healer, a God?"

Bob just swung his chair around and handed me Tillich's *The Courage to Be*. "Why don't you try to read this today?" he asked.

That man of God knew no shibboleth . . . no magic password to the heart of God . . . no Open Sesame to his storehouse. But he cared. Every hour or so he stopped to be with us for a few minutes. He made sure we had dimes to call him should he be at home when the time came. For a year I kept Bob Davis's dime taped to the inside of my billfold.

I think I expected Stephen to die on February 4. It was appalling to discover how thin my veneer of civilization was. Scratch my Christianity and superstition oozed through; a tiny rent revealed the remnants of an ancient animism. There had been too many parallels in the lives of Stephen and my young brother Alan for me not to fear parallels in death, also.

Sunday, February 3, when none of my family were there and I could not see Steve, I went to the chapel. Instantly, I felt caught in a web of fate—I, who believed free will to be the evidence of the love of Him in whom we live and move and have our being. The scripture being read described the raising of Jairus's daughter and ended with that triumphant pronouncement, "The child is not dead, but asleep. *Talitha cum,* Get up my child."

That was the exact lesson for Sunday, February 4, 1951, the day Alan Dale had died.

Yet, the day came and went. Slowly, even that day's night yielded to the sunrise.

There was no change.

Sometimes Steve's respirator would be turned on to increase the percentage of oxygen he got. Occasionally there was evidence that he had had to be suctioned—evidence that I trained my eyes to avoid. Often, his lips were so parched and cracked that I would get a warm cloth and try to wipe them clean—to leave them moistened. Sometimes, if I had not had time to grab a washcloth, I would bend down and, in the guise of kissing, him I'd run my tongue over Steve's parched and blood-tinged lips.

Years later I find it incomprehensible that I was afraid of "getting caught" ministering to my child.

I am angry that, in my stupidity, I stooped to subterfuge.

But sometimes, even as I wet Steve's lips, I almost smiled. I remembered him as a little boy, fussing and fuming, writhing to escape a "spit bath."

Once I took in a segment of orange, hidden in Kleenex, to press against Steve's lips—to touch his tongue. It had been a long time since the fried chicken supper of January 23—a long time since he had tasted a flavor. Another time I smuggled in a piece of peppermint, to try to summon him back to the world of color and flavor—to coax him from that web of Morpheus into a red and white candy-cane world where a sugar plum fairy danced about a Christmas tree and a babe lay in a manger—a babe born with healing in His wings.

One night I saw orange sherbet on the trays in the hall and begged Peggy to give Steve just the tiniest taste. She didn't think he could handle it, but she said she would try. Late that night she brought some grape juice, and with the tip of a spoon she put some in his mouth. It rolled out the corner and onto the pillow, mute evidence of Steve's terrible weakness—his undone condition. It stained the white linen like communion wine. Oh Agnes Dei; Oh, Lamb of God.

On Tuesday, February 6, I wrote to Betty and Lee Moorehead again:

For a long time we have been on the brink of death and each day the brink wears a little thinner. Of course, we have not thought of anyone eulogizing Steve but you, Lee. Eulogize! How Steve would scoff at that word.

I have not been able to awaken him all day, though I saw him move both feet when I touched his toes.

I trust the rest of us will somehow live again. Sara Teasdale writes that when she heard the wood thrush through the dusk,

"I snatched life back against my breast
And kissed it, scars and all."

Once I looked out the tenth floor window and saw an ice-covered tree and its shadow. It was beautiful, and I could *see* its beauty. I know we shall live again, but what answer can I have for our darling Stephen. How can life have meaning if his life is to be snuffed out?

This has opened old wounds for Mama and Daddy, whose own boy died in February when Kathy was a baby. Dave says as soon as he gets anything dirty he rushes it over to Mama to wash so she can have something to do.

It is a blessing to have friends. They have offered their service as well as money. I was shocked at the first money gift, when friends came and put a check for a hundred dollars in our hands.

The Johnston City church sent a note, "After all, Steve is our baby you know," with their check. Dave put it succinctly when he said, "Two things amaze me about money. First that so many people want to give it, and second that we just reach out and take it." Everybody offers to help, but nothing helps. I feel with Frances Gunther, "They (doctors) were helpless, and we were helpless, and in His way, God, standing by us in our hour of need, God in His omnipotence, was helpless too."

Right now, nothing makes sense. I think that's my problem—I still expect things to make sense and the world to be just.

Suddenly, on Thursday evening, February 7, Dr. Racheson appeared at our side in the ICU as Bill and I stood by Steve's bed.

"I can wait no longer. I am going to put in the shunt tomorrow," he said abruptly. He added, almost as if he were talking to himself, "I dare not go into that precious skull one more time."

He explained, as much as we could understand, about an *abdominal* shunt. Its valve would trap the fluid as it built up in Steve's spinal cord and empty it into his abdominal cavity. That would relieve the cranial pressure that was so disorienting and so deadly.

Again, the rocks almost got off the ground. Again, the puny crumbs were gleaned and made into a whole loaf by our very longing. Something was going to be done for Steve. He had not yet reached the end of his tether. There was still hope.

Dave came up Friday morning, before Steve's surgery. We stood, huddled close together and close to Stephen in the ICU cubicle. We followed him to the same room where he had waited for other surgeries. It was untenable that this could be happening for the seventh time. It was incomprehensible that he could withstand such an onslaught.

There was little talk. Just the aching, the yearning, the tremulous hope. Just love.

Unbelievably, as the orderlies wheeled him away, William Stephen Warner-—Lucky, Plucky Steverino, the kid with the derring-do—raised his hand in a graceful, almost jaunty good-bye.

Who can remember the hours anymore? Who can keep anything straight? It's been so long since anything was straight. He's in recovery.
They're bringing him up.
"He's doing as well as can be expected."
"You may go in and see Stephen now."
We have heard this same sequence so many times.

We were told that Steve came through the operation well. The nurses were optimistic. All his vital signs were good. He seemed stronger.

The head nurse, a woman with two teenage sons of her own, told us that Steve seemed better that night than he had in weeks. The next morning, the nurses' answers seemed guarded, but we saw no difference in him when we visited him in the afternoon. It was Saturday, and Bill had gone home for Sunday services. David and I sat alone in the lounge.

We slipped in several times in the afternoon to talk to Steve, to touch him and soothe him. Around six o'clock, when we called to see if we could come in, the nurses told us to come ahead. Then, in an exact replay of January 27, they called back and told us not to come.

Again, the coded signals flashed over the intercom. Of course it was Steve. There was no need even to ask. The rocks plummeted from the sky and sank. Others must have been in that hated lounge, but I was aware of no one but us—David and me. We sat numbly, waiting to be told what we already knew. For if Stephen was worse, he was dead.

About eight o'clock, we saw Dr. Racheson striding down the hall. He wore a red plaid sport coat. He was on his way to a party. I will never forgive him for stopping—on his way to a Valentine's party—to tell me that my son was dead.

"Stephen is going to die," he said. There was no need for preliminaries.

He mumbled something about Steve's blood pressure being wildly out of control all day—something else about Steve having trouble with his breathing. Something about irreversible damage before they found him.

Again!
Damn them!
They let it happen again!

I don't know when we stood up. I just remember standing beside my other son, our arms around each other, saying, "Oh, doctor—such a boy! If you'd only known him. If you only knew what you've been fighting for. He is such a wonderful boy!" The words tumbled from our lips.

"They all are." Doctor Racheson sighed with weary resignation. "They're all wonderful."

We tried to believe that, but privately we protested, "But not like Stephen—not like Steve!"

Dr. Racheson could not be sure when Stephen would die—he was sure only about the certainty—the irreversibility.

"You should go home now and get some rest," he admonished.

I felt he was really saying, "Get the hell out of here! Go home and don't come back. I can't stand the sight of your pleading faces, constant reminders of my failure. Sitting there, day after day, week after week, month after month, begging for cures I can't bring about, expecting miracles I can't perform."

It was hard to remember that the *disease* was the real enemy—not the people who could not cure Steve. Sometimes I hated every doctor who'd ever touched Steve. I hated them for not knowing instantly what was wrong and how to cure him. Most of all I hated us because of crass carelessness—to let him slip through our fingers like that. You *lose* a dime or a watch. You don't *lose* a child.

Dr. Smith, Steve's doctor back home had promised he would come to St. Louis to visit, but a busy practice, the horrible weather, his family—all these—had prevented his coming. That night, ironically, he came with his wife and two young daughters and stayed until Bill got back.

"Wouldn't Beth and Sarah like to wait in another lounge or even on another floor?" I suggested.

I'll always remember Alice's reply. "No, they have writing materials and coloring books. They know Stephen, and they know their daddy's a doctor. They need to know it sometimes ends like this. This is what it's all about."

IF IT SHOULD HAPPEN TO THEE

I sat in the corner chair of the ICU Lounge—mine by squatter's rights—my eyes glued on the corridor ahead. At times my consciousness seemed an elongated cord that reached to the far end of the unit—to infinity. It was like an invisible but almost tangible umbilical cord stretching from me to Steve. It had been that way for weeks.

I crocheted furiously—a stupid robot with hands shaking so that I could hardly hit the spaces with my doubles and my singles.

I tried to close out the chatter. It was distracting, though it was kindly meant and seemed to relieve Bill.

What else did I do? I looked at David and saw him as infinitely precious and an exquisitely painful reminder of what was ebbing away in a room down the hall.

It will soon be morning.

Perhaps "today" is to be the "tomorrow" I worried about yesterday. Perhaps it is the "tomorrow" I have worried about ever since Steve entered the hospital. Perhaps "today" will be the day I've dreaded since February 4, 1951, when my young brother had died. I had cradled Kathy in my arms and prayed, "Oh Lord, anything but that! Place any burden on me—poverty, ill health—anything but the death of a child. That I cannot bear."

Morning is breaking.

It will never be morning.

For a week before the final surgery to implant the abdominal shunt, we'd begged for Steve to be moved from ICU to a private room so we could sit by his side. We pleaded, "If he must die, then let him die with his family."

Once, when Dr. Racheson started a conversation with, "Now, I'm a practical man, and . . . " I deliberately stilled my heart, steeling myself to hear him say: "You are right. There is no point in keeping him in ICU any longer. We're moving him into a room."

But instead, his welcome words were, "Now, I'm a practical man, and I think he has a chance." That was forty-eight hours ago, the day before the abdominal shunt.

I have such a horror of the forced and prolonged isolation Steve has undergone that I think, "Never again. Never again will 'they' persuade me to consign my love to an ICU." But even as I vow this, I'm aware that I do not know whether it is a vow I could keep. If "they" said "chance vs. no-chance," I might still throw in with "chance," though the odds be infinitesimal.

Late at night, on January 27, I had pleaded with Frank, "Don't hurt him anymore if there's no hope." When Dr. Worth had ordered the cobalt therapy, and again when Dr. Racheson had recommended this shunt operation, we'd stood helpless and naked before them and begged for their best advice. Each had said, "If it were my son, I'd give him a chance. He has none the other way." They said thoughtfully and, we felt, truthfully.

So each time, rightly or wrongly, we'd gone with "chance." If I had it to do over again. . . . "If I Had It To Do Over Again" is a futile pointless game that everyone plays. We all have 20-20 vision—hindsight. If we'd known, we'd never have had the surgery in the first place. We'd have gone on our trip to Mexico or the Himalayas or Timbuctoo, and maybe if Steve had been lucky his foot would have slipped, or his rope would have broken and he'd have fallen to a clean death on a rock ledge a thousand feet below. He had planned to dive at Acapulco (I think he truly planned to travel to the moon someday). I had worried about his diving such a distance, but no death could have been worse than this.

If we had it to do over again, we'd have let the kids from church and school come to see him. We'd have encouraged them to come and sit and laugh and weep and rage away the hours with him—to show their love for this "tender life, wounded in every breath, sustaining for a while without defense, the enormous assaults of the universe." A friend gave me a sampler with those awesome words. The author was anonymous. That must mean they had been written by Everyman, Everywhere, Whensoever. I think now it might have eased his agony at having to quit life so soon to have such evidence of their caring. Because we discouraged it, only a handful came after that grand going-away party on December 16. Maybe we were wrong.

If death had been a gentleman. . . . If, for one moment after Stephen and he became engaged in this grisly *pas de deux*, death had let Steve come up for air . . . just one time, after they locked horns in this *guerre a mort* he'd have given him his turn at bat, if just once, in this mismatched life-and-death struggle, death had played fair, given him a sporting chance, I believe Steve could have handled it. Just as in the note in which he said he'd accepted the fact that he would be blind but "after a great deal of thinking and much PRAYER [sic], I think I can handle it," I believe he could have come to terms with his dying.

Perhaps in the locked fastnesses of his soul he *was* able to handle it. If we could have talked, perhaps he could have helped me "handle" what was before us.

I remembered our conversation the past summer when I'd asked, "In a relay race, which is most important—the torch or the runner."

He had said, "Mom, I believe the torch is the most important." When I'd protested a little, he added, "Yes, each runner's important, but the torch is the thing."

Perhaps it was because they expected him to die each hour that they did not move him into a room. Now they let us come in often and stay for twenty or thirty minutes at a time. Ironically, when to every appearance Steve did not know we were there, we could sit by his side for long periods of time.

Tuesday morning, February 12, we looked up to see a nurse and a group of orderlies trundling his bed down the corridor toward a room. We had asked for this. It was what we wanted. Wanted? That's a word as ambiguous as "fair" or "right" or "just." We had never been granted any approximation of what we *wanted*. But it was what we'd asked for—to have him where we could sit beside him every moment and could die in each others arms—but it was harder than we'd expected. We knew this room would be the last.

He is now like a wax figure. Beautiful. Inert. Oh, so still. Since Saturday night his stillness has been like that of a wooden table or the inanimate bed on which he lies.

Three or four years before, just to see if it would work, he lay for a couple of hours on our coffee table while I tried to make a wax casting of his face. I remember he breathed through a soda straw until the wax hardened.

Now there is no evidence of breathing except that the respirator keeps sighing. It will stop when he no longer triggers it.

I found these words I had scribbled on the back of a menu:

February 12, 1974
     Your presence still permeates the room. At least this first day out of ICU your essence, normal and whole, is so real to me as to be uncanny. I have the distinct feeling that you are by my side—sort of at my left shoulder—and together we are looking down at the poor maimed form on the bed—grieving, remorseful that such a tragedy should have befallen it. Already I feel that you and this beloved body that housed you, are separate.

Time seemed to stand still. Hopelessness is a land of no color, no motion.
     A minister friend who often came to sit with us had said, "When there is no hope, I'll not be able to come." But he did. He came and sat beside us, sharing in our grief. Occasionally Steve choked and had to have help. Once David quickly sprang to his side and pulled the long strings from his throat. One evening he choked so badly that the resident was sent for. For forty-five minutes David, the

chaplain, and I stood in the hall expecting to be told it was all over. However, when the door was opened we were told, "You may go in now."

When David left, I began to write:

February 12, 1974

Detachment

The name of the hospital gift shop is "The Wishing Well." In this highly sensitized state, where I see symbolism in every word, this is a wry misnomer. When the kindly ladies from The Wishing Well—that fabled place of wishes granted, and dreams come true—ask, "May I help you?" I must always repress, "Oh yes, I've come to have my son made well, if you please, Ma'am." I say instead, "Is the 69-cent jar the only size you have?"

They were featuring autumn leaves when we came, and now it's Valentine's Day and they are featuring a pair of cuddly teddy bears locked in close embrace. The red one is hugging the bejabbers out of the white one and the white one is kissing a red plush cheek. The bears are delightfully cunning, until one sees the startling tag, "To detach, simply unsnap the fasteners." The simulated love is caused by gripper snaps strategically placed in paws and body fur. "Unsnap to detach."

I haven't wanted anyone operating on Steve with tear-dimmed eyes, but how glad I am for the nurses and doctors who still risk the ache that inevitably comes with identifying with our beautiful dying Stephen. A few have mingled their tears with mine and they somehow give me a little hope in this whole unreal, cock-eyed hopeless experience—someone cares. It is frightfully important to me that human beings still weep and rage at injustice and unfairness. Others have built a wall around the deep place of the heart. They have made themselves invulnerable. When we meet in the hall or share an elevator they look the other way. Our eyes never meet. I have no reason to doubt their skill but they have detached the gripper snaps.

What *are* the bonds of love? The glad affirmation that reassures me now is that they are as natural as the next breath and as constant as a heartbeat! Not to have wondered about them but just to have had them and accepted them is a testament to the depth and reality of those bonds.

And now I find that death itself cannot break those bonds of love. Detachment? Impossible! I could no more detach myself from Steve than I could remove my heart from my breast. I will always hate the word "died," but I find the euphemism "lost" equally repulsive. *Lose* Stephen? Never! He is inextricably bound in the hearts of each of us and will flow through us, enriching us forever. Love finds no alteration. The little teddy-bears are literally cute, but how meaningless is an embrace that depends on gripper snaps.

Steve had fought for so long. How could it not be rewarded? It had been sixty days since that first awful day-long brain surgery when we each had charged him with a desperate urgency to "Hang on. Remember now, hang on. You can do it. You know you're the kid who never gives up." Finally, it seemed that Steve could not loose the tenacious grasp he had on that life he loved so much. The day before they moved him out of ICU, David whispered, "Mama, I cannot ask him to hang on any longer. I've felt guilty every time I've said it for two weeks."

I did not go into the ICU with him that time but left them alone for a last sacred moment together. David and Stephen, Steve and Dave. Twins in so many ways who just happened to be born three years apart. Closer brothers because they were friends, dearer friends because they were brothers.

As he stumbled out of the intensive care unit for the last time David sobbed, "I couldn't ask him to hang on any longer. I just said, 'Go in peace, my Brother.'"

Much later he told me that during that time together with his
beloved brother he whispered these words of an ancient prayer, that
poignant blessing:

May the Lord bless thee and keep thee
May the Lord make his face to shine upon thee
May the Lord lift up his countenance and give thee peace
And give thee peace,
Stephen, my brother.

Kathy and the grandparents came Wednesday. Kathy looked so
broken, so sad. She could still scarcely believe the mute evidence
before her.

We admonished her not to remove the heavy moist gauze eye
patches. We did not want her to see his eyes. When they allowed
him to stop breathing in ICU, the oxygen starvation had drawn the
pupils almost into pin points. They did not look like Steve's eyes.

It was hard not to read a personal vindictiveness—some
deliberate despoilment of all the gifts we gloried in. Usually I could
keep those banshees at bay, but sometimes it was hard to remain
rational about the savage eradication of all Steve's graces—his
dexterity, coordination, quick-silver motion, nimble wit, discourse.
Finally, his eyes. He had been able to hold a stare longer than
anyone, unless it was Julie, our American Field Service student from
Australia, who lived with us when Steve was eleven. Just watching
their staring contests caused my eyes to sting.

Now he cannot blink. Now he makes no tears.

Steve had the glistening, dewy eyes that cosmetic manufacturers
promise. Also, he had eyes in which tears were quick to form in
response to any moving incident. Often he would have to tip his
head back to keep them from spilling over. Once that past summer
he'd flung back his head in annoyance and said, "When am I going
to stop crying like this?"

"Don't you know that's one of your charms?" we asked. "That tough and realistic as you are, you can still cry?"

"But Mom, I'm almost seventeen!"

Close on the heels of that warming conversation, we'd had an argument, over something long since forgotten, and I'd said angrily, "I don't think I have to take that from a snot-nosed kid!"

Steve flashed back, "And I don't think I deserve to be called a snot-nosed kid, either!"

I said, "You know, I think you're right!" And we touched and laughed and it was over.

Kathy holds his hands—smooths them. We can do nothing. But what we can do, we do. She moves his hands from time to time, being careful the fingers are not left crimped. His beautiful hands with the long, sensitive fingers she places on a little pillow so they will not swell.

A philosophy professor, from Carbondale, and his wife, a renowned sculptor, spent many hours with us that week.

"His hands," the sculptor said. "I've never seen such lovely hands. I must try to get sketches of them soon."

His hands looked like Bill's did when I first met him—long and graceful. The summer before, at an ecumenical youth retreat, Niki, his summer love, fell asleep in a wheelbarrow during a long midnight rap session, and as Steve was trying to spirit her away (what a joke to have her wake up in the cafeteria) he slipped going down the ramp and chipped a tooth and broke a bone in his hand. The fracture healed and the tooth was capped. The dentist said it would have to be redone when he was fully grown.

Once Kathy turned to me fiercely and, in a voice ragged with grief, said, "One thing! We'll never let him become just a picture on the piano! Not Stephen!"

Bill's sister Marguerite came from New Jersey and went home with my parents and Kathy. David told us he was not coming back.

I could not read. I could no longer work puzzles or crochet. But I wrote. My letters to Steve seemed not much different than the pitiful monologues I'd done for the last sixty days.

My Dearest Steve,
If you ever hear these words, you are already receiving them in that spirit world that each of us hardly dares believe in. Yet, as I see you, inert but beautiful despite the ghastly tubes and merciful eye patches, I feel communion—a sort of spirit bearing witness to spirit—that is comforting and real.
How can we live without you? I have no idea. Our minds recoil at the enormity of our loss. Please, Stephen, let's keep in touch. Bless us with your warmth and humor. May our lives be enriched for as long as we live because you shared life with us for seventeen years. Dr. Racheson told me to go home and regroup my family. Son, I don't know how to do that—not without you.
Darling, when I'm an old lady I want your wit and charm still to be fresh in my memory. Your quick anger when you saw something was unfair, your speedy forgiveness, your fierce (if sometimes I thought misplaced) loyalty, your utter tenderness toward all things little and wild, your awed respect for the spaceship Earth and your steadfast determination to leave it in all ways better than you found it—how can I possibly enumerate the things that make you unique?
I recall odd things as I sit here beside you. Perhaps I should have my mind on spiritual things, but instead I'm remembering the day you came home from church camp and found that tree frogs had taken up housekeeping in your wren house. You said, "No one had ever told them it was a restricted area—Aves only."
You were so tired that you fell asleep in the tub that night, and woke to see us all peering down at your weary floating body. "Some family!" you snorted, as you sat up. "It's got to be some kind of weird family that would come in

and look at a guy lying here naked and asleep in the tub! I've got a weird family!" You weren't really angry, for you realized that when we no longer heard singing or splashing, we'd come in to investigate, and had stayed to smile and sympathize with your weariness. You looked so young and vulnerable. You were thirteen. We were glad to have you back. You'd been gone a whole week.

I've always loved the looks of you. Your large angular knees and elbows, and your long, long arms ending in those big handsome hands, lent you an awkward grace. All the parts still a little ungainly with adolescence, but when put together, they become a symphony of rhythm and grace. A running giraffe is like that, too.

I would keep the agony of my heart forever green rather than lose those glad gifts of your spirit from my life.

Oh, Stephen, how can we let you go ahead of us? How can we let you cross the vastness by yourself?

I remember Emily Dickenson's lines:

"I believe in immortality
But oh, I would have tried it first,
Before entrusting him."

Most of the families we had grown close to were gone by the second week of February, but still there were always people. During those last days, one lady in the hospital walked up and down that corridor all day long, exercising her new hip joint. On every lap she'd stop and ask, "And how is your son today?" Each time we'd tell her the same thing, but on each lap she would ask again. Did she think we'd have used a filthy word like "dying" if it were not true? We avoided her if at all possible. We also tried to avoid a lady who kept drifting up and down the corridor saying of her dying husband, "This is his crowning day. You should think of it as Steve's also." That day her remarks were utterly inane. Stephen was not ready for a crown; he was saving his money for a kayak!

Another little hurt was tobacco. At that time Barnes made no accommodation for nonsmokers, and Steve, who had never liked smoke, tolerated it even less now. As long as he could talk he asked for a room with a nonsmoking partner, but he shared this very last room with an inveterate pipe smoker. As long as we were there the roommate went out in the hall to smoke, but if we came in unexpectedly the blue smoke would be circling Steve's bed.

When we came in Thursday morning, we saw on the windowsill the Valentine candy Mama left for me and Bill to give each other. We'd forgotten it was Valentine's Day. (One day Bill had forgotten it was Sunday!) But Mama said from her own hard-earned wisdom, "Now you still have each other. You mustn't forget that." We picked up the little red boxes and gave them to each other.

It was Valentine's Day, and our child, our baby born of our love, lay mortally wounded. He did not look like he was killed; he looked like a beautiful Prince Charming, put under a curse, waiting for a magic kiss to bring him back to life. Alas, we were so helpless, so impotent, so sorry.

There was an odd slipping in and out of reality as we waited for his death. Past, present, and future became distorted and juxtaposed. It takes a long time to grasp a future so drastically changed. A future where every table will be set with broken plates.

Valentine's Day—a day for lovers. He had not dated a great deal yet, but I found myself—then and long afterward—looking at cute girls and thinking just for an instant, "Now, Stephen will be interested in her." Then the present and the future hit me smack in the face. There will be no love affairs, no waiting at an altar, no holding a son's trusting hand as he pours into him the distilled lore of the ages—no more of life's experiences for Stephen—ever!

Yet, in an hour or so I would think of all his medals and some of his favorite things which I must save for his children. The topaz ring made from the stone a friend brought him from Nepal—I must save that ring for his daughter!

I had hardly seen Steve naked since he'd been a little boy, and yet these last two months when I would bathe and clothe him, I would look at his beautiful body, all promise and no fulfillment, and think I'd never seen anything so beautiful and sad. These thoughts would come to me when I'd see the horrible misuse and literal prostitution imposed by the tubes, catheters, and hurtful tape—"misuse," in the sense that he had all that marvelous mechanism that was never to be used. That scrotal sac, as beautiful on his emaciated frame as on a Greek statue, filled with genes that would never be reproduced. Yet even as I wept over his open but unseeing eyes and his inert frame, I'd catch myself promising, "But darling, maybe your daughters will have eyes and lashes like this," or "Sweetheart, I hope one of your sons will have dark hair that grows just like yours—so thick and shiny. I love your 'drakes tail' in the back."

Ah—Bonnie Prince Charlie, the father of marvelous children destined to remain unborn.

Dr. Racheson changed from taciturn and brusque to very gentle. He even put his hand on my shoulder as he told me again, "Mrs. Warner, you must go home and begin to regroup your family. We cannot tell you any time schedule. Stephen's body was wound up to go a hundred years. It may be a long time."

Shortly after that, Bill and I turned to each other and said, "We have two sons. One will be twenty-one tomorrow. We must go home to be with him." We called two friends nearby who could come and sit beside Steve from nine until nine—the hours we could have been with him—and then made plans to leave.

Sometime in the early evening, after supper, I left Bill with Stephen and slipped away once more to talk to the hospital chaplain.

When I came back Bill asked a little tremulously, "Have you gotten any response from him lately?"

Not wanting to see the hope rise again in his face I quickly answered, "Oh, no. There's been no response of any kind since last Saturday. There can't be any, Honey. The doctor said the damage was irreversible. I've watched him as immobile as that table for the last six days."

"But I think . . . I'm positive he moved for me." Bill insisted.

"No. There's no real movement." I was the voice of insufferable authority. "Sometimes I've been fooled, too, and thought he moved," I continued. Its just gravity that causes his hand to slide down—you know, the weight and drag of his arms."

Sometimes we'd lift those Neanderthal arms and lay them across our shoulders in simulated embraces. As they clung there briefly, their weight felt a little like a hug—a remnant of the energy spells that could be spent only in quick hard hugs for everyone. Sometimes the reflex movement of his fingers as we gently squeezed and massaged them just *seemed* to be volitional responses—a tiny shred of the "love message" he always sent around the circle of our held hands as we said (or sang) grace at the table. In fifth grade Kathy had discovered a table grace that we loved to sing as a round. A quickly squeezed love message had become the coda to our "Amen."

All the time I was talking, his Daddy was holding his dear right hand while saying softly, "Squeeze my hand, Steve. Squeeze my hand if you can hear me."

"Come here," Bill called excitedly, and I leaped to the bed. I seized Steve's hand and watched unbelievingly as he *did* squeeze in response!

Then Bill touched the one foot that had had limited movement until a week ago, and said, "Can you move your toes, Son?"

We saw Steve move his toes! They moved about one-half inch!

Laughing and crying, Bill said, "Move them again, Son. Mama doesn't believe you are doing it."

Immediately Steve moved his toes until they were nearly crimped! What feeling swept over us for nearly an hour! I thought I had long ago given up any hope of a take-up-your-bed-and-walk miracle, but I was wrong. In those moments I thought, "This is what God has been waiting for! He was only testing us! Naturally he would choose a flamboyant miracle to use with Stephen! Our son is not going to die, he's just been put through some horrible trial so that in some inscrutable way that beggars comprehension, "His Name might be glorified." God is going to raise Lazarus again! Any minute now he'll say, "Talitha cum."

One of us ran out to get a nurse and the little curly-haired intern to come and see what was happening! Neither of them came into the room, although these reactions kept up for nearly an hour. We assumed they thought it was involuntary muscle twitching—their manner was humoring, almost patronizing. That seemed a logical explanation, but there had been absolutely none of that for a week. Nothing will ever make me or Bill believe anything but that in some almost suprahuman way, Steve rallied for about forty-five minutes. He was conscious of his parents, bending over him in love, and the kid who hung on longer than anybody else, the kid with the derring-do had pulled himself out of the jaws of death to tell us good-bye.

We did not take our eyes off him until we left him about ten o'clock that night, but there was never any further sign of consciousness.

February 15, David's birthday. Once I told Steve, "We'll have his birthday party in a downtown restaurant. Won't you look elegant observing, just this once, all the festivities from your wheelchair?" That was in early January. Later we planned to have this party for Dave's twenty-first birthday right in Steve's room. But it would be complete with presents and guests and candles and everything, right in that hospital room.

Our friend Georgia came about nine to stay until five; Another, friend, Virginia would come then and stay until closing hours. Those friends had loved him in the days of his sunshine and somehow we felt we could let them stay beside him in the time of his journey into the valley of the shadow.

After several attempts to leave, we gave Steve one final hug, one final I-love-you squeeze, and we walked out.

Many birthdays had been celebrated at Grandma's, but never one as sad as that one. Every attempt at gaiety made the "celebration" more macabre. It was a heavy burden for David, the birthday boy. Having Aunt Marguerite, slightly outside our inmost circle, made it a little more bearable.

Sometime after ten o'clock, Bill and I left to go across the woods to our house. Kathy and Russ came with us, but David was going to stay at Grandpa's. It was with a sense of sharing that we left him there. Kathy and Russ decided they'd rather sleep in their own bed after all, but it seemed we could not bear to part. We stood on the stairs by the front door and talked for an hour about Steve—Steve, that part of us that was apart and yet so terribly near. Finally, they left.

Within minutes of their leaving, the phone rang. We flew to answer it. For a moment the call could not get through. There must be a slew of gadfly imps who ice up windshields and scramble emergency phone calls. The operator kept saying, "But who is going to pay for this call? Is it a collect call? Which party is to pay? I must know if it is to be billed as a collect call."

All the time one of us on each extension was saying, "We'll pay. Yes! Make it to us! Make it collect!"

Finally, the operator connected us and we heard the voice of Dr. Brumbaugh, the cadaverous looking interne who long ago had warned us not to feel guilty. Tonight he said only, "Mrs. Warner, Stephen has melted away. It happened about 11:15 tonight."

He repeated the highly unmedical terminology, "Stephen has just melted away."

The telling took so few words.

When Grandma heard it minutes later, she put into words the sigh of us all, "Well, thank the Lord."

What a precipitous cliff we had been clinging to for four and one-half months. We started with great hopes and lost ground step by step, inch by inch, until our most viable option was to be thankful for Steve's release at last.

The next day I wrote simply:

February 16, 1974
Stephen died last night, but by God, by all that men call holy anywhere, it took a big one and it took a long time.

INTERIM

I would prefer to whiz-bang around for a hundred years and then just disintegrate like Holmes's "Wonderful One-Hoss Shay" into some neat and dry (but very celestial) dust. Very likely I shall not be that tidy. Abhorrent and unacceptable as they were, decisions about funerals were now ours to make.

We found many of the customs and mores of our neighborhood comforting. The flowers were testimonials of caring, and more too—they were fragile blossoms honoring the fragile flesh that binds us all. There were huge, splashy bouquets of red and white carnations the florists had had in stock from the Valentine's Day Dance—those were chosen by the young people themselves. That would have pleased Steve. Food was a love offering that said, "We wanted to do so much that was impossible, so please let us do this." As the third ham was brought in, the thought flashed through my mind, "Well, Steve will surely get his fill of ham for once." Later in the evening, I was startled by the thought that I hadn't any idea what Steve would wear the next day! My mind could not grasp the idea that we were having a "party" without him.

His beautiful burgundy velvet sport coat—the first one he ever bought with his own money—needed a pale, pale pink shirt. He had had a shirt like that for Kathy's wedding, but somehow he lost it the same week at a cast party for "My Fair Lady." That spring, instead of buying a new shirt, I'd tinted one of his many white ones. It looked fine, but how obscene to have him wear a dyed, make-do shirt for a big prom and then buy a lovely new one for such as this.

In some way during that interim he "appeared" to Kathy in a way that she could not share with us except to say, "After that, nothing can ever shake my faith that life goes on—after that, I will never be afraid to die."

While we were still in the hospital, Bill and I decided that we wanted Steve buried in our woods, in spite of all kinds of advice to the contrary. After we learned that we could do that legally, we told our plans to Kathy and David. We both thought we detected a momentary start before they agreed. Kathy and David were the ones to be considered then; if they had the slightest reservation we would change our plans. In case of grandchildren, we would not want a place that was hallowed and still—maybe even "scary"—in the woods. That was not the way Steve must be remembered.

We would have preferred it and have great empathy as we read about archeological digs where the little skeletons of the babies and small children were buried around the hearth or somewhere near the living quarters. However, we chose a windswept hillside in an old country cemetery where his greatgrandparents are buried, beside the church I attended until I was married. Overlooking a small lake, it would have been a perfect place to pitch a tent.

Once Steve had said, "Grandma, I just love to go to your church. I like it better than the town church."

"Why?" we asked, wondering what simplicity of worship had spoken to his little heart. How we laughed at his answer.

"It's because of all the wasps. While the preacher is preaching I can make the time go fast by watching the wasps in the ceiling!"

It is tradition in our area to have a "viewing," and so we did that. We had seen the disease take its relentless toll for such a long time that we did not realize how shocking Steve must have appeared to those who had not watched that ravage.

Someone whispered, "Why didn't you put a wig on him?"

"A wig? Stephen? Why that's enough to make him turn over in his grave!"

For me, there was another harder-to-define reason for an open casket. Even in this gesture, there was the desire to strike a blow for realism. I wanted to say, *This* is the way life is sometimes! It's not a fairy tale. Everything does not end happily ever after. All winners do not win—at least not by earthly standards. All our love and all Steve's courage were brought to naught by the ugly reality of death and disease.

Years later, when I saw pictures of the stark chimney at Belsen, that replica of the ugly smokestack from which belched the stench of the burning bodies of the holocaust, erected by the surviving Jews "so that man will not forget," I knew instantly that that was what I'd wanted to say with the open casket. Look! Observe! This is what can happen. You must never forget. If it could happen to Steve, it can happen to any of us. Regard with utter awe and respect the gift of life.

Although the hundreds of friends who streamed by that night were somehow a comfort to me and to Bill and Kathy, David found the thought of greeting people intolerable. He stayed shut in his room for two days, with only one or two friends beside him.

Even the flowers we chose were eloquent in their symbolism—tulips, daffodils, hyacinths, tiny Dutch iris—beauty springing forth from apparently "dead" bulbs. For David it had to be something else. A little while before the funeral, he charged out of the house. When he came back he held in his hand a small clump of life everlasting, that tiny wild flower, sometimes called Eterna, that dried into clusters of tiny off-white stars. He had twigs of Grandma's soft maple already showing red with swollen buds, and he found a lovely piece of rough bark and some lush green moss under the white oak tree in our woods. He put these together in a sparse but eloquent arrangement. A piece of driftwood from one of the canoe trips on the Current River was an appropriate container. For Stephen and David, it was right.

In *The Summer of the Great-Grandmother*, Madeleine L'Engle wrote, "We grossly underestimate the capacity for the realism in the mourner." Sometime that summer I wrote:

Time was
I'd see a grave—
A tiny grave ringed with shells
Or bits of bright blue bottle—
And think
"How quaint,
How primitive,
How simplistic in their grief."

But now—
Now that I have moved
From novitiate to mother superior
In this ancient Order of Niobe,
I do not smile a knowing smile
But wipe a tear,
As strewing nuts upon the ground
I try to coax the squirrels near—
'Twould make him laugh, you know—
And turn away from lilies white

And bring a turtle rescued
From the road
Instead.

The funeral was held in the church where his father and I had been married, where his sister had been married, where his father ministered and where Steve and Dave and our entire family had worshipped during an important segment of our lives. When his death became imminent, Kathy somehow calmed her spirit and chose special musical selections; then she contacted his choirs at both school and church. We are forever indebted to her for that expression of her love, and to the young people who came in droves to pay that tribute to Steve.

A woodwind quintet played Debussy's "Arabesque," and the Band Ensemble played Bach's "Chorale Prelude." The Youth Choir, of which Steve was also the assistant director, sang "Long Live God" from *Godspell.* The combined choirs sang Handel's "Since by Man Came Death," from *The Messiah,* which Steve had loved since he was a little boy. As his high school chorus sang selections from *Jesus Christ Superstar,* I remembered a party at our house the summer before, when Steve took his record player outside and our woods fairly reverberated with that same music. Once or twice I caught myself looking for him in the choirs.

We clutched to our hearts certain phrases of Dr. Lee Moorehead's eulogy. "Stephen Warner lived for seventeen years of joy and delight." "One reaches out to catch a free spirit, to hold him close and think of him as Steve Warner." "We were freshened with delight when Steve spent the night with our family."

Lee told us later he was a little startled as a ripple of laughter spread over the congregation when he said, "Someone asked his mother one day if Steve had ever been normal. She said that she just smiled and said, 'Yes,' but confided, 'Inside I was screaming, Normal? Stephen? No. He was *never normal*. Wild? Yes. Exuberant? Yes. Sometimes heedless? Yes. Brilliant? Yes. Fiercely loyal? Ruthless with bigotry and snobbery? Independent? Stubborn? Always stretching for more? Yes. But normal? No, I don't really think you could say Stephen had ever been just normal. . . . He was a joy always, and it did not take this calamity to make us aware of it."

That spontaneous laughter—laughter from those who knew and loved Steve best—was healing and hopeful. It was a tribute with a rare poignant beauty.

Lee went on to explain that just that week an announcement came saying that Steve's college entrance exam had placed him in the top three percent across the nation. He continued, "Stephen Warner was, indeed, an extraordinary boy whose death diminishes all of us. This gathered throng silently declares that today, the bell tolls for us all."

In the grossly mismatched battle, where Steve did unceasing combat with so formidable a foe, he had been catapulted ruthlessly from boyhood to adulthood. But the rest of us, too, had been forced to face a stark reality that aged us all. It was not the coming-of-age birthday that had made David a man. Some of his anguish was shared as Lee read portions of a letter Dave had written shortly after that first dreadful brain surgery.

Dear Stephen,

The last few months have been hard on all of us, but I can't imagine the physical pain and emotional strain that has been placed on you. It is difficult to accept my life without the companionship, friendship, and love that have made my life enjoyable. Whenever I'd think of times in the future if you would die, I keep catching myself thinking, "But things will be back to normal when Steve comes back." I couldn't really imagine life without you, only if you were gone on a long trip—but not dead.

. . . the regular grind of school, work and chores keeps life going on and covers the fact that you are gone. But gnawing away at my stomach and the back of my mind is the truth that you are suffering and not with us.

I had not known the real meaning of brotherly love until the past two years or so. About the time we moved to Carbondale, or a year or so later, we grew closer and closer until we became friends, companions, comrades as well, and true brothers instead of just siblings.

I wish I could have suffered for you because you have suffered too much . . . you are alive, and recovering. . . . You may still have a long way to go before you can again enjoy life to its fullest, but you will attain this goal. At this point I don't know, no one knows what permanent impairment you may have, if any, but let me say, blind, uncoordinated men can enjoy the taste of a fresh mountain stream and appreciate the complex beauty of nature and all of God's creation. All obstacles can be overcome somehow and you have the strength and courage to overcome them. I pray that God will aid you in any way possible in this fight and that he can make me useful in helping you recover. I long for the time we can again enjoy a field of winter wheat under a blue sky, with a taste of spring water on our lips and a pleasant feeling of aching, tired and successful muscles in our limbs.

God has granted my prayer that you survive the operation with a sound mind and now we must fight for recovery and accept any infirmities that cannot be overcome. . . . You *live,* and we thank God for this.

As I look on you now, wild-eyed, fearful, bony, shaved, and partially paralyzed, I can't help but long for the past when you were whole. But the alternative to being sick now, is death, so we must struggle on. . . .

Now, I can live a life with you around, even if you were to be confined to a wheelchair, which I don't expect, but I could not live a full life, ever, if you were to die. These thoughts are always on my mind these days, and sometime I will have you read them or tell you my feelings while we overlook a valley of grasses as the wind appears in waves across the floor of the valley. I can carry you on my back so that you can enjoy these sights with me until you are well enough to walk.

For now, my Brother, these thoughts remain trapped in my heart and on this page. May we soon be really together once again.

Your brother, David

The memorial ended with, "Let no one arise to offer a cliche-ridden explanation. Let no one come forth with well-worn phrases, no conventional wisdom . . . for none of us can bear the tyranny of triviality. . . . Whatever doubts or questions there might still be . . . one truth is magnificently manifest: Though love is a mystery too, that never in this world finally yields all its secrets, there never was a day in the life of William Stephen Warner when he did not know and experience love, when he did not know that he was loved. This was the ultimate gift given him by his family, his church, and his friends. He knew, too, I believe, that despite all the torment, that he was loved by God, for God is Love."

As the people in the sanctuary stood and sang, "Be Thou My Vision," that ancient Irish hymn, my faith which flew in the teeth of the obvious, was strong, and I sang too, almost with a glad, mad defiance:

"Heart of my own heart, whatever befall,
Still be my Vision, O Ruler of all."

In the act of singing this hymn, I was throwing in with faith—betting my life on God. My voice seemed joined to—yea, lost in—that resounding swell which has come down to us from a mighty host, filtering through the smoke of kindling faggots, carrying over the screams of angry mobs, prevailing despite the unholy chants from the Coliseum, saying simply, under the most improbable circumstances, "Yea, though He slay me, yet will I trust Him."

After a ten-mile ride, six of his young friends carried Steve's casket under the pines and over the winter stubble to a corner of the plot of ground overlooking a lake. There was a redbud close by and a dogwood whose buds were plump like the ones Steve and I had seen magnified the winter before by the ice and sleet. It truly would have been a good place for weary back packers to pitch a tent.

It was there that I especially remember Bill, crushed and heartbroken himself, giving comfort and help to the many young people who flung themselves sobbing into his arms. More than any words, there was just the sharing of frustration and grief—a mingling of tears and a daring to express hope. A hope that whatever marvelous forces that had come together to form Stephen Warner could never be eradicated. One boy stumbled toward the long line of cars, then ran back to us and said, "I just wanted to tell you. Well—Well, that boy of yours—Well, he was crazy. That's what he was." We all laughed with him at his tribute. All of us knew what he meant.

The young people started it. Then, huddled there on the gentle hillside, the rest of us joined our voices to the strains of "Long Live God, Long Live God." It started like a dirge, sad and moving but gradually the tempo and volume increased until, once more flying in the teeth of all reason, beside an open grave, the song became a hope that swelled to an affirmation. For a moment, life did not seem wild and bereft of reason, but a part of a whole—and Steve had come full circle.

Later, David wrote, "Our thoughts are that he would have made a large contribution to the world and it is sadly diminished by his death. However, when we see the host of friends of all ages who mourn him, we are aware that he has already made a great contribution."

Kathy said, "He romped through seventeen years of life—Giving and receiving much love."

He did. These words were engraved on the stone that marks Stephen's gravesite.

The Blessing of Aaron

> The Lord bless thee, The Lord keep thee,
> Make his face to shine upon thee,
> And be gracious unto thee.
> The Lord lift up his Countenance upon Thee,
> And give thee peace,
> And give thee peace.

—Ramsey

Amen

NEVERTHELESS: AN EPILOGUE

Stretched somewhere between our dreams of how we think things are going to be and the harsh realities of things as we find them is a bridge that each of us must cross. That bridge, paved with stones stamped "however" and "nevertheless," is the arena where the drama of our lives unfolds. In the years during which I wrote this book, I became intimately acquainted with that bridge and eternally grateful for the stepping stones.

Why have I written?

Pen and paper have been such an extension of my mind that not to have written would have been abnormal. The challenge of putting nebulous thoughts into words that can be shared has always beguiled me. I have written prayers to God, love letters to my husband, cherishing notes to my children. Why should I stop now?

When I felt my entire psyche scattering like a drop of water on a hot griddle, I would come together again if I could write. I called them poems—those things that dripped from my finger tips, those thoughts wrung from my heart continually. A friend who also lost a son thinks poetry must be a gift from God, given to man to keep his heart from breaking.

I could not keep from writing. For a while I had the uncanny feeling that by my words I could keep Steve alive. What I could not do with my ministrations and my prayers, I could do in a greatly diminished way with my pen. In college, "A's" were the result of hard work. Shouldn't life be as logical? I was driven by the subconscious feeling that my reward for a super colossal job would be Stephen, alive and well again.

It took a long time to realize and accept the irreversibility of death. And it was almost two years after Stephen's death before I could write coherent prose—ordinary sentences, where subjects preceded verbs and the modifiers stayed modestly in their places.

Elie Wiesel wrote from the flames of the Holocaust, "I write in order to understand as much as to be understood."

When I read his words, I recognized my own compulsion. Yet, having written, there is much I will never understand. In retrospect, it seems vain and egotistical, but for a while I truly had the conviction that I would find an answer to the agony that swept over us and sweeps over the world. Although later, weary with the search, I realized it was naive and even arrogant to think I would be given the answer to the riddle of pain and suffering, at that time it seemed plausible that some great lesson, some great truth must be exchanged for such a price. I was crazed in my search for meaning and suffering.

Longing for the great truths that great travail purportedly teaches I searched through the lessons of my sorrow and learned only a wry twisted thing. If I fixed my eyes on some distant point and twitched my nose as I applied pressure to my upper lip, as if averting a sneeze, I would not cry—in public. That was a small bit of knowledge for the price paid.

Once, when the irony of trying to make words on paper be a puny substitute for my son became obvious, I wrote:

I sag
With the realization,
That if I could lend his name
To all the redwood groves in California,
Could christen every constellation
In his honor,
Could etch his name
Upon the very rainbow's path,
It would be so pitiable a thing
Compared to the splendor
That was him.

Occasionally I still write a letter to Stephen, years after his death. To me, this is natural, though I'm sure it might cause raised eyebrows and knowing glances from those who've had one course in abnormal psychology. When should I have stopped? Certainly not when he entered the hospital, nor when he lost his voice, nor when he was isolated in ICU for so long. Should I have stopped when he went into a coma? There seemed such a little difference when at last his great heart stopped beating. The relationship has not changed, so occasionally I still write—perhaps on his birthday or Christmas. Martha Whitmore Hickman says in her book *Love Speaks It's Voice:*

> In every life there is a watershed experience—an event by which time in that life is forever marked, as having taken place before, or after, that significant event. For me, that event took place on the afternoon of July 20, 1974, when my daughter fell from a horse and died. She would have been seventeen in another two weeks.
>
> With that event the coloration of my life has become radically different—almost as though the sky were brown, and the earth blue, or as though the alphabet of our daily life were wrought from different symbols . . . it is as though a slash mark was cut through time, my time, and the two worlds, while they have the same cast of characters—even to her, for she is, in a way, still here—are also different worlds, as if a wall were built across the tunnel of life at that instant. The wall is transparent, but it is sealed to the edges and in the middle of it is her death—as flowers are fixed in a circle of resin. To look back . . . before that death one must look through that resin film; to move in the present at all is to move in the rays projecting from that great event.

I believe there is a great universality in grief. At least two years before I read these words I had written, "It is incongruous to compare the life we now lead to our life before Steve died. There is no frame of reference. It is like asking, "Which is heavier, lead or lavender?" or "If you have two oranges and one lemon, how many children do you have?"

Ah, "Watershed"—I have a picture of our three children standing beside a sign that read "The Great Divide." Without realizing we were approaching it, I had reached the great divide in my life.

It was wasted breath and thought to bemoan the fact that things would never be the same again. Of course they wouldn't. It would be macabre if things had remained the same. Of course Christmas would never be the same. Nor vacations. Nor family picnics. Nor our faith, nor our outlook on life, nor our priorities.

One well-meaning friend said, "I'll be so glad when you're like you used to be."

That can never be. We are not necessarily lesser people than we were, but we can never be the same.

For a long time I felt that I, too, was dead. At least I thought I would never live again. A couple of times that first summer I caught myself speaking about myself in past tense. Nothing was pertinent to me. Life was happening for someone else. Always there was a deep, overall ache—the profound remorse that Steve had to die—punctuated by a poignancy—the pain of things remembered. As I had yearned to kiss away his sickness, so now I yearned to hold him, caress him, and kiss away even his death. I was his mother—I should have known a way.

For a while I was cruelly haunted by the idea that I had not been a good mother. All I could remember were times when I had not been patient or understanding; times when I had said harsh things to Stephen; times when I had been too demanding or selfish or picky; times when I had not gone with him when he'd wanted me to go; times I'd not made transportation easy for him because of our too-tight scheduling. Most of all, I rued the time I had given to my job and other lesser things—time that now I wished I had to pour at his feet.

I grieved over different aspects of Steve's death at various times. For a couple of weeks, maybe a month, I would become obsessed with some guilt or a particular ambition of his that would never be realized. A calm I had arrived at one day might have flown completely the next.

Sometimes I tortured myself with, "What year, what day, what hour did the thing begin to grow?" "Was there ever an instant when

I could have stopped it?" "Was it some fault on my part, or his dad's?

I agonized over all the time that was wasted from October to December when the doctors were toying around with a wrong and relatively minor diagnosis.

Finally my mother said, "Honey, if they had found it sooner, we would have lost him sooner."

Her matter-of-fact, straightforward, probably clinically accurate, words helped me get off that particular treadmill of recrimination. Bereavement is a time when guilt and recrimination can run rampant. In our case there could be no guilt or fault assigned, unless it was a corporate inability to recognize fleeting symptoms and even then it would have been too late to have thwarted tragedy.

As I went through the motions of living, I recalled the words of dear friends, whose five-year-old elfin sprite, Galen, had lost her battle with leukemia: "It will be like you are recuperating very slowly from a terrible illness."

Gradually becoming aware again of my physical senses was strange, like learning to walk after a long hospitalization. It was with actual shock one day that I realized the yellow flowers in our yard were chrysanthemums and not daffodils. I had been numb those many months.

My family helped me live again. They brought little gifts—a burr oak acorn from David, burgundy roses that are the blooms of the paw-paw from my father. Slowly I began to write of the things I had seen or felt or heard, trying to capture in words all the wonder and beauty of the ordinary. What I wrote I stuffed under the bed in a box labeled "Mizpah," a Hebrew word that, loosely translated, means "May the Lord be with thee and with me while we are absent one from the other." David commented wryly that Hebrew must be a very efficient language.

We found joy in little things we did for each other and things we did for Steve. One of my joyous moments was when David came striding across a frozen field saying, "Mom, come out and look at the sunset." Within five minutes, I had two phone calls—one from Bill and one from Kathy—urging me to hurry outside and look at the sunset! I felt Steve, too, wanted us to see it and declare it beautiful!

Once I had said to Bill, "We have watched Steve die for so long that surely when the time actually comes it can be no worse."

He cautioned, "Oh yes, it will be worse. Nothing will be as bad as his actual death."

I'm not sure that Bill was right, but the finality was suffocating. Every parent must have some dread of a child's dying, but we spit out the bitter taste of that fear and savor the elixir of life when we feel the infant roll beneath our flesh, or later sigh with relief as a hand quickly thrust into the bassinet detects a gentle breathing. Regardless of all the whispered horrors that the Furies in Hell tell us it will be, the actual loss of a child is worse. Yet to enter into the agreement of parenthood is to accept this vulnerability. To accept birth is also to accept death. To enter any love relationship is also to enter into a pact where the heart is laid wide open.

Our value systems reflect what is hardest to live without. After persons, I list joy and beauty and purpose. The lethargy and the absence of joy that crept into everything were devastating. Never before had I realized how crucial a thing was joy. That first Christmas, I thought I would break in two if I could not sing "Joy to the World." Finally I sang softly, tunelessly, and without much assurance, but I found I could not live without some joy.

February 18, when we came home from Steve's funeral, we had spotted a yellow crocus blooming, despite chilling winds and frozen ground. If a flower blooms it always blooms despite—despite winds or heat, gophers, moles, aphids, trampling feet, blight, stones, or disease. That crocus was symbolic for me. Common wayside flowers suffer from frequent mowing and lack of care, yet they bloom. If they could still be beautiful, maybe my life might yet be meaningful, too.

The things that first appear beautiful are personal for each grieving person. For me they were tangible, earthy things like cloud formations and smooth brown stones—tactile things, things of substance. Except for the yellow crocus, flowers did nothing for me that first year. When I saw them I did not care whether they lived or died, and I watched dispassionately as they withered during a long drought. The plants in the garden dried up and even the weeds in the woods shriveled and turned gray. Suddenly one afternoon I looked out and saw them dying—dying, when life was so precious! Like a crazed person, time and time again, I carried buckets of water to ragweeds, Jimson weeds, Jerusalem Oak, and every common weed in the edge of our woods. That obsession was irrational and certainly illogical, but that day, to me, it made sense. Many things became metaphor for Stephen, and most of them were beautiful—a butterfly that lit on my shoulder, a white feather outside the back door one Christmas morning. Then there was an indigo bunting dead beside the road.

Years later, David and I sorrowed to see another dead Indigo Bunting. That one killed himself by flying into our patio doors. As we watched, another bunting, a brilliant male flew down and tried in vain to coax the dead bird to fly away with him. Apparently oblivious to our nearness, he repeatedly flew to his fallen comrade, nudging and tweaking him and finally taking his wing in his beak and pulling him several inches. Finally, David said quietly, "I know just how he feels."

Studies have shown that an appalling number of marriages break up after the death of a child. From an outsider's viewpoint that must be hard to understand—surely the greatest of tragedies should draw couples together, not split them apart. But it was not hard for Bill and me to see why that was so. Grief is so personal that the way another person handles his own sorrow may seem crazed or demented or else callous or insensitive to another—even to a spouse. When my brother died, I remember wanting my mother to kiss me. I wanted her to kiss me on the mouth, though I don't remember her ever having done that before. Somehow it seemed to me that although I was twenty-seven years old, if she would kiss me fiercely and intimately it would wipe away the sorrow. Somehow the heartache would go away like the pain from a skinned knee under her kiss.

In retrospect, I think it must have been a similar longing to touch good things again that made my husband want to make love. I remember being appalled at his callousness. How dare he enjoy the delights of the body when his son had died! Perhaps our situation was not unique, but for four months we had slept in separate beds or had huddled scared and fearful in someone else's borrowed bed, listening for the phone to ring. Getting together again was a little difficult. I remember the first time we made love after the funeral and what I remember most about it was weeping as I heard David driving down the lane alone—coming into the house—alone. No chatter, no brotherly talk—just silence. I also remember feeling very sorry for my husband. I cared for him. We cared for each other. Perhaps it is this caring for others that pulls one back into a viable life again.

In the first two years after Steve's death, many joys had come into our lives, the greatest being a grandson, William Jacob Tate. Lesser joys also brought many happy moments. Kathy seemed to demonstrate that life must be stronger than death as she was determined to go about her life, her marriage, and her baby boy. Every member of my family helped me; I'm not sure I helped anyone.

The second Christmas my mother wrote a little note on my card. "Darling, I know you are heartbroken and nothing will ever be the same without Stephen, but we have all been hurt and it seems we all need each other so much." My mother was a wise and wonderful woman.

Bill did not express his doubt and rage as loudly as I did, but he struggled just the same. He listened to me in all the stages of my sorrow and never preached or criticized. Someone said they hoped the Warners could come out of their grief with some affirmations. Once Bill said quietly, "Some days, just to get up in the morning is an affirmation." I understood. Just to go on was saying yes to life.

Of all the emotions involved in the death of a child, anger—bitter rage that something so filthy and so final should besmirch such innocence—is the common denominator. That rage that intermingled with our sorrow was awesome—frightening as well as liberating. I think before Steve's illness, the pattern for my behavior was the model of Gentle Jesus, Meek and Mild. My anger (and in fifty years I'd seen things to be angry about) had found ways to work itself out in research, study, forums, boycotts, stand-ins, speeches, and letters to congressmen, editors, etc. That anger that came with Stephen's death was different, not only in degree but in kind.

The death of a child is the ultimate unacceptability. It is an anger that spins itself in impotence. There is nobody to hate. Nobody to blame. Nobody to hit.

Charles Schultz, who dares to touch on all our problems through the actions of his little people, has a sequence where Good Old Charlie Brown is sick. Eventually he has to go to the hospital. After many days, during which there have been various theological pronouncements that make little sense and give little comfort, we see the character Lucy, saying in her customary strident voice, "It is wrong. It is crazy for someone like Charlie Brown to get sick and not get better." She protests, "Something is wrong with a world like this." The strip finishes with her gritting her teeth, seething with rage, still proclaiming, "There ought to be somebody to hit."

But there was more to come. On January 13, 1975, the school secretary once again came to my room to tell me my husband was on the phone. I remembered the summons just eleven months before when he had called to tell me of the tumor—that he and Stephen would not be coming home. Surely, nothing so hellish could be in store for us again. However, there was still Kathy—still David—still Mama and Daddy. My hands shook as I picked up the phone.

"Honey."

Bill's voice was shaking. So it was not a routine call to announce a schedule change. He paused to regain composure.

"Honey, our house has just burned to the ground."

I could hardly comprehend what he was saying. A whole house could not be gone just like that. Houses do not burn in broad daylight without a reason. As Bill's words slowly sank in, I tried to picture nothing—smoldering, smoking, nothing. Nothing where this morning there had been a beautiful big white house largely wrought by our own labor. So much labor. So much money and time. So many dreams. Suddenly I was angry.

I turned to the secretary and blurted out, "I don't know what God is trying to teach me, but I wish I would hurry and learn it." Silly talk, for I no more believed that God had burned my house than I believed he had killed my boy, but the vernacular of accepted thought is easy to slip into.

I had two strange and eerie sensations the night of the fire and part of the next day, when we stayed with my parents. During that time I experienced an odd free-floating, not-belonging feeling that I think came from not having any material possessions—nothing to wash, nothing to cook, nothing to wear. It was frightening, but it was also liberating. I had no possessions, but I was still me. Also, for a few hours I had the irrational sensation that the sacrifice of our house was the penance required, and now at last, everything would be right again. Something—Fate or God—would accept our house for the return of our son.

Steve's get-well cards, which filled two big boxes, were all gone, as well as the dear funny little notes he'd written to friends who'd given them back to us. The bushel of Christmas gifts he'd never let us open was in his room, still carefully wrapped. The white elephant Dave had bought at the Cub Scout meeting for my birthday did survive—it was made of iron—but I could find no trace of the exquisite Venetian beads. The big suitcase holding our accumulation of Halloween gear burned without ever being opened again. I'm glad. We were all so different that attempting the same disguises would have seemed pitifully counterfeit.

For a while I think we felt like characters in one of Camus' novels—damned without knowing why, and so besmirched by bad luck that normal people might not want to associate with us. It was perhaps logical that many people would link the fire and Steve's death, and they would exclaim sympathetically about what bad luck we had had, but the remark was always unsettling. For the two events even to be mentioned in the same breath—for them to be considered together as if they were tragedies of the same kind—was repugnant and intolerable! Had we lost the house first, we would have thought it a great loss, but put into perspective by Steve's death, it was a minor bit of bad luck—nothing that could not be remedied.

For Bill, the planning and rebuilding of another house was therapy. Although he worked until he was lean of frame and grey of face, still it was healthful, welcome weariness. Though I helped in planning and buying furniture for the new house, my main concern that summer was the relentless search for answers to the questions that beset me.

When fruitless unanswerable questions threatened, and when endless flagellation wooed me to the edge of hysteria, it was always hard, basic, cold facts that settled me. After Steve died, I wrote Dr. Guise, the neurosurgeon who had given me such joy when he assured us that Steve's trouble was only sinus. Dr. Guise wrote me a sympathetic letter, saying that, in his wide experience, he had found the tumor, epindomoma, to be "catastrophic and irreversible."

Curiously, those words, along with the cold gray stone of Dr. Racheson's "Stephen is going to die," jerked me to reality at times when otherwise I might have found a way of escape. Stephen had died. Nothing could be worse. If I had lived through that, I could surely get through the rest of my life. Small comfort, but it settled me.

I had always wrestled with the meaning of life, but after Steve's death, I had a compulsion to find what there was to believe. I felt as committed to finding answers as I think doctors are to finding cures. Gradually, after two or three years, a wave of despair swept over me, and I thought, "Who do you think you are? Do you think you'll find answers when man for a million years has not been able to understand?" It had not seemed presumptuous to think that Steve's life could have brought such revelation, but slowly my conviction that God had been waiting since the beginning of time to reveal this truth to some waiting heart faded, and one night with great reluctance I wrote, "You are going to bang your head against a solid wall every day for the rest of your life and still you're not going to learn anything. You'll just get a bruised and battered and bloody head."

I grabbed books—religious books, philosophy books, books of psychology and para-psychology—and turned to the index to look for "death" or "survival." If a book did not speak of those things, it could not speak to me. I suspect I was equally ruthless with people and institutions.

Although I no longer expected to find THE ANSWER written in tablets of stone at my doorstep, I kept on seeking. I could not give up God. If I did, I'd be totally alone—and so would Steve. We had done all we could and it had not been enough. All human effort had been to no avail. If my swashbuckling Bonnie Prince Charlie continues it is because of God. My arms were too short to help him, but my wild desire for his existence could not tolerate the thought that he was over—that *he* had been obliterated, as had his body.

In March, our friend Naomi wrote from California: "God has never promised us that we would understand life . . . and all of life's happenings. He promised only that as we trust, He will provide peace and joy that passes all understanding. . . . Grief is normal, but Jesus will take this grief and replace it with peace and joy, 'though not understanding.'"

I scanned the letter, than crumpled it and put it down. The same old scriptural mish-mash. The words were so ambiguous as to be meaningless. I'd trusted them before.

Days later I picked up the letter again and smoothed it out, for she had also written:

I have suffered much this past year—these past five years—but I never felt the suffering until I reached the door of death. It's frightening but the fear leaves as I rely on Jesus. I have lost my hair. I have lost my larynx and because my lungs are filled with fluid . . . I don't have much breath. I'm taking many stabs at writing this letter. How I praise the Lord for his peace and joy through it all. . . . I have never written so much to anyone else about my illness, and I write to you only to make you aware of how short life really is. Please don't let grief rob you of your zest for life and your beautiful family.

I love you both so much that I share in your grief over
Stephen. My eyes are wet with tears. Tears of love . . . of
God's promise of life.

I did not throw the letter away, but slipped it in the shelf of a
bookcase. We were living in a trailer parked in our drive, and as I
worked in the unaccustomed cramped quarters, I could not avoid
seeing her letter folded there. Although I could not accept for myself
the unquestioning faith that gave Naomi strength, I did not repudiate
it either. Her husband, Danny, the barber who had given Stephen his
first haircut, had died three years ago, and now there she was, still
a young woman and so very ill. One does not scoff at a faith that
flies like a banner over one's head as one is being dragged to the
gallows.

After Steve's death I had come downstairs one morning to
apparently dead ashes in the fireplace, but as I stood and stared
dumbly at the grate, a bit of the gray fell away and I could see a faint
pink, a tiny ember still glowing. I became obsessed with saving that
spark—using it to kindle a great roaring fire in the fireplace. I
wanted to bring the fire back to life because the tiny glow had
become Stephen and I was fighting for his life all over again. As I
blew and fanned and watched the grey turn pink, I became aware of
the upward pull of the chimney and I hated God as I sobbed, "That's
what made the difference. You didn't do your part. Never one time
was there an updraft, never did we get any help from above. Here
these blasted ashes have turned to leaping flames—all because of the
chimney. All because of the updraft." In my mind I harangued like
a fishwife, "Where were you, God? Are you even there at all?
Anywhere? Looks like in four months you could have made yourself
known! Not a glimmer did we see. Not an inkling."

Then I remembered the people. All the people. Family. Friends.
Strangers.

In all my sense of betrayal by the doctrine of the church, I must
never forget the overwhelming love and caring by the people. Our
friends both within and outside the organized church ministered to
us in every way possible during Stephen's illness and after the fire.

The sharing came from everywhere. It is hard to explain, even now, that murmur, that susurrus that seemed to spring from the earth itself. As many persons grieved and raged and mourned (all facets of the same emotion), we experienced an almost scriptural "laying on of hands" that was significant in our healing. One of the things that had caused Steve to chuckle during those dark weeks in January was a cartoon in a St. Louis paper about the fifty-five mile speed limit. Months later I wrote to the editor in search of it. He thought it might be one of Jules Feiffer's, but along with the cartoonist's address the editor told me of the tragedy of his own son. Soon afterward came the cartoon with a warm letter from Mr. Feiffer. The woman at the dry-goods counter told me of her nephew; the policeman told me of his little girl; the hairdresser about her niece.

In January 1976, Bill and I led a work crew to Guatemala to help rebuild one of the villages that had tumbled down the mountain-side in the grip of a fierce earthquake. As I stood among all the ruin and desolation, I felt a kinship with the whole of mankind. I worked side by side with people who had known great loss—people who were as fragile and as marvelous and as vulnerable as ourselves.

There in Guatemala I saw the same compassion on a wider scale. We worked with crews from many states, and we used money sent by many countries. There, amidst all that wreckage, I felt an acknowledgement of the old phrase from our church membership ritual, "Brethren, the Church is of God." There, in an alien culture, far away from home, I felt my faith strengthened.

I had felt this quickening of my spirit at other times as well. I pay homage to the unquestioning faith of my parents and to that of Naomi as she wrote from her deathbed. I believe some of the fantastic evidences that other people have received from a life Beyond. If there is any sense to life at all, there must be a Love that loves us despite. . . . I am wont to believe Paul when he said, "Nothing can separate me from the love of God . . . neither death nor any other creature."

In the spring of 1976 two events occurred that were pivotal in my healing. Lee Moorehead, with whom I'd exchanged many letters during the last two years, called to tell us he was coming from Green Bay, Wisconsin to spend the day with our family. It was not a social call and no one else in town was to know he was coming; he was coming seven hundred miles to make a pastoral call for us. Kathy, Russ, David, Bill, and I sat and talked for eight hours with this man whom we all loved and respected. During that long session every fear and every doubt, as well as every tenuous hope, was discussed. In some ways we were a sounding board for each other, with Lee there as a loving friend and seeker more than an authority.

His help came not in ecclesiastical pronouncements, but in listening and talking and letting us see that he, too, struggled daily with our same question. Whatever we believed—whether we chose chaos or a Loving Creator who was also the yearning Father—there would always be loose ends that did not seem to fit in either system.

I seem to remember his saying, "If I choose chaos it leads only to bitterness and despair, but if I choose faith, it points to a way that has sustained me all my life." The God who loved Steve for seventeen years would not abandon him at his death. That day was a milestone.

That same week, we went to Southern Illinois University, where the Catholic Student Center was sponsoring a day-long seminar, "Death and Dying," with Elizabeth Kubler-Ross as the resource person. As Kathy and David and Bill and I listened throughout that morning, I felt the presence of a fifth person with us, too. After a quick lunch, we hurried back to the auditorium, hoping to have a private word with Dr. Kubler-Ross.

While dozens of other people had had the same idea, intuition, or God, or her own sensitivity caused Ms. Kubler-Ross to turn in our direction and ask quietly, "How can I help you?"

Bill said, "Is there somewhere we could talk to you just a few minutes?"

Without hesitation she murmured, "Here's a side door."

As we went out, she slipped off her shoe and put it in the door lest it close and lock us out. There was a little run in her stocking.

"I am expected back there in a few moments," she said, her Swiss accent still thick after many years in the United States.

She sat on the steps of the little side entry and the four of us clustered around her—a tiny, unassuming woman with a run in her stocking. I had to ask my awful question one more time: "Do you believe our son continues?"

She grasped my hands in hers, looked intently into my eyes and said, "I don't believe it; I know it." At that, tears flowed from the eyes of the two parents and a grown-up brother and sister. Ms. Kubler-Ross talked a little more and told us other things, but it seemed to us that in that first pronouncement we had heard a voice of authority.

Another thing I remember—just before we started inside, she said, "Mother, don't tether a butterfly."

For me, that occasion marked the beginning of a time of letting go. For the first time it felt like release and not abandonment. The bad days were not over. The doubts were not all gone. But the direction of my path had changed from down to up.

It dawned on me slowly that I could not claw Stephen even a toehold into the future, but that Steve, dancing at the head of the parade, could lead *me* as the future unfolded. It is hard for a parent to live up to seventeen, even for one year, but here are we, in joyous lock-step with the fierce and terrible scrutiny of seventeen, forever. Seventeen. Was there ever an age so crammed with promise, so on tip-toe with expectancy and yet so naked in its vulnerability? Seventeen is anticipation without fulfillment. It is like the old man Moses being led to the pinnacle that overlooked the Promised Land. Seventeen's eye is not jaundiced nor is its outlook jaded. Seventeen is a hard age to live up to. Attempting to do so by trying to understand the young, trying not to let ourselves get set and stolid and perhaps wrong in our thinking gives an air of serendipity that brings pleasure to our lives now.

Steve met everything with such exuberance and exultation. He always had. We went to Florida when he was two, and although the ocean seemed frigid to me, when he saw it he started to walk and waded right in, laughing, with arms outstretched. Bill leaped to get

him, calling, "He'll walk all the way to Cuba if I don't catch him."
We all loved the movie of him wading in, joyously, unafraid, with
the waves sucking at his little white underpants. Oceans still beckon
on every hand, but there's no Willie Steve to embrace them.
Stephen had a way of thinking and speaking that was inimitably
his own. I must not forget that. In affirming that our lives can be a
beautiful etude again, lending breadth and timbre and fidelity to the
total symphony, let no one think that I am saying that time heals, or
that life goes on as usual. It does not. Death is not like a broken
bone that heals and leaves the owner no worse than before. Death
is a fearful amputation, and nothing is ever the same. Since it must
be endured, it must be woven into the strains of the entire work
where its minor chords will change the mood in the entire concert
hall.

Thus Steve's verve and effervescence helped us even to survive
his death. The bottom line must be joy. It would be a sin—our
sin—if we let the event that was William Stephen Warner leave the
world sadder and worse for his having occurred.

Once I saw the caterpillar of a monarch butterfly swagger across
the floor, swinging his head in mock ferocity. He looked fierce and
not too lovely, but I smiled, for I knew he was headed for a grand
metamorphosis. I grabbed my pen and wrote:

Metamorphosis

God
If his caterpillar
was William Stephen Warner,
What must his butterfly be?

W. H. Auden charges us not to sermonize or theorize but to tell
"particular stories of particular people," and that is what I have tried
to do in my writing. There was no way we could plan or prepare for
such a life-changing event as Steve's death. All we could do was
simply live through it.

Alan Paton, in his book, *For You Departed,* written after the death of his wife, says, "Something within me is waking from long sleep and I want to live and move again. Some zest is returning to me, some immense gratefulness for those who love me, some strong wish to love them also. . . . Writing this book has taught me to accept the joys and vicissitudes of life and to fall in love again with its strangeness and beauty and terror."

I had never doubted that when my hour of trial came, in some way God's Everlasting Arms would bear me up. This did not come as I had expected it, but somehow I was sustained. I did not fall down and lie there. I did not keep walking out into the depths of the water. At first the entire picture of our lives appeared black, but other joys did come. Bleakness did not take up all the landscape. Life broke through, with seasons both full and empty.

There are four grandchildren now, for David and his lovely wife Ann have Emily and Caleb Stephen, and Kathy has Katie and Jacob. Other delights appliqued themselves to the black background until eventually the picture became beautiful again—always different, perhaps bearing no resemblance to what might have been, but a thing of worth, nevertheless.

Dylan Thomas says, "After the first death there is no other." I feel that Stephen's was my first and only death. Nothing else will ever be accompanied by such soul crush and such anguish. Through him I learned of Death. There could be no escape.

When David learned to fly he wanted to take his father and me for a ride, so I asked, "Kathy, would you rather the three of us not ride in the same plane? We're about all the family you have left."

She answered, "No, Mama. After watching Steve die, I believe everyone I know could die and it would not hurt me that much ever again."

I don't know, for now she has her children.

I look about me at the faces of the young and the beautiful faces of the elderly, and I cannot believe that life has no meaning. It cannot be a tale told by an idiot. Surely my love must be rooted and grounded in a Being whose very name is Love. I have been made to realize that every man truly must sign his name to surrender. Even Stephen. Even his mother.

But somehow I can believe a young son spoke to me and said, "Mama, did you think dying would kill me?" So I can believe that surrender is not defeat.

I see a design written into the universe, and I dimly grasp that without a Designer there is no Design. I acknowledge Design—not a design that tells me what clothes to wear, or what city to live in. And I acknowledge a Designer—not one that snatches my child from the path of a speeding car—but One whose inner core is Goodness and whose ultimate design will not be thwarted.

I still wrestle with immortality, but I am reassured by Leslie Weatherhead's words:

> It would seem irrational to produce, on one of the minor planets, after millions of years, a being of immense possibilities called "man," who realized that those possibilities are never ended by the time he dies and that some of them . . . have just begun to function, and then to deny expression to those possibilities by extinction. . . . It would be the same kind of irrationality as if every baby died at birth. Within the foetus are the structures of ear and eye, of taste and smell, harbingers of a fuller life beyond the gates of birth. . . . They cry out for a far wider context. . . . Whenever we attend the funeral of a loved one we feel that man cannot be just an animal that dies alone in a hole.

It has not seemed blasphemous to have let the words of Mary's Magnificat lave my mind during labor, nor to have announced my children's births with those words of Isaiah, "Unto us a child is born, unto us a son/daughter is given," nor to have echoed God himself as I looked at our children and murmured to myself, and I hope occasionally to them, "This is my son/daughter in whom I am well pleased." After Stephen died, the words of John 3:16, "For God so loved the world that he gave his only son . . ." had a jarring effect. In some twisted way they angered me, even while they strengthened my belief. I could not have done it. Not for the World could I have given Stephen. Myself? I think so. But not Stephen. Not my Steverino. That is not human. That took God.

And you did it because you loved us God? Love us even now despite the relentless hammer blows that fall upon us without cause? Oh, God, if you loved him—if you *love him*—maybe I can love you again. Help me to love you a little.

Help me to love you for love's sake, without expecting benefit or advantage. The author of the Old Testament book, Habbakuk, avows that tho' the fig does not blossom, tho' the brooks dry up and the kine die, yet will he rejoice in the Lord. When storms and blizzard raged outside, and the children were still so small that I heard their prayers, we would thank God for shelter, a fire, a warm clean bed, but always followed with, "But God if the time ever comes when we are freezing, and sick and alone with no shelter, help us still not to doubt thy presence and thy love." That time came for all of us.

When the Biblical Stephen was thrown to the ground and lay there with the stones raining about his head, breaking his body and taking away his life as the crowd "gnashed on him with their teeth, he, being full of the Holy Ghost,looked up steadfastly into heaven, and saw the glory of God, and Jesus standing on the right hand of God, and said, 'Behold, I see the heavens opened, and the Son of Man standing on the right hand of God. . . . Lord Jesus, receive my spirit.'"

Against any evidence to the contrary, I dare to hope that this also happened for our Stephen. That for the little boy who carried in stones and gravel to have an object lesson beside his bed, with his Bible opened to this passage, the heavens also opened up and he beheld the Glory of God. That would be enough. That would be God.

His last year, the youth choir had learned a new benediction and often sang it in closing:

God Be In My Head
God, be in my head, and in my understanding;

God, be in mine eyes, and in my looking;
God, be in my mouth, and in my speaking;
God, be in my heart, and in my thinking;
God, be at mine end, and at my departing.

—Henry Walford Davies, 1869–1940

SOMEDAYS I AM SO CERTAIN

Once,
I watched a funny green worm
With ferocious eyes
Crawl across the floor,
Swinging his head to and fro
In mock ferocity–
The larva of a swallowtail butterfly.

I knew he was headed
For a glorious metamorphosis.

Did he worry?
Or fret?
Or did he simply trust God?
Or Nature?
Or a Benign Process to care for him?

Grabbing my pen,
I wrote:

Oh, but Oh–
If his caterpillar was William Stephen Warner,
Think what his butterfly must be!

"To Life , to Life, L'Chaim"
Nevertheless, L'Chaim.
Amen.